The Will
to Live On

Books by Herman Wouk

NOVELS

Aurora Dawn
City Boy
The Caine Mutiny
Marjorie Morningstar
Youngblood Hawke
Don't Stop the Carnival
The Winds of War
War and Remembrance
Inside, Outside
The Hope
The Glory

NONFICTION

This Is My God
The Will to Live On

PLAYS

The Traitor
The Caine Mutiny Court-Martial
Nature's Way

For Stephen Freidhes
on his ben mitzvah

HERMAN
WOUK

בכל טוב

Herman Wouk

June 2000

The Will to Live On

THIS IS OUR HERITAGE

Cliff Street Books
An Imprint of HarperCollins*Publishers*

HarperCollins books may be purchased for educational, business, or sales promotional use. For information please write: Special Markets Department, HarperCollins Publishers, Inc., 10 East 53rd Street, New York, NY 10022.

FIRST EDITION

Designed by Nancy B. Field

Library of Congress Cataloging-in-Publication Data has been applied for.

ISBN 0-06-019608-4

00 01 02 03 04 ❖/RRD 10 9 8 7 6 5 4 3 2

For my grandchildren

Stephanie   Barak   Zohar

with love

ושננתם לבניך

Teach these things diligently to your children.
—MOSES, DEUTERONOMY 6:7

CONTENTS

PROLOGUE

Now my hand slows. The task needed an Ezra, and it found only this poor pen. I have done the best I could to tell my brothers that our law of Moses is great and honorable, now as when it first came to us.

This is my God, and I will praise him; the God of my father, and I will exalt him.

S o reads the last page of a book I wrote forty years ago. At the time I was something of a freak in American literary circles: a youngish novelist and playwright, subject of a *Time* cover story, who kept kosher, observed the Sabbath, and studied the Talmud. I wrote *This Is My God* more or less to explain myself. By then I had published *The Caine Mutiny,* in which a Jewish lawyer expressed nonconformist views on the military, and *Marjorie Morningstar,* a controversial novel about New York Jewish life. So my book was bound to attract some attention. To my genuine and gratified surprise, it became a truly popular long-lived work, still read nowadays. There was evidently a need which the book met.

Decade after decade since then, I have been writing afterwords and epilogues to successive editions, trying to keep abreast of the earthquake shocks in Jewish current events. That expedient has run out. For a long time I have sensed that another very different book is called for, to deal with our apocalyptic twentieth-century experiences—the reborn Jewish State, the prodigious yet precarious American diaspora, and the deepening religious schisms, and overshadowing all, the German massacre of Europe's Jews, called the Holocaust. The Torah and the Talmud are timeless, so in that regard *This Is My God* may continue to be useful. The state of our people worldwide, however, has meantime been utterly revolutionized. It is that revolution, and its effect on our heritage, that I have written about here.

The Gathering of the Great

The theme of this book broke into the light when my wife and I were in Jerusalem, awaiting the birth of a grandson. Late one evening I had downed whiskey to combat jet lag. After an hour I snapped awake, turned on the TV, and saw confused pictures of agitated crowds and racing, screaming police cars, while the Hebrew commentator was saying in a shaking voice that Prime Minister Yitzhak Rabin had been shot at a peace rally, and was dying or dead.

The stunned country went into mourning. The hysterical national discord over the peace process died down. Early next day, outside the gates of the Knesset where the slain Prime Minister was lying in state, masses of Israelis queued up to do him reverence, and I got into the line. I had come to know Rabin well when he was the Israeli ambassador in Washington, and I loved the man. After hours of slow shuffling, still nowhere near the gate, I sadly gave up and returned to my hotel, where a message from an old friend, a retired Israeli army general, summoned me to come with him to the funeral. Police and army security outside the stadium was several layers thick, but at each checkpoint the general's car got a salute and a wave-through. So it happened that I was present at the gathering of forty-four kings, presidents, and prime ministers, with foreign ministers from forty more nations, to honor a murdered Jewish leader.

Egypt's Mubarak was there, rubbing shoulders with three American presidents, Clinton, Bush, and Carter; with the prime ministers of Russia, Germany, France, and Britain, with Shimon Peres and Ezer Weizman of Israel. There was something eerie in this concourse of recognizable faces, seen not up close on television screens as usual, but at a distance, very small and human under a gray November sky. Though there was no sun at all, the Israeli elite and high diplomats crowding the stadium wore blue caps handed out as sun shields, in lieu of too-ethnic yarmulkes.

Among the many eulogies, the late King Hussein of Jordan, in red-checked head cloth, spoke with moving eloquence about the soldier who had seized the West Bank from him in the Six-Day War, and then worked with him in the cause of peace. Rabin's granddaughter, with a few beautiful clear words in Hebrew about the grandpa she loved, stole the show, if the phrase is not incongruous. In one sense it was indeed a show, a show of world sympathy, an international political spectacle seldom matched in modern history.

Such an event, in its sheer magnitude, defeats and numbs the mind. At the time, as I sat among Israel's senior army officers, we chatted idly between the tributes, and as we left we were comparing notes on the speakers, President Clinton getting the best marks "after the girl and the King." Outside the stadium I encountered the chief rabbi of Haifa, a teacher and friend for many years. "*Tzome Gedaliah*," I said to him. Without a word in reply he nodded, and we parted.

Gedaliah was the governor of Judaea, appointed by Nebuchadnezzar after the fall of the First Temple. A moderate Jewish leader, Gedaliah had favored making peace with the besieging Babylonians. His regime was brief, as the Bible relates. Within months, a cabal of dissenters from his peace policy murdered him. Our religious calendar marks this occurrence with a fast day (*tzome*), still observed by the devout. The death of no other Scriptural personage, not even Moses, is so commemorated. Rabin's fate resonates back twenty-five hundred years to *Tzome Gedaliah*, the unique annual lament for a murdered man of peace. This awesome depth of Jewish experience is something I explore here in my book.

The full impact of Rabin's assassination has been a while sinking in. In truth, it drew the great of the earth to Jerusalem because it was a tragedy of majestic, of biblical consequence. The journalism has faded, the historians have yet to cope with it, but the remembrance will endure. It is graven in the Jewish soul. The lone assassin was a young Talmud scholar, psychopathic but sane, who was against Rabin's peace policy, and justified his act by morbidly misquoting the Talmud. Jews like me who love the Talmud and study it daily must live with that knowledge, and come to terms with that challenge.

Point of View

Let me make clear where I stand today on the religion. Not long ago a popular photographer put out a picture book of Jewish writers. There I was at my desk in a yarmulke, with a brief quote underneath from a scene in *Marjorie Morningstar*, where Marjorie's raffish seducer, Noel Airman, persuades her to eat a lobster. "This is how the author layers his religion into his novels," the photographer commented. She took a good picture of me, but she missed the point of that little scene. Where my fiction deals with moral or religious questions, I leave the resolutions to the reader. Were the *Caine* officers right or wrong to depose Captain Queeg? Is Marjorie's final contentment as a kosher suburban housewife a sad ending, or the artistic truth about her? The lobster moment in her growing-up story is funny, truthful, and revealing of both protagonists, young New York Jews in the 1930s. It does not layer in a dire warning to nice Jewish girls, who aspire to be actresses and experiment with seafood. The kosher rules are fair game in literature for any writer, religious or not, as colorful shorthand for Jewish identity.

Saul Bellow opens *To Jerusalem and Back*, a short vivid book of reportage written many years ago, with an engaging episode about the dietary laws. He is bound for Israel in a plane crowded with ultra-religious Hasidim, and he converses in Yiddish with a Hasid seated beside him until the lunch comes; a glatt kosher meal for the Hasid, airline chicken for Bellow. The Hasid, scandalized at such laxness in a nice Yiddish-speaking Jew, offers to send Saul Bellow fifteen dollars a week for the rest of his life, if he will pledge never to eat unkosher food again. With this wry beginning the author defines himself as a detached humanist, and his critical yet subtly admiring account of Israel becomes the more convincing.

In *The Merchant of Venice* when Shylock first appears, the merchant Bassanio, needing a large loan, invites the Hebrew moneylender to dine. Shylock roughly replies:

> Yes, to smell pork; to eat of the habitation which your prophet the Nazarite conjured the devil into. I will buy with you, sell with you, talk with you, walk with you, and so following, but I will not eat with you. . . .

So Shakespeare provides a strong abrasive entrance for the one unforgettable character of this minor comedy. Shylock bursts from the Jew stereotype of the Renaissance to command the stage almost with the pathos of a Lear, and he defines himself at the outset with his barbed refusal to eat airline chicken.

In short, I treat of Jewish matters in my books and plays like other authors, not to persuade but to delineate. Among Jewish writers of the day I remain odd man out in point of view, of that I am well aware. In some of them I think I discern rueful second thoughts about religion, but any relevance of eschewing lobsters to the grand question of man's fate, in a vast baffling universe, may well seem to them a persisting petty absurdity. On that I have had my say in *This Is My God*, where I lay out my cards face up, and there an end.

In this book, as in all my works, I have no religious ax to grind, nothing to "layer in." The Orthodox will not be happy with some things I say here. As for the rest of world Jewry, estimated today at eighty or even ninety percent, I value them every bit as highly as I do my relatively few observant fellow believers. In fact, I write mainly for the others, as I did in *This Is My God*, and I write in a personal vein, as I did in that book, because I do not pretend to scholarly authority, and can put things only as I myself have come to see them. A lifetime of living and studying Judaism has only taught me how little I know; but that little I would share with others who love our people, who are concerned by the changes sweeping over Jewry, and who would welcome a few thoughts from one who has reached a great age still studying.

Structure of the Work

There are three parts to this book. Part 1 briefly explores the turbulent aftermath of the Holocaust, against our historical background of recurring catastrophe, survival, and resurgence over three millennia. I call this part SEARCHING THE WRECKAGE.

Part 2 surveys our history and our sacred literature: Bible, Talmud, Kabbalah, titans like Rashi and Maimonides, and the rise of modern Zionism. This is the meat of the book, and I call it THE HERITAGE, OR THE POWER OF A DREAM.

Part 3 examines the present world scene of Jewry, the troubled wonder of Israel, and the remarkable though dwindling American diaspora. I call this part THE JEWISH RESURGENCE.

The Jewish way of life is in wild flux nowadays. We all know that. If my book attracts attention, the picture drawn here may provoke strong disagreement or even anger. What I am after here is the truth, as I am given to see it. For more than a quarter of a century I have avoided television and print journalism; not that my ideas are sensational or even newsy, but they are my own, they are serious, and hardly to be conveyed in interviews. I have kept my distance from the media, held my peace, and stuck to my work. The deep-running controversies in Jewish life are there, nevertheless, challenging insight and honesty, and having taken up my pen, I will do my best to deal with them.

For some readers I am writing about very familiar things. For others, many terms will be new and puzzling, unless I clarify them as I go. I risk, therefore, being either too obvious or too obscure. A glossary and some amplifying notes appear at the end of the volume. In the book itself I have tried to steer a middle course, aiming above all at clarity.

I dedicate *The Will to Live On* to the memory of two of my teachers: Moshe Feinstein, the Torah master of the age, at whose feet I learned Talmud, and my deeply mourned friend, Yitzhak Rabin, who taught me in his life and in his death that the Talmud was not enough.

Part I

SEARCHING THE WRECKAGE

We owe to the Jews a system of ethics which, even if it were
entirely separated from the supernatural, would be the most
precious possession of mankind, worth, in fact, the fruit of
all other wisdom and learning together.

—WINSTON CHURCHILL

One

THE REBBE AND THE HISTORIAN

In **Palm Springs** where I live nowadays, I go to a Hasidic synagogue. I am not at all a Hasid, but it is a reasonably short Sabbath walk. Later in my book I write a lot about this mystic pietist movement, which arose in eastern Europe around 1700, and still flourishes worldwide. Our likable young American-born rabbi—lean, tall, long brown beard—settled here years ago. In this desert town of golfing and sun his intensive Orthodoxy has proven a hard sell, and his family is large and growing, so he perforce doubles as a prison chaplain. Now and then after a taxing week, he asks me to give the Sabbath sermon. I try to fill in with a few plain words about the week's Torah portion, and that once led to a bizarre incident which can serve as a topic sentence for this book.

In the summer, the little congregation can shrivel below the ten men needed for a minyan, a prayer quorum, but come winter the place is packed with black-clad fur-hatted Hasidim of varied allegiance, known like their Rebbes by the ghost names of their destroyed shtetls—"little towns"—Lubavitchers, Satmarers, Belzers, Gerers, Bobovers, and so on. One Rebbe, who comes himself with his followers to warm up, is the *Munkatcher*, a grizzled imposing personage in his Shabbat garb of white stockings, dark knee breeches, and black or gold-embroidered long coat. As I was holding forth one Shabbat on a verse in Exodus, the Munkatcher Rebbe suddenly rose to his feet and stalked out into the sunshine, considerably disconcerting me. I had been citing a comment by Ibn Ezra, the twelfth-century exegete who strongly influenced Spinoza, and had I made reference to Spinoza I might have understood the Munkatcher's walkout. But I had not, and Ibn Ezra is a classic authority accepted by all.

The comment I was quoting was on the laws of the Hebrew bondman, the *eved ivri*. This passage in Exodus precedes the law on murder. Ibn Ezra observes that the sequence is proper, because freedom is more to be prized than life itself. Israel's first Prime Minister, David Ben-Gurion, once said something like that to me, and I was mentioning this when the Munkatcher Rebbe, upon hearing the name "Ben-Gurion," got up and left the synagogue.

There is more to the story, but let me first explain what it was that Ben-Gurion said.

The Encounter with Ben-Gurion

"What took you so long?" Ben-Gurion asked me when we first met, during the intermission of a performance in Hebrew of my *Caine Mutiny Court-Martial*, at the Habimah Theatre in Tel Aviv. It was a gala evening, laid on in honor of the playwright, a newcomer to Israel, so even the informal Israelis were somewhat dressed up; but the squat paunchy Zionist leader, instantly recognizable by the floating wings of white hair on his tanned balding head, wore a khaki open-neck shirt and pants. My wife and I had been out at sea with the fledgling Jewish navy, had docked late in Haifa, and had been rocketed to Tel Aviv in a military car, barely in time for the second act. So his inquiry might have been a gentle twitting about that, but it was not what he meant, and I understood him.

"I'm not here yet," I replied, adopting his allusive style.

He grinned and invited Sarah and me to his home in the Negev desert. Next day we came to the Sde Boker (Fields of Morning) kibbutz in a command car escorted by a jeep with a mounted machine gun, for back in 1955 the raw little country was being bloodily harassed in broad daylight by *fedayeen*, terrorists from Egypt and Gaza. Ben-Gurion was out of office and working on his memoirs, so he discoursed in long Churchillian style on history, politics, philosophy, and literature until the sun was low. His wife Paula, seeing that he was enjoying himself, invited us to stay for dinner.

"No, no, they're kosher," said Ben-Gurion.

"So I'll make them hard-boiled eggs and salad."

"Paula, they have to get back to Tel Aviv before dark."

When we were leaving he came out with his straight Zionist line, no more hints. "You must return here to live," he said. "This is the only place for Jews like you. Here you will be free."

"Free?" I ventured to reply. "Free? With enemy armies ringing you, with their leaders publicly threatening to wipe out 'the Zionist entity,' with your roads impassable after sundown—free?"

"I did not say *safe*," the old man retorted, "I said *free*."

That was how I happened, nearly forty years later, to mention him and outrage the Munkatcher Rebbe.

Digression on the Shtetl

Ben-Gurion once wrote in an irritable outburst, "What is all this sentimental nonsense about the shtetl? We *fled* from the shtetl!"

So the Zionists did, and they revived in the Holy Land the first independent Jewish State in two thousand years, renowned today for armed prowess and economic vigor. Back then, however, the scrawny, new mini-country was tottering under the imposed load of more than a half million refugees, driven out of Arab lands after the Jewish victory in the War of Independence, while the overburdened Israelis themselves numbered less than a million. Except for the inspiring holy places, and the romantic biblical landscapes, restored Zion was a letdown, a transplanted beleaguered shtetl on a strip of Mediterranean coast not unlike Southern California. True, it was an armed shtetl, and the Jewish military forces were an exciting novelty, but hardly more than that to a veteran of Pacific campaigns.

And yet that evening, as we went bumping back to Tel Aviv in the twilight on unpaved tracks through Negev sands, I found myself somehow hooked by Ben-Gurion's parting words. A native-born, successful American author, I was not aware of having felt unfree in the land of the free. It was here rather, in this bizarre little place called Israel, amid its harried bristling Hebrew-speaking Jews, at once so familiar and so different, so proud and yet so defensive, that I felt uneasy and hemmed in. How then had Ben-Gurion snared my attention? Something unexpected had been happening to me in Israel which the old Zionist lion had probably discerned; an atavism in a Bronx-born boy, one generation removed from the shtetl fugitives who by the millions had thronged through Ellis Island to form the bulk of today's American Jewry. Actually, both my parents came from Minsk, not at all a shtetl, except that the word has come to stand for all of the east European Yiddishkeit that is gone.

The Jews of that vanished diaspora, scattered over several countries, were riven in religion between the Hasidim and their opponents, and raucous with political splintering among the secularists; but Yiddish was the tongue in which they all clashed, hot in dispute but homogeneous in heritage. Believers and unbelievers alike were immersed in Yiddishkeit, a mother's milk Jewishness. There is no such homogeneity here, no such thing yet as American Yiddishkeit. That is the tax paid for the admirable tolerance of the Melting Pot; that, and the constant subconscious nag at all points: *"What will the goyim think?"* In Israel I found myself losing this wariness, in a way I can best suggest in navy terms. My radar had shut down.

Bellow's *To Jerusalem and Back* is a self-portrait of a tough-minded American intellectual, not in the least hooked by Israel, however sympathetic. When he and I were scholars-in-residence together at a summer retreat in Aspen, we discovered a shared love for Yiddish, so we conversed in that wonderful tongue on long trail climbs, and Israel hardly came up at all. Our celebrated contemporary, Norman Mailer, has not been there yet; I know this because his Israeli relatives have grumbled to me about it. As for me, I have lived in Israel for more than a year at a time, I have spent months there off and on, and I have long since lost count of my shorter visits. My two grandsons have been growing up there, my sons and I are fluent in Hebrew, and they ran a business in Eilat for a while. You might say that with my family Ben-Gurion more or less carried his point.

One recent Shabbat as I came into the synagogue, a warning whisper from the young rabbi greeted me. *"The Munkatcher is here again."* There he stood at a prayer stand by the eastern wall, donning a magnificent silver-collared tallis, prayer shawl. I was putting on my tallis when he left his stand, approached me, and startled me more than he had with his walkout, by offering his hand. You have to understand how odd this was. Services had not begun. Strict synagogue custom defers greetings by word or gesture until the time of the Torah reading, a rule neglected by the laity but not by Rebbes. Nor do Rebbes approach plain Jews like me. If certain of your welcome, you humbly approach the Rebbe. Yet here came the Munkatcher, and his handshake was not the soft formal palm-to-palm touch one expects from a Rebbe. It was a firm amiable grip, as though to say, *"Nothing personal last time, you understand."*

The Pessimistic Historian

By chance an Israeli historian, an old friend, came to lecture in Palm Springs a few days after this, and I recounted to him the whole strange business of the walkout and the handshake. "Oh, the *Munkatcher*!" he exclaimed. "No wonder!" And he proceeded to enlighten me about Munkatch and the Munkatchers.

Munkatch is a town in the Carpathian foothills. Before the German massacre, it was a Hasidic stronghold for more than a century, shuttling between Hungarian and Czech rule. The Munkatcher Rebbes were noted for their absolute unrelenting opposition to modernity. They were not only against secular studies in Jewish schools, they opposed teaching and conversing in Hebrew as a profane use of the holy tongue, and with the Zionist movement they would have no truck whatever. Even as the Nazi doom was coming on, they excoriated the small super-pious Agudat Israel party for joining the atheistical Zionists in rescue work. Such was the background of the Munkatcher, and so his walkout, if not his handshake, stood explained.

My learned friend turned out to be as hardheaded a secularist as the Munkatcher was a pietist. Our breakfast talk in the coffee shop of his hotel went on for a long time, and his critique of some aspects of Hasidism was harsh. I did not argue. I held my peace and listened, though my grandfather, a major influence in my life, was a Lubavitcher Hasid, as is our Palm Springs rabbi.

Shutting up when talking to an authority is not a bad rule. While doing research on the atom bomb for my novel, *War and Remembrance*, I consulted a supreme mental giant of the century, the physicist Richard Feynman. I had barely told him what I wanted of him when he broke in, "You know, while you're talking, you're not learning anything." There I heard a book of wisdom compressed to a calculus formula, so I shut up and listened, and learned something. With my historian friend that day in the coffee shop, by shutting up and listening, I learned a great deal.

After his diatribe against the Hasidim, he had sobering words to say about American Jewry, putting familiar things into grim focus; to wit, that strict observance of the faith is unmistakably going down, that most young Jews year by year show less and less interest in the Holocaust and in Israel, and that intermarriage is alarmingly on the increase. Such has been the litany of our hand-wringers in pulpits, journalism, and doomsaying books. Cheery by nature, I have been taking note of some counter-indications. Judaic Studies, for instance, are certainly trendy at the universities. American Jewish publishing seems to expand and prosper. Even the offering of kosher products in supermarkets is up, or so my wife tells me. My old synagogue in Washington, where we sometimes had trouble making a minyan, is packed not only on High Holy Days but on ordinary Sabbaths. Altogether, I have been nursing the notion that there are two sides to the picture.

Not for my historian. He would have none of it. *"American Jewry is dying."* He spoke the words flat out. Coming from him this jarred me, bringing unpleasantly to mind something a Reform rabbi had told me not long before, when I came to his temple to give a talk. "I'm glad if one couple out of five that I marry are both Jews," he said bitterly. "American Judaism is hemorrhaging." He himself wears a yarmulke, and he sends his children to a Lubavitch school in another town. A good-looking thoughtful man, he struck me as desperately unhappy in his work. I know Conservative and Orthodox rabbis not much happier, if less vocally despondent.

My historian had numbers at his fingertips to validate his views and their fears. Setting aside entirely the drastic drain by intermarriage, the rate of reproduction of American Jewish families is today 1.4 souls, he informed me, and the minimum survival rate of an ethnic group is 2.1. Since we are as yet more than five million, the shrinkage will take a while before it becomes critical and frightening, but to this dour realist's sharp eyes, the handwriting already glares on the wall.

"Keep Writing"

As he was sketching this lugubrious picture, his handsome red-headed wife, a professional musician, joined us. "Well, it's good to see you again," she said to me, when he paused to drink coffee. "What do you think of his ideas?"

"I don't know anything. He is the scholar."

"Nonsense."

"Come on," he said. "You're an American, a Jew, and a good observer. Do you disagree with me?"

I paused before answering. "Are we dying? No. Not yet. Running on empty, perhaps, as the phrase goes."

He flashed an acerbic scholar's smile. "Explain yourself."

Now I was at a seminar, so I did my best at some length. I spoke of familiar contrasts in American Jewish life—the peaks of achievement in the sciences, the arts, and the business world against the sharp slump in Yiddishkeit; the awareness of waning identity versus the instinct to cling to roots, and my own view that any hope for our long future lay in a massive return to our sources in faith, literature, and history. He nodded and nodded, she fixed me with alert blue-gray eyes, and neither interrupted. When I finished the wife said, "You must write that."

"I've written enough," I said.

I meant it. For the past thirty years I have been writing uninterruptedly on Jewish themes. Even the television serials which I dramatized from my war novels turned on the Holocaust. I have since published *The Hope* and *The Glory,* two long novels about Israel's wars. Enough already!

My historian shook his head. "Not if you have more to say."

This was a cue, and I drew a typewritten sheet from my pocket. "Very well. I want you to listen to this, that's why I brought it." I read aloud without emotion, "'*Eichmann was absolutely convinced that if he could succeed in destroying the biological basis of Jewry in the*

East by complete extermination, then Jewry as a whole would never recover from the blow. The assimilated Jews of the West, including America, would be in no position (and would have no desire) to make good this enormous loss of blood, and there would therefore be no future generation worth mentioning.'"

"Where did you get that?" he asked. Both their faces were sad and hard. "Did you write it yourself?"

"The commandant of Auschwitz wrote it."

"Rudolf Hoess wrote that?"

"Right. In the book of memoirs he finished in prison, just before he was hanged."

"I read that book," said the historian. "I don't remember the passage."

"How could you forget it?" asked his wife.

"I copied it down," I said. "I've read it over and over, year in and year out. What do you say to it?"

"Do you know how I end the lecture I give on this tour?" retorted the historian. "I ask the audience, *'Has Hitler won his war against the Jews?'* Those are my last words, and I sit down. It's a jolt. The question and answer period after that gets lively."

"But what about Israel?" I said. "That's the area where I'm still groping. Eichmann never foresaw Israel."

A worried glance passed between the two Israelis. "Do you think it's any better there?" she asked.

"It *is* better," he contradicted her. "A bit better. The Israeli rate of reproduction is about 2.4 today. That's a survival margin, anyway."

"And the rate of reproduction of the Arabs?" Her tone became faintly agitated. "And the young people who go traveling when they finish the military, and never come back? And the ignorance, *the ignorance?* And the crazy Americanizing? And the consuls, the attachés, the businessmen, the scientists, the entertainers, the doctors who marry outside and stay outside? And what about the post-Zionists, who want to forget the whole thing once for all?"

"Ah! Tell me about these post-Zionists," I said to him. "The more I read about them, the more they puzzle me. Aren't some of them professors at the Hebrew University? What are they getting at? *Forget the whole thing*? Surely not."

"That's a long story," he said, "and I have to speak to the temple men's club now, then fly to San Francisco."

"I'll drive you to the airport, and you'll tell me about the post-Zionists."

"A deal." He signaled to the waitress for the check.

"Meantime," I added, "let me say a word about the Hasidim."

"Shoot."

I told him about my grandfather, and reminded him of the intense clandestine rescue and education efforts by the Lubavitchers, often at the risk of prison or death, in the darkest days of the defunct Soviet Union. "You can't wave that aside," I said, "nor the way they send young men all over the world today, even to Tasmania—why, even to Palm Springs—to give Jews a place to pray and learn some Yiddishkeit."

"All true, they do many fine things, but their outlook is obsessively backward, and I can't forgive the Lubavitcher Rebbe for a passage in his book *Emuna Umada* (*Faith and Science*), about the Holocaust, comparing it to radical surgery that cut off a poisoned limb, so that the whole body could grow healthy again."

"Did he write that? He couldn't have. Surely not *poisoned*," I said. "The limb was sick, that's true."

He replied with asperity, "Who isn't sick nowadays?"

"The million children weren't sick," said his wife. "They were pure."

That ended the conversation. He got up to pay the check, and she walked out into the lobby with me. "Keep writing," she said. "*Keep writing*. What you write is plain and clear. That's important."

"Retrospect"

Not long afterward, my wife and I spent some time in the Georgetown house we acquired when I was working on my World War II novels. Most of our possessions are still there. Late one night, on a totally random impulse, I took down from my library shelf the fifth and last volume of Heinrich Graetz's *History of the Jews*. After reading in it for hours, I decided to do as the historian's wife said, and to try to write this book.

Graetz was an old-fashioned "narrative historian," as the condescending critical term goes nowadays, so he sweeps you along in a gigantic tale as absorbing as fiction, yet meticulously true to all the facts known when he wrote. His epilogue, called "Retrospect," compresses into twenty-six pages the three thousand years of the Jewish past. "Retrospect" comes down only to the 1880s, for Graetz died in 1891. His entire account of the Jewish saga is therefore short by more than a hundred years. It cries for continuation.

So much has happened since then that a serious historian could hardly bring the story up to the present in a single book. What I offer here, at any rate, is certainly not such a book. My life work has been in fiction and drama, and if it has contained much history, that is because the essence of the narrative art—in novel, play, or film—is conflict, and the great conflicts of our time have been on the world stage. What I am essaying here is only a summary picture of where Jewry stands today, a century after Graetz.

Has Hitler Won His War Against the Jews?

Inevitably, therefore, I must face my historian's mordant question. There is no need to peek at my last pages for my conclusion. I do not for a moment accept that the three-thousand-year miracle of God's people in history may be ending, but then I am a believer. I

know all too well that some of the cleverest, best, and most powerful Jews are skeptics or non-believers, and that nevertheless I must
engage their interest, if not their assent.

In the half century since the Holocaust, the decimated Jews of
the world have already proven themselves a generation worth mentioning, by creating and supporting Israel. About our generation,
which is passing, Eichmann was wrong. The open question is
about the generations of the year 2000 and beyond. This question
confronts every living Jew, Israeli or not, religious or not, Zionist or
not, married to another Jew or not; it confronts, in fact, every non-
Jewish spouse of a Jew, and I sense that the question—faced or
not—lives in the hearts of all of them. Most of all it will confront
their children, and they are pure.

The Brackets

I understand why the Munkatcher walked out on me. But why did
he approach me and shake my hand? Did he know that I once
wrote *This Is My God*, and did he approve of that simple essay? Or
was it because he had seen that, without black garments and a fur
hat, dressed in light desert garb, I could discuss the Torah and its
commentators? The last thing my historian said to me at the airport was, "If there's any real hope, it lies in the very violence of the
conflicts among us. We are a cauldron of passionate contradictions,
and to that extent we are still the Jews of the Talmud."

I am a Jew of the Talmud. It is my heritage, and perhaps the
Munkatcher perceived that. My stand-up study desk occupies a
corner of my little office in Palm Springs. On the wall facing me as
I con my daily Talmud page is a bronzed picture of a Merkava, the
first-line battle tank that the Israelis had to develop, because no
major power would sell them any. Those are the outer brackets of
the time we Jews now live in: the Talmud and the tank.

Two

RUNNING ON EMPTY

Early on a Sunday morning after the historian's visit, I am chatting over bagels and lox with the temple's earnest woman president, who chaired his lecture.

"Was the fellow trying to be clever? Sensational? '*American Jewry is dying*'! Right! And meantime we poor dying American Jews fly him coast to coast and pay him fat fees to talk his foolishness! Why doesn't he come once to a national leadership conference, and meet the thousands of men and women who work their hearts out all year long for the Jewish people, and try that stuff on them?"

"Why don't you invite him?"

"Ha. They would string me up! '*Has Hitler won his war against the Jews?*' Irresponsible scaremongering! I wrote a blistering letter to his lecture agent, let me tell you."

"He's a major scholar. I have profound regard for his views."

"You *agree* with him?"

"I didn't say that."

Whereupon I tell her pretty much what I told the historian and his wife in the coffee shop. She listens intently, and as I speak it seems to me that her eyes start to moisten.

The Moon Module

All those leaders at her annual conclave—leaders of federations, councils, congresses, committees, institutes, lodges, leagues, temples, synagogues, united appeals, and so on—might well string her up for inviting this Israeli Jeremiah. Then again, some might be braced by the cold douse of his warnings. Her indignation tells me that the lecture gave her a qualm, that she hates the qualm, and that therefore she hates the messenger. Her impression of a strong active American Jewry is accurate as far as it goes, but in my judgment it is misleading.

Two psychic forces have been infusing American Jewry with amazing vitality since the Second World War, the energy of guilt and the energy of pride. Both are waning, and neither is likely to fuel this great diaspora far beyond the year 2000. Such is my view, and that is all I mean by the stock phrase "running on empty." The guilt is about the Holocaust. The pride is about Israel. If not for those two nearly simultaneous hammer strokes of history, which rang alarms and struck sparks in our souls, I believe we might even now be withering below the survival margin, for all to see. Except in enclaves of the observant, the religion which has preserved our folk down the ages is undeniably at an ebb. From Bible days onward Jewry has experienced lapses and revivals of faith, but this decline among America's Jews is steep, and the bottom is as yet not discernible.

Nor is that hard to understand. Among immigrants like my mother and father, early in the century, there was a byword, *"When you get halfway across the Atlantic, throw overboard your prayer shawl and phylacteries."* One couldn't observe the religion in the *Goldena Medina* and make a living, it was said; and anyway, here was the chance to shrug off the musty ways of the shtetl and its Torah—from which, as Ben-Gurion rightly put it, they were fleeing—and to start life in a pristine new identity as AMERICANS. I am a product of a household that resisted this byword, yet I well know how it almost entirely overwhelmed the old Yiddishkeit.

Hitler's leap to power was an electric shock to the drifters, as well as to the more established and assimilated Jews of earlier migrations. When twelve years later the truth emerged of his vast secret slaughter of the six million behind the smoke of war, not only was American Jewry stunned, the whole world was. That was the decisive reason for the United Nations vote in 1947, which enabled Israel to run up its flag, for since then such votes have tended to go lopsidedly against Israel. But this miraculous rebirth of the ancient nation in the Holy Land did not at first greatly stir the American Jewish heart. To most, Zionism had always been a dreamy notion, to some even odious, raising the old specter of dual loyalty; and Palestine was no place to visit, let alone to live.

The Palestine wrested by the British from the Turks, during the First World War, was still the sad disease-ridden Ottoman province of ancient ruins, described by Mark Twain in *Innocents Abroad*. The scattered settlements of *halutzim*, pioneers from eastern Europe, plus the old very small religious enclaves, were a mere marginal fragment of world Jewry. For wartime reasons of state, the British in 1917 issued the famous Balfour Declaration, the enabling document of Zionism:

> His Majesty's Government view with favour the establishment in Palestine of a national home for the Jewish people, and will use their best endeavours to facilitate the achievement of this object, it being clearly understood that nothing shall be done which may prejudice the civil and religious rights of existing non-Jewish communities in Palestine, or the rights and political status enjoyed by Jews in any other country.

So modern Jewish history takes a sharp turn. In my chapter on Zionism I discuss with some care this momentous, complicated, and decidedly equivocal single sentence. At the time, the American Jewish reaction, by and large, was a shrug. Only with the Six-Day War in 1967, fifty years after the Balfour Declaration, did there come the abrupt mass turn to Zionism. At that time the threat to Israel by Egypt and Syria, acting together and heavily armed by Russia with tanks, artillery, and combat aircraft, wore the aspect of a second Holocaust; and the surprise triumph of Israel's armed forces against such odds created a mighty awakening in American Jewry. The sudden outpouring of support—financial, political, emotional—was unparalleled, unforeseen, and fantastic.

An odd analogy comes to my mind, the Apollo lunar landing module. The spidery little machine, when it soared off the airless moon with the astronauts, was powered by two chemicals which flowed together at liftoff; once combined, they shot the module skyward to the command vehicle in a burst of terrific propulsion. So, in those historic six days, guilt about the Holocaust and pride in the new Jewish military prowess flowed together, as it were; and the ensuing explosive synergy of ethnic force has been carrying our community ever since toward the twenty-first century. Israel has had its subsequent ups and downs in peace and war, and in its approval rating among journalists, politicians, and academics, but the American Jews have remained, as one Israeli general has put it, Israel's strategic depth.

Still, I do not forget another thing Ben-Gurion said to me: "Nothing is permanent in history."

Running on Empty

So it seems to be working out. That explosive synergistic force is largely spent. The module is back on earth, so to say, mission accomplished. For the rising generation of American Jews, mostly born after the Yom Kippur War, Israel is a robust modern country in no danger, an established patch of global geography that has always been there, a sort of rowdy Jewish Denmark on the Mediterranean, and—what with the Lebanon War, the intifada, and the leftist tilt on campuses—hardly an unchallengeable source of pride.

Jewish collegians have no memories, as their elders do, of hanging sleepless on the news bulletins in 1973, as Syria and Egypt attacked and for three harrowing days appeared to be crushing out the life of the new Jewish State. Of the earthshaking glory of the Six-Day War they know nothing but words in books—like my novel *The Hope*, if they bother to read it—and more words of rabbis, parents, and lecturers. As for the War of Independence of 1948, they have enough trouble relating to the American Revolution, let alone to those ancient doings in the Middle East. The Zionist few among them who care about such matters not only encounter apathy, they risk being considered—ultimate campus disgrace—uncool.

Shortly after the Six-Day War, Prime Minister Levi Eshkol said to his ambassador returning to Washington, "You have a hard job now, you have to represent a nebbish Samson." Nebbish has made it into *Webster's* like other Yiddishisms: "nebbish: a timid, meek, or ineffectual person." The whole present Jewish image problem is there in Eshkol's sardonic oxymoron. What sort of Jew lives among the nations today, anyway? The nebbish Eternal Wanderer who docilely climbed into the German trains, or the New Jew manning the formidable Israeli air force and tank columns?

Apathy and Holocaust

"The first thing Israel has to do to achieve a normal existence is to tear down Yad Vashem," an eminent American correspondent said to me, as we lunched in a balcony alcove of a little dairy restaurant overlooking the majestic Old City walls. He is a Jew who spent his boyhood summers in Zionist camps, and today writes bestsellers on the Middle East. I was taken aback, to say the least. *Yad Vashem*, a phrase from Isaiah, means a memorial; literally, "a pillar and a name." Yad Vashem is Israel's great Holocaust museum, where no dignitary who visits Jerusalem fails to be photographed, bowing his head. Few tourists omit at least one brief awed stop at Yad Vashem. For Israel's children it is a perpetual must. For scholars no Holocaust archive touches it. *Tear down Yad Vashem??*

On what I might call the Feynman rule, I shut up and let him explain. His point was sharp and simple. Present-day Jews, he said, Israelis most of all, have to stop thinking of themselves as victims. That part of Jewish history is over. Erase the nebbish, we are New Jews. Today the victim frame of mind is obsolete, paranoiac, and conducive to misguided policies. He was as good a talker as he is a writer, and obviously the war in Lebanon and his noted writings about it had much shaped his own frame of mind. When he finished, I gestured at the view. "Do you know what Ben-Gurion said after the Six-Day War? He was out of power, so he could speak freely. 'The first thing Israel must do now,' he said, 'is tear down the walls of the Old City.'"

The correspondent looked a bit startled, then conceded with a wry grin, "Well, all right, don't tear down Yad Vashem. But at least limit schoolchildren's visits to once a year."

Tearing down Yad Vashem was of course just a conversational ploy. Yet he truly seemed convinced that we Jews should put behind us the Holocaust, the pogroms, the Inquisition, the Crusades, the entire blood-soaked nineteen centuries of Jewish suffering in exile, and rethink our history, starting with Israel. Very well, but what about Israel? There, on a spring day in the Hebrew calendar—Yom Hashoah, Holocaust Day—a siren sounds in midmorning, and all foot and motor traffic stops. I once saw from my window in the Tel Aviv Hilton two players freeze on a tennis court far below. Until the siren died off, neither man moved. Then one of them wiped his eyes, threw up a ball, and slammed a serve.

Israelis have a gut sense that in every new office building that rises in Tel Aviv there is a trace of Auschwitz ash. In Israel that siren sounds every year, bewailing the destruction of the European Jews. I do not think it will cease to sound while Israel exists. To some of us, Yom Hashoah in itself is a sufficient raison d'être for a Jewish State.

The Man on the Cruise Ship

One summer when Palm Springs was sizzling, my wife and I took an arctic cruise. On that ship a total stranger said to me out of the blue, "You know something? The Holocaust was worse than Tisha B'Av." Tisha B'Av is our annual fast day mourning the destruction of the First and Second Temples; for by an eerie coincidence, or a veiled decree of Providence, both occurred on the ninth (*Tisha*) day of the month of Av, some six centuries apart.

I had glimpsed this gentleman at a brief Friday evening service led by the ship's social director, a jolly youngster who knew a few Hebrew words. Now we stood on deck in a pleasant morning breeze, looking out at the green crags and blue water of a Norwegian fjord. A sight-seeing tour was the day's program, but evidently like me he would not ride a bus on Saturday. Except for our wives and the crew, we were on a deserted ship. To call a historical event worse than Tisha B'Av was clearly a ploy, like advocating the demolition of Yad Vashem. "How so?" I inquired, then shut up and let him talk.

He began with a story. He and his brother were survivors whose parents perished in the Holocaust. These two men, successful Los Angeles real estate developers, tracked down details of their parents' last days, so as to locate and honor their remains. They traveled to the site of an enormous mass grave in Poland where the mother and father were almost certainly buried, intending to raise a memorial stone in that place. To their horror they found that grave robbers had been at work there, digging for "Jewish valuables." The ground was in disorder, some corpses gruesomely exposed. The brothers obtained the Polish government's permission to pave over the huge site with acres of thick cement, and they did it at their own high cost.

"All these Holocaust museums and memorials will one day be empty buildings, and all these Holocaust studies will be passing talk," he harshly asserted, "unless the rabbis put into the religious calendar some remembrance of what happened. That is how the memory will last, not otherwise. Only we Jews can keep it alive." He paused, then broke out angrily, "How many Jews died, after all, when the Temples were destroyed? A hundred thousand each time? Two, three, *five* hundred thousand, a million? Is there any comparison to the six million? But they have no vision, the rabbis. It isn't happening. I'm afraid it won't happen, and the memory will die out. What does the rest of the world care?"

Tisha B'Av usually falls in August, when synagogue attendance wanes and many temples are closed. Nowadays it tends to be a neglected, not to say a forgotten, observance. There are some who even say that it is out of date. For those who do keep it up, this holy day is hard going. Services night and day are protracted, the liturgy is loaded with difficult medieval poetry, and more punishing even than Yom Kippur is the twenty-four-hour thirst of a midsummer fast. All during the Tisha B'Av services that year, I kept thinking about the man on the cruise ship. In the anguished blurt of a son's grief over his murdered mother and father, I had heard a new chapter of the Book of Lamentations.

Graetz, himself a German, narrated nothing in all his vast work to compare to the massacre of 1941–45. His graphic pictures of the horrors of the Spanish Inquisition, protracted through three centuries, still freeze the reader's blood, and his ever-recurring accounts of mass killings all over Christian Europe, generation after generation, end by deadening the mind. Yet even Graetz gave not the slightest hint that he foresaw this Third Destruction. Indeed, his last volume ends on a note of guarded optimism, a sense that the worst may be over, that the Jews of Europe are at last finding their strength and their voice. The irony is bitter beyond expression.

Tent and Sarcophagus

While my television serial, *War and Remembrance,* was being filmed in Yugoslavia, the Chernobyl reactor exploded and sent poisonous clouds drifting over Poland. The scenes in Auschwitz had not yet been shot, and there was talk of shutting down the production. I was scheduled to observe the filming there. When the director made the decision to proceed—thereby losing a number of his actors—my wife and I flew to Poland and joined the company in nearby Katowice. We had visited Auschwitz twice before in researching my novel, and this was the third time my feet walked that cursed and sacred ground. It was perhaps the strangest experience of my life.

I came there toward evening when the director, Dan Curtis, was filming the arrival of the train, timed for what he called "the magic hour" of best natural light. Over and over the train arrived, passed through the infamous arched entrance, backed out, and arrived again. When he was satisfied, the cars rolled ahead to the selection ramp, which was lined by actors in SS uniforms, complete with barking dogs. A mob in shabby yellow-starred clothing tumbled out of the cars under glaring floodlights, the whole familiar scene re-created with macabre accuracy. As the men and women lined up separately, Curtis told me that since these hundreds of extras were all Poles, he had had to import a few real Jews from Austria to make the first rows look right.

We walked to a large nearby tent during a break. Inside at a long buffet, performers in costume were helping themselves to appetizing cold and hot food, natty SS officers elbow to elbow with ragged camp slaves, for movie companies on location are provided with excellent catering. I took some tuna salad and rye bread, Curtis and I sat down at a table, and as we ate we discussed possible script changes in a forth-coming Battle of Midway sequence. What with such talk and the phantasmagoria of the whole scene, Auschwitz had for me become a movie lot, as it has since become a museum. Where uncounted Jews died from starvation, there I was having a nice snack.

I cannot shake the memory. But is that not mere bathos? If films are to be made about the Holocaust, no Hollywood-constructed Auschwitz can equal the actual ground. The Polish government is acquiescent, no doubt quite pleased with the fees charged for such usage, and with the flow of income to Polish performers. If the pro-duction is to be done in Auschwitz, there has to be a catering tent. That being granted, what would I have? Could my Jewish director observe a month-long fast during the filming? Preposterous notion. Still, I did not have to eat in Auschwitz.

It sometimes seems to me that all the Holocaust museums, movies, plays, novels, lectures, and college courses are happening, one way or another, with a catering tent. It is inevitable. We are in another time, and cannot bring back the dead and relieve their starving agony by feeding them a film caterer's buffet. Surely their sufferings should continue to be memorialized, however inadequately, in every way that a shamed humanity can devise, even a TV serial. Yet I will always wish I had thought of not eating in Auschwitz, though nowadays German tourists routinely picnic there when lunchtime comes.

The Chernobyl fallout did brush Auschwitz and Cracow, but if there were ill effects, I have not felt them. Today the ruined reactor is encased in a gigantic cement block called the "sarcophagus," inside which the fire burns on, and the poisonous radioactivity gnaws and leaks. So the Holocaust is now encased, one might say, in a vast sar-cophagus of contrite world recognition, shading into exploitation;

but within there is the smoldering residue of a runaway explosion of evil at the core of human nature, contained but unmastered.

In short, mankind may have adopted "Holocaust" as a catchword for ultimate evil, but it cannot adopt or handle our tragedy. The bereavement is ours as a people, to cope with as we can. The Jewish genius transformed the burning of the First Temple into the granite poetry of Jeremiah and Lamentations. It transcended the Second Temple's fall by creating the Talmud, the lifeblood of our scattered folk for nineteen centuries. Today the challenge is to come to grips with the Third Destruction, beginning with calling it by its right name. The converse of Santayana's apothegm is just as true; those who remember history may be empowered to surmount it.

Patent of Nobility

The task begins by analyzing how our forebears accomplished the miracle of surviving two apparently irreversible national Destructions. That calls for a backward glance over thousands of years. In doing this, I can offer brevity and attempt clarity, but I know well that all too many Americans are not grabbed by history. Huckleberry Finn, the truest literary voice of our land, expressed this in his plain way.

> . . . She learned me about Moses and the Bulrushers, and I was in a sweat to find out all about him; but by and by she let it out that he had been dead for a considerable long time; so then I didn't care no more about him, because I don't take no stock in dead people.

History buffs in one or another field abound among us, to be sure, and our university history departments are ably manned; withal, Huckleberry speaks a down-home view which Henry Ford put somewhat more tersely: "History is more or less bunk."

Nor is the resistance to history just American. It is a self-protective shell of youth everywhere. The life of the moment sweetly beckons, the freedom, the kisses, the fast cars, the rock music, whereas the graybeards and the purse-mouthed grandmothers would shackle golden lads and lasses to a dragging chain of the past. For the Jewish young, that means three thousand years of chain. Straight through college, history was my own worst subject. I was bored by it, I detested it, and my imperviousness to history killed my average. I had to marry a Phi Bete key. I write these words then, with a vivid recollection of my own youth, and some understanding of youngsters today.

All the same, from my present perspective I would suggest that there is a special way of looking at Jewish history. Let us suppose that a fortune of millions is left to one in youth by an almost forgotten uncle in a foreign land, an uncle who turns out to be a baron, and who with the money bequeaths his patent of nobility, so that one becomes a baron or baroness. Who would decline such a bequest as a mere drag to a free spirit eager for wine and roses? "I may be young," would be the comment, "but I'm not that stupid."

There are no such baronial uncles, of course; just another ploy, like tearing down Yad Vashem. But I would argue a bit about the patent of nobility, that is, a document attesting to one's wellborn origins. Such a document does exist for us Jews. It is called the Bible. The world acknowledges it as the greatest Book ever written, and in eastern European Jewry, every child was taught it as his or her natural heritage. To what extent that heritage is retrievable is the crux of this simple work. We can at least search the wreckage of European Jewry—the broken walls, the scorched timbers, the wide expanses of rubble, the overgrown graveyards with the toppled tombstones—for Jewish valuables. Is it conceivable that we may also find glowing whispering embers, which can rekindle in us some of the fire of old Yiddishkeit?

Three

THE FIRST DESTRUCTION

The Crown Jewel

Among the papers of Blaise Pascal, the great seventeenth-century French thinker—mathematician, theologian, experimental scientist—this scrawled fragment was found, after his death:

> The God of Abraham, Isaac, and Jacob, not the
> God of the philosophers and scholars . . .

About the time he wrote that, his Jewish contemporary, Baruch Spinoza, was breaking from the faith of his fathers, casting aside the God of Abraham, Isaac, and Jacob for an abstruse, pantheist deity of his own devising, and bringing the voice of skeptical modernism into western religious discourse. He was excommunicated, in consequence, by the nervous Jewish community of Amsterdam. Yet even as he was departing once for all from classic Judaism, his intellectual peer, Pascal, was arguing forcibly in his *Pensées* for the essential truth of the Jewish religion, failing which his own Christian faith would be baseless. In a day when the burning of the Talmud and even of Jews was still going on, such praise of things Hebrew was risky and rare. Pascal's insights into our heritage, and his acknowledgment of what Christianity owes to it, are notable even today. As for Spinoza, Albert Einstein called himself a Spinozist, and the philosopher's difficult works endure in controversy.

Not less than Christianity's debt to our heritage is surely that of Islam. The biblical content of the Koran, which I have read in translation with care, is self-evident. The voice of Mohammed speaking as Allah's prophet is new and powerful, and the emphasis in the narrative sequences often differs; for example, the story of Joseph in Egypt, as compared to the Genesis account, is colorfully expanded. Mohammed himself freely cites the Torah and the Hebrew prophets. Where the Koran and the Bible are at variance, Islamic authorities hold by dogma that the Koran is the pure light and our Scripture is unreliable. Let it be so for them. I simply note here that a second great religion, numbering almost a billion adherents, to an indisputable extent is rooted in our Bible.

Hebrew Scripture has thus inspired, in two faiths of later beginnings, the present religious life of half the human race. The original Book is still in our hands, still the crown jewel of our heritage. Surely we may take pride in possessing that Book, even before we open it again in our quest for guidance on where we stand today as Jews.

God's Eternal Present

Parts of the Bible fall in Homeric times, but when I read about Achilles fighting Hector outside the walls of Troy, I plunge across a vast black space of history to a world as remote as the moon. The Bible to me is all different, possibly because, as a Bronx boy of five, I was dragged in from a street game of one-a-cat or marbles several times a week, to study the Torah with a Mr. Horowitz. Ever since, Abraham, Isaac, and Jacob have seemed almost a part of my recent past, and I hardly exaggerate. Years later, when I was studying Talmud with my grandfather, I expressed boyish skepticism about the Revelation on Sinai. Unperturbed, my grandfather said, "Of course it happened. My father was there, and he told me about it."

"Oh, Zaideh, your *father*?" I protested. "Come on."

"Well, then, my grandfather or my great-grandfather, same thing," said Zaideh. "And would he lie to me?"

Zaideh knew all the rabbinic masters, with their dates, going back to Second Temple times. This mind-boggling collapsing of time was pure old Yiddishkeit. One finds the same time collapse in even starker form at the heart of the Passover Haggadah. *"In every generation a man is obligated to regard himself as having personally come out of Egypt, for it is written, 'And you shall tell your son, this is what God did for me when I left Egypt.'"* God's eternal present, as one might call such a notion of time, sounds through the Bible and the Talmud. It certainly jars the modern mind, and let me make plain that it is not a mystical idea. Jewish mysticism, which we will look at too, is something quite different. This eternal present is the everyday common sense of my Zaideh, of Mr. Horowitz, and of the Book of Isaiah. It takes some getting used to.

Now in our more familiar thinking about time, we can call up the words "three thousand years" on the computer screen with a flick of fingers, but the trouble is, no real meaning is conveyed. The phrase is too worn, the quantity too big. In high school texts, moreover, and in popular science writing, we are drowned in billions of years, dating back to the "big bang" of Creation, and to the evolving of life forms from a "primordial soup"; while we learn that the universe spans billions of "light-years," the light-year being the distance light travels during 365 days of ticking seconds, at nearly 200,000 miles per second. Such concepts and such figures leave us stupefied, and if we really think about them, frightened, we who live an eye blink of seventy or eighty earthly years. We shrug all that off and click on the TV, for a little distraction before bedtime.

That turnaway frame of mind we must here resist. Our aim in opening the Bible again is to unfold thirty telescoped centuries. We are not going back to Adam and Eve, nor to Abraham, Isaac, and Jacob, but to the First Destruction. In his vivid account of it, Graetz had to draw on the Bible as his primary source. For the Second Destruction, by contrast, there are numerous literary sources. There is even visible evidence. The Temple menorah juts from the frieze of the Arch of Titus in Rome, showing a triumphal procession carrying loot from fallen Jerusalem.

The First Destruction

Our folding telescope opens up to about twelve hundred years before the birth of a Jewish baby in Bethlehem, from which occurrence most of mankind dates its present history and business, so that a most uncommon calendar year ending in three zeros looms as I write. At that far reach in pre-Christian times, archaeologists have tried to dig up, and still argue about, traces of Joshua's conquest of Canaan. The Temple of Solomon was built a couple of centuries after Joshua's time, and until then Israel worshiped at a curtained Tabernacle in Shiloh, a few miles north of a mountainous site which later became Jerusalem. Solomon's Temple stood for four centuries.

Now six hundred years—Shiloh, plus the Temple—is a mighty long time, longer than the time from today back to Columbus. During that long stretch, as the Bible tells us, the Israelites endured invasions, waged wars of conquest, experienced victories and defeats, suffered internal dissension and treachery, and eventually split into two kingdoms, the North seceding from the South. The break happened in the reign of Solomon's unwise son, Rehoboam, when ten tribes revolted from the Davidic dynasty, formed a new monarchy and a new sacrificial cult, and cut themselves off from the central Temple worship in Jerusalem.

The Bible thereafter tracks the fortunes of both kingdoms, a sine curve of narrative, alternating piety and transgression, backsliding and repentance, godly kings and evil kings, return to the

Lord and falling away to strange gods. When peace smiles on the Israelites, paganism tends to seduce them. In disaster they cry out to the true God, and he sends a deliverer, as humble as Jephthah or as magnificent—for all his terrible failings—as David. Yet a slide to idol worship proceeds in both domains. Cabals and murders weaken internal coherence. Inept political policies provoke invasions, and eventual conquest, by the great powers of old.

The populous northern kingdom falls first to the Assyrians, and the Ten Tribes are carried into exile. Thereafter they figure largely in legend, placed now in remote Asia, now in dark Africa, and one account even makes them the red men of North America. In fact, most of them simply assimilate and disappear, though some mingle with later exiles. The rump southern kingdom, called Judaea and comprising only the tribe of Judah and a shrunken Benjamin, lasts another hundred thirty-six years, until the First Destruction by the Babylonians.

Why the main body of Israel vanished while Judaea survived and, though exiled, continues in life to the present hour—the hand moving this pen being that of a Judaean, i.e., a Jew—is one of the questions we are exploring. Studying this part of the Bible in English, one runs an obstacle course of numbered verses and strange names, especially once the Ten Tribes secede. The effort is worth it. These narratives are replete with unforgettable personalities—Deborah, Samson, David, Absalom, Ahab, Jezebel, Elijah, Elisha—brilliantly delineated in spare strong action scenes. While they play out the high drama, the common people work the holy soil, fight in the wars, live out their lives, and despite lapses serve their God, until the Babylonians break into Jerusalem to conquer a hostile Judaea once for all. They destroy the Temple and the capital city and carry Jerusalem's populace off into exile, leaving an abandoned waste where the seat of David's monarchy had been, a heap of stones inhabited by foxes and ghosts.

This happened almost six hundred years before the birth of the baby in Bethlehem.

The Return

That should have been the end of Jewish history. Conquest, collapse, exile, and dissolution were the usual fate of peoples in the region. The Bible tells of dwellers in Canaan who ceased to exist long before the Israelites came—Anakim, Emim, Refaim—displaced by Hittites, Ammonites, Moabites, and Amorites, who also eventually disappeared. Great empires like Assyria, Babylonia, and Egypt rose, fell, and expired, leaving only shards of their culture, with indecipherable inscriptions in forgotten writing. Once a nation had been routed and plundered, and the temples of their gods destroyed, that was that. Their gods were weak gods or no gods, that people's tale was finished, their culture withered, and they faded from the scene. The Judaeans broke the mold. Instead of melting away in exile they returned to Zion after some seventy years, as their prophet Jeremiah had predicted. They made the wasteland green and fruitful again, and built the Second Temple, which lasted close to six more centuries; and their alphabet, contemporaneous with Babylonian cuneiform and Egyptian hieroglyphics, is in print in Tel Aviv's morning papers.

This Return was not accomplished with Mosaic signs and wonders; no pillar of fire, no splitting of the sea, no manna from Heaven. It played out, in fact, in a way quite recognizable to us American Jews. Most of the exiles in prosperous Babylon just stayed there. The few thousand zealots who trekked back to the land were believers, aboriginal Zionists, for whom the Jewish God had not failed at all. Rather, in the Temple's destruction, they saw his hand made visible in history, even as it had been at the Red Sea. The Torah had taught, after all, that the One God had chosen Israel as his holy people, had given them his Law, and had promised them the land of Canaan on condition that they keep that Law, failing which, "the land would vomit them forth," as it had the previous iniquitous inhabitants. Their prophets had echoed the warning down the generations, his people had not listened, and it had all come to pass.

The Torah had also predicted that God would not wholly abandon them after the downfall, that a remnant would return and restore the Promised Land to its lost glory. These returners needed no second Moses to urge Cyrus the Great, the Persian conqueror of Babylon, to let his people go. Despite the fall of Jerusalem, Israel's God still commanded awe in the region. "The Lord God of Heaven," Cyrus proclaimed, using the Torah name for God, "has given me all the kingdoms of earth, and has commanded me to build him a House in Jerusalem, that is in Judaea." He encouraged the exiles to go back, and his successor, Darius, underwrote from the royal treasury the cost of rebuilding the Second Temple.

Abandoning to philosophers the thickets of theology about the ways of God in such complicated matters, let us look straight at what the Bible is here telling us about the ways of the Jews. The Torah had been Israel's heritage for hundreds and hundreds of years. In two shattering dithyrambs of warning in Leviticus and Deuteronomy, Moses had predicted the straying after other gods, the downfall, the exile, and the return of a remnant. How was it that the people of God, knowing the Mosaic Law and its warnings, drifted time and again into idolatry and disaster, to be rescued by judges like Gideon and Samuel, or restored for a while to the true faith by the great prophets, until after many centuries God's forbearance—or their luck—ran out?

A Kind Word for Paganism

The gods of the ancients have been extinct for so long that it is hard to think seriously of them as deities. The Greek and Roman pantheons still figure in poetry and drama, but it never crosses anybody's mind to bow down to Minerva or Jupiter. The wonderfully preserved

Egyptian wall paintings and sculptures, first exhumed from the sand dunes of the ages by Napoleon, show the gods as animistic monsters, figments of a nightmarish religion. The idols of Canaan were worse yet, according to the Bible, their modes of worship sometimes gruesome, sometimes depraved; and little survives of Canaanite religion, comparable to the monumental art of Egypt, and the beautiful works of Greece. What then possessed our ancestors, who had in hand the Torah of Moses, and teachers like Amos, Isaiah, and Jeremiah, to depart from their advanced faith to serve these relatively crude Canaanite fetishes?

We have light on this perplexity from Hollywood. I am perfectly serious about this. The Bible is an inexhaustible mine for film-making, calling as it does for much warlike action, lavish pagan revels involving lots of nearly naked dancing women, and an invariable spectacular disaster demonstrating God's wrath. "Wall to wall production values," they say out there. The Golden Calf story, the *locus classicus* of such films, provided the climax for two Cecil B. De Mille blockbusters, both called *The Ten Commandments*, produced thirty-three years apart.

In this genre, a lesser-known film called *Sodom and Gomorrah* is worth noting here. *Sodom and Gomorrah* presents Abraham's nephew Lot as a sort of weak-kneed, middle-aged Moses, vainly cautioning the cavorting ladies of Sodom and their mocking half-nude queen that God is going to punish them for their wicked ways. This has nothing whatever to do with the Bible narrative, but the production values are all there, wall to wall. The unfortunate actor who plays Lot, reading his lines as though under a court order to do so, finally is too repelled by all the debauchery to hang around any longer, so he leads the Jewish people (who will not exist until several centuries later) out of Sodom, whereupon lightning strikes the evil city, the buildings fall down, and his wife duly gets coated over with salt.

Kidding the movies is no trick. My sole point here is that even in an idiocy like *Sodom and Gomorrah* Hollywood has got paganism right. Paganism was blatant, sensual, usually drunken, often obscene, and above all tangible, visible, eye-catching. In Solomon's awesome Temple there was gorgeous pageantry, to be sure, but it was all very solemn; ranks of robed Levites blowing trumpets, playing ancient instruments, and chanting psalms during somber sacrificial ceremonies, not a half-dressed dancer of either sex in sight. What was missing above all, and what paganism always offered, was an Image; a colossal figure to bow down to, a Dagon, an Astarte, a Baal, a Bel, at least a Calf. The second commandment was stark:

> Thou shalt not make for thyself any carved idol or any likeness of any thing that is in heaven above, or that is in the earth beneath, or that is in the water under the earth; thou shalt not bow down to them, nor serve them.

The idea of an unseen Creator of the fathomless universe who interested himself in human affairs, loved mankind, and chose a people to be his witness on earth, was tough to grasp then as now, compared to the digestible attractions of paganism. The local movie house, after all, still outdraws the church and synagogue ten to one, and for the indolent and lax among us, there are always the couch, the tube, and the remote control for tuning in on *Sodom and Gomorrah*.

The Second Temple Rises

Our time telescope is still almost fully extended. Now we collapse it through five centuries, which will bring us down about to the murder of Julius Caesar in 44 B.C. If I have been beating this telescope metaphor into the ground, I now fold it up for good. I am only trying to convey the long time-spread of the Jewish experience, the depths of our roots in the human story. For if nothing else, this awareness can bring us some strength to confront the open question that prompted this book. After the stupendous bloodletting of the German massacre, has Hitler in fact prevailed, so that there can be no future Jewish generations worth mentioning?

The Hebrew Bible's history ends with the Return to a much diminished Zion, enfeebled by skepticism, quarreling factions, and intermarriage. Yet in seven years, the Temple is rebuilt under the patronage of the Persian monarchy, despite slanderous reports sent to the Persian court by hostile local inhabitants, intended to cut off what we would today call foreign aid. Two master spirits, Ezra and Nehemiah, come up from Persia to inspire a religious revival, and the reconstruction of Jerusalem's walls. This work goes on under constant armed attack by what we would today call terrorists. The last prophets picture a Messianic age to come, mingling their reproofs with a word of comfort for a troubled dark present. Despite all the gloom, something irreversible has happened to the Jews. The agonizing lesson of the First Destruction has sunk in. Backsliders may long abound, but the brutal surgery has excised idol worship, the near-fatal cancer of Abraham's people, once for all.

One lesson having been learned, however, another harder one awaits. It will take all six centuries of the Second Temple era for it to register.

Four

THE SECOND DESTRUCTION

Hebraism and Hellenism

That rich tapestry of antiquity, the Second Temple time, is a treasure trove of plots and characters for novelists yet unborn, and of grist for future films and TV specials. I offer here only a glimpse, no more, of a tumultuous era that shook and eventually tumbled down the ancient world, a brawling crucible of history in which giants stride across the Judaean stage.

The eminent Victorian critic and poet Matthew Arnold, in a passage of his *Culture and Anarchy,* throws oblique light on the Second Temple and its fall:

> Hebraism and Hellenism—between these two points of influence moves our world. The uppermost idea with Hellenism is to see things as they really are; the uppermost idea with Hebraism is conduct and obedience. Nothing can do away with this ineffaceable difference.

Both polar terms are borrowed from the writings of the apostate Jew Heinrich Heine. Arnold's actual subject, in a chapter called "Hebraism and Hellenism," is the dwindling of the Christian faith in his own spirit, and—as he sees it—in all modern culture. "Hebraism" was Heine's literary locution for what we call today "Judeo-Christian values," though in my view this melding blurs a schism which produced a new religion. By Hellenism he simply meant Greek rationalism and Greek civilization, borne on the crest of conquest throughout the Middle East by Alexander the Great.

Marching into Judaea, Alexander of Macedon found a peculiar people living by a decidedly peculiar Law, the Mosaic heritage, transmitted by the prophets to a religious council called the Men of the Great Assembly, *Anshei Knesset Hagdolah*. By this time the Judaism we know was taking discernible shape. The punctilious ceremonial forms, the general order of prayer, the prescriptions for daily, weekly, and festival practice, were the common way of life in the land. This all-embracing religious structure, called the Halakhah—literally, The Way—had emerged as the pristine form of what observant Jews today still practice. The conqueror demanded no change in that Way, only fealty to his rule, which the Judaeans willingly granted. And so it was that the two great cultures which, according to Matthew Arnold, shaped the Western world, met head on.

When Greek Meets Jew

Alexander the Great's tutor, Aristotle, was the pupil of Plato, who recorded and immortalized the philosophy of Socrates. The Greeks were certainly pagans, but an ironic attitude toward their gods, for which Socrates was in fact condemned to die, already pervaded serious Greek thought. Aristotle's Supreme Being, the unmoved prime mover of the universe, was a far cry from Zeus. In his rarefied metaphysics the prudent Aristotle let the divinities of Mount Olympus alone, possibly with the fate of Socrates in mind. Plato too is gingerly about the gods, though in the *Crito*, he has the dying

Socrates instruct a disciple to "pay a cock to Aesculapius," the god of healing. So the master of Greek wisdom departs this life, leaving thinkers down the ages to make what they will of the pious gesture, whether it really happened that way, or Plato as a dramatic writer gave his teacher that unforgettable exit.

Matthew Arnold presents Hebraism and Hellenism as equals, almost as thesis and antithesis, the synthesis of which produced modern culture. Perhaps the encounter of Greece and Judaea was not one of equals but rather of incommensurables. Take Greek religion at any level—the popular worship of beautiful sculptures personifying the Olympian deities, or Socrates' relentless probing for final truth behind the shadows of human existence, or Aristotle's arid pursuit of cause and effect to the Uncaused Cause—and one is in a different universe of perception from Bible and Talmud. If Hebraism and Hellenism are in any sense equal, it is only in that both are enduring systems of thought and action encompassing all human experience. Otherwise, the gap is not only ineffaceable, as Arnold declared. It is bottomless.

Between Mosaic religion and early paganism there was also a total gap. When the children of Abraham worshiped Baal, they were falling from an exalted faith to primitive local cults. Yet the encounter with Hellenism was of another order. While many Jews of the time were repelled by what they perceived as abominations in Greek beliefs and ways, there were those who felt that in the people of Euclid and Archimedes they were confronting a superior wisdom and culture. The Talmud expresses all this with customary pith: *"If they tell you there is wisdom in the Greeks, believe it; if they tell you there is holiness in the Greeks, do not believe it."*

Hellas had many charms new to Jewry besides its science and philosophy. It offered the architecture and sculpture which still awe the world, the theater of Aeschylus, Sophocles, Euripides, and Aristophanes, the hedonistic lifestyle, and the glorifying of the human body in magnificent quasi-religious athletic games. Withal, it was the mind of Greece which really hit Jewry where it lived. The power of the Oral Law lay in the intellectual muscle of Talmudic process, the intricacy, the subtlety, the rigor with which each nuance of the Bible was drawn out and linked with every other, so that the whole formed one supernal design, interwoven of forcible human thinking and Godly revelation. When Greek wisdom burst on the Judaean scene with the coming of Alexander, this very excellence of Talmudism became a vulnerability. The Hebrew genius for profound and exact thought seemed to some to be meeting its match.

To the Jewish Hellenizers, this encounter brought liberation and enlightenment, an opportunity to loosen or shrug off the yoke of the Law, and to rejoice in the sunlit pleasures of epicurean Greece. A new word of the blackest opprobrium now entered the old Hebrew tongue. One can hear it today, hurled in the yeshiva at a boyish scoffer: *apikoros.* More than *heretic,* more than *unbeliever,* more even than *atheist, apikoros*—in Yiddish, *apikayress*—is a term for an aggressively and irredeemably Godless person. Never mind that Epicurus himself took an easier view of religion, amounting to a mild skepticism bordering on indifference, and that his was an elevated philosophy of enjoyment of life's transient good things, in a detached spirit more intellectual than fleshly. That was an overlooked subtlety. For the Hellenizers, and for the halakhic faithful whom they offended and infuriated, Epicureanism simply and baldly meant a free life of wine, women, and song, of the pleasures of the table, the pleasures of sport, the pleasures of the theater and the arena, the pleasures of art and the dance, in short the indulgence in all earthly pleasures, perhaps even including the pleasure of Temple-going, providing it did not imply a killjoy commitment to the dour restrictions of the Halakhah.

Here is Graetz on what ensued. I cannot put it more succinctly, nor improve upon it.

> As has repeatedly occurred in the history of thinking nations, lack of moderation on the one side brought forth exaggeration on the other. Those Judaeans who saw with pain and rage the

attempts of the Hellenists, grouped themselves into a party which clung desperately to the Law and the customs of their fathers. . . . Every religious custom was to them of inviolable sanctity. A more complete contrast than was presented by these two parties can hardly be imagined. They understood each other as little as if they had not been sons of the same tribe, people of the same nation.

Plus ça change! As my historian said, if there is any hope for us, it is that we remain a people of passionate contradictions.

That perfervid break never closed, never healed, never scarred over during the long Second Temple era. Throughout Judaea's vicissitudes in politics and war, as a province under Greek and then Roman rule, it persisted fresh and sore, sometimes inflamed and dangerous.

The conflict peaked in Alexander's fragmented empire a hundred fifty years after his death, under a Syriac Greek monarch, Antiochus Epiphanes, descended from one of his generals. Antiochus set out to eradicate the Hebrew religion—circumcision, Torah, and all—and in its place to force the Greek gods upon Judaea. This seemed the final triumph of the Hellenizers. In the way of such things, the faithful reacted by rising in the famous Hasmonean revolt, sparked by an old priest of that family. The brilliant military victories of Judah Maccabee and his brothers halted the Hellenizing excesses, restored the desecrated Temple, and reestablished Judaea as a free country until the Roman legions came, and with them the procurators. The memory of that relatively brief glory, perhaps a hundred years in all, lives on in the holiday of Hanukkah. No later event as yet holds a place in our liturgy, though the Second Destruction merges with the First in the mourning ceremonies of Tisha B'Av.

The Septuagint

One momentous accomplishment of Hellenism was beyond reversal by the Maccabees. By hands unknown, at a time undetermined, our Torah was translated into Greek. Tradition has it that a Ptolemaic dynast summoned seventy-two scholars to Alexandria, and put them to translating the Torah, each in a separate chamber, possibly so as to catch them in inconsistencies. By divine inspiration, all their versions came out identical, down to thirteen variant readings intended to forestall pagan questions or jeers. Such is a Talmudic account, and Hebrew scholarship calls this work *Targum Ha'shivim,* that is, the Translation of the Seventy.

Later, book by book, the whole Hebrew Bible was rendered into Greek, and the world knows this version by the Latin word for seventy, the *Septuagint.* When Constantine turned his empire toward Christianity, the Septuagint became, with the Gospels in their original Greek, the Holy Scripture of the Roman world. It remains that today in the Greek Orthodox Church. Subsequent famous translations of our Scriptures—the Latin Vulgate of Jerome, the German of Luther, the King James Bible that one finds in American hotel rooms—may have drawn on the canonical Septuagint, but all three emphasize that their source is, in Jerome's phrase, the *Hebraica veritas,* the original text of the Jews.

The discovery of the Dead Sea scrolls gave Bible scholarship a jolt of fresh energy. Minute study still goes on, checking our Bible and the Septuagint against the scrolls. The Hebrew text is emerging remarkably confirmed. The Septuagint also comes off well, and modern criticism speculates that it was produced by teams of scholars in Egypt, working over a hundred years or so. The job was masterful whoever did it, for the Septuagint was the delayed-action bomb that blew up paganism. Once the minds of Greece and Rome had been opened to the revelation of the God of the Jews, there was no ultimate retreat from conversion. The old gods slowly crumbled, shallow outdated metaphors.

Christian scholarship acknowledges, indeed teaches, that the Septuagint prepared the way for the Gospels, and that may partly account for the equivocal present status of the Greek translation in our faith. The Talmud in tractate *Megillah* (Scroll), which deals with liturgical readings, endorses the Septuagint as an inspired work. The story of the seventy-two scholars is there given in full with the variant readings, and the rabbis concur that Greek, as "the most beautiful of the Japheth tongues," is suitable even for writing a Torah scroll. Yet the liturgy of a minor fast, the Tenth of Tevet, includes the translation of the Torah into Greek among our national calamities. What happened, to make of the Septuagint a *b'khiah l'dorot*, a weeping for the generations?

The American Jews of Alexandria

At the death of Alexander, his empire was partitioned by his generals, and two rival dynasties arose, the Seleucids in Syria and the Ptolemies in Egypt. Whenever these two countries warred, Judaea endured times of trouble, clamped between them by geography as Israel is today. Meantime, the Hebrew diasporas in Babylon and Egypt flourished. The Babylonian Talmud affords us encyclopedic knowledge of that community, but about the Egyptian Jews we know strangely little. They have faded from our historic awareness, except for scholars who study their great Alexandrian thinker, Philo.

Yet they were a prosperous, powerful, and in some ways unique Jewry, for they not only spoke everyday Greek, they may actually have read the Torah in the synagogue on Shabbat in the Septuagint. To us that is unthinkable, but not only had they apparently lost Aramaic, the lingua franca of dispersed Jewry—the Yiddish of ancient times—it seems that they knew little Hebrew. Even Philo's Scriptural citations appear to come from the Septuagint.

The rabbis of the Talmud regarded the Egyptian Jews with a

touch of awe at their affluence, much as Israelis today tend to think about American Jews. Their synagogue in Alexandria was so huge, the Talmud tells us, that liturgical responses had to be signaled to the rear reaches of the congregation with a system of colored flags! They maintained regular contact with the Holy Land, and were scrupulous about Temple contributions. Though thoroughly Hellenized, and well aware of Greek philosophy and culture, they nevertheless as a body staunchly kept up the traditions of their fathers for centuries: the dietary laws, the Sabbath, the regular learning, the festivals, and the limits on relations with the heathens.

Philo does record, nevertheless, in sorrow and anger, the occurrence of apostasy, and he lists three sorts of defectors: those overcome by the desire for banned foods and pagan women, which he severely calls, "yielding to the belly and to organs beneath"; prosperous climbers eager to be accepted in high Egyptian social circles, to achieve which they shed Judaic ways and even identity; and "uprooted individuals," torn loose from their traditions by the thought and art of Greece, to become rebellious mockers of Jewish beliefs, traditions, and their own kin.

Perhaps the fast of the Tenth of Tevet deplores the spread of another faith through the medium of our Hebrew Scripture, in the Septuagint translation, or perhaps it is only a muffled threnody over the vanished American Jews of Alexandria.

The Second Destruction

Coleridge once said that the only subject left for epic poetry was the fall of Jerusalem. The catastrophe does offer characters, scenes, and themes of awesome grandeur: three ancient great powers, Egypt, Babylon, and Rome, in action; the blinding figure of Yeshu, the Galilean baby, grown up and commencing his conquest of the Roman soul; the devil's brew of Jerusalem's court politics under

Herod the Great, spiced with royal murders and erotic intrigue; and thrown in for dramatic subplots, the assassination of Caesar and the passions of Antony and Cleopatra.

All this awaits some young poet eager to take on Homer and Milton, but we are here seeking only to understand how our forebears survived the Second Destruction. After all, Ptolemaic Egypt is long gone, and an Arabic Egypt flourishes in its ruins; Seleucid Greek Syria is obscure dusty history; Babylon is gone, and where the world once marveled at its hanging gardens, Saddam Hussein conceals his mass slaughter weapons; and the Roman Empire is gone, entombed in Gibbon. Yet an independent Judaea, two millennia after the Hasmoneans, once more flies its flag in Jerusalem. This seems worth looking into.

For a prose narrative of the Second Fall, nothing matches the work of the historian Josephus. Himself a commander in the battles, though hardly an admirable one, this Jerusalem Jew settled in Rome and wrote his history hoping to obtain the approval of the emperor Vespasian. Graetz takes his account with skeptical hostility, despising his fellow author for the equivocal part he played in that ancient war. But there is no denying the classic force with which Josephus depicts the three-year battle of the religious rebels, called Kanaim, roughly Zealots, against Rome. For all ages, he portrays the final crushing advance of Titus's army through Jerusalem's walls, and the fearful last hours of the Second Temple in flames and collapse.

Josephus exonerates Titus of the torching, ascribing it to an excess of the rampaging soldiers, but any competent military commander would have known that destroying the Sanctuary would probably break the back of a religious uprising. So it did. Titus's recorded cruelties do not jibe with any tenderness about burning the Temple. A futile flare of Zealot resistance was snuffed out at Masada, in the year 73 A.D., in a mass suicide. The crushing of a briefly successful revolt against Roman rule under Bar Kokhba, in the year 135, ended the Jewish role in political history for eighteen hundred years. Josephus, incidentally, got the emperor's imprimatur. Peace to his dust.

Yavneh

In the Second Temple time, prophecy and prophets had long ceased, but master spirits had not. Even as Jeremiah had prophesied unheeded against defying Babylon before the First Temple's fall, six centuries later a master spirit, Rabbi Jochanan ben Zakkai, vainly advocated compliance with Roman rule. This time there was no magnanimous conqueror like Cyrus to help the Jews rebuild the Temple. This was Rome. The Temple was gone. But Jochanan ben Zakkai acted in time, even while the siege of Jerusalem was at its worst, to preserve Jewry.

The details are shrouded in conflicting accounts. We know that he escaped the beleaguered capital and obtained permission from the Roman besiegers to open a Talmudical academy at Yavneh, a small coastal town west of Jerusalem, and to bring scholars there to carry on the Pharisaic teachings. One story goes that before Jerusalem fell he was smuggled out in a coffin, against the orders of the Zealot defenders, and brought to the Roman commander, who granted this insignificant boon because Jochanan had been a known peace advocate. When the Temple was a heap of cooling ashes, Torah learning was already going on at a new spiritual center in the Holy Land. In time, a new Sanhedrin, a supreme council of scholars, was convened at Yavneh, to replace the Sanhedrin that had sat in the Temple's Hewn Stone Chamber. Thus Jochanan ben Zakkai in the last agonizing hours of the Second Temple, improvised a new structure of Judaism which has sustained the folk to this day; a moveable civilization, with an eternal constitution in the Torah, and an enduring portable culture in the Talmud.

Other factors may have seemed more important at the time, but this proved the key to the scattered nation's remarkable survival. All around the Roman-ruled Mediterranean littoral, and in far-flung inland places as well, Jewish communities had existed since the first exile. The most advanced of these was in Babylon, a great seat of Jewish learning and commerce, safe from Rome in the Parthian kingdom far to the east. The Egyptian diaspora, on the other hand, though populous and strong, suffered much by recurrent anti-Jewish riots and pogroms. This once resplendent Jewry, reduced by Hellenistic penetration, imperial Roman disfavor, and the hostility of the heathens, slowly died off. But the other communities hung on and on, long after the fall of Rome, and crucial to their vitality was awareness of, and contact with, a center of Judaic learning and spirit in the Holy Land.

In a word, Jochanan ben Zakkai brought off a miracle of restoration, perhaps greater than Darius's financing of the Second Temple. He moved Jewish central worship from Jerusalem, where it had been sited for a thousand years, to the Jewish brain.

Five

THE THIRD DESTRUCTION: I

The Enlightenment

Pledged to brevity in searching the past, this account now traverses a time tunnel of mind-numbing length—no less than one thousand seven hundred years—hurrying toward a gleam at the end called the Enlightenment, which dazzles eyes emerging from the Dark Ages. In general culture the term *Enlightenment* implies the shaking-off of Church scholasticism and dogma, the leap from medievalism to the new thinking of Bacon, Newton, Locke, and Voltaire, a passage of the human spirit from darkness to day. Gradually one discerns, blinking in the glare of this new light, that God's people are still around, practicing their religion very much as taught at Yavneh, though Yavneh itself has sunk from sight many centuries ago, as have the Egyptian and Babylonian diasporas, while Judaea has declined to a thinly settled stony desolation, a mere patch of a Syriac province under the Ottoman Turks, where some Jews still cling to the desiccated land, maintaining in Safed a stubborn core of great scholars.

There are now adventurous Jews to be found from the frozen reaches of Czarist Russia to the raw European lodgments in the Americas. Most of the nation-in-exile lives in two vigorous diasporas, the Sephardim of Mediterranean lands and the Ashkenazim of northern, central, and eastern Europe. An enormous rabbinic literature has grown up in these two traditions, differing in detail but agreeing in the large. The Kabbalistic mysticism rooted in Safed is spreading. The dispersed body of the folk—in the warm modern Hebrew term, *Amkha*, "Your people"—displaced from the sacred soil, and like as not forbidden to own land elsewhere, wrests a living from shopkeeping, skilled labor, moneylending, or whatever other modes of breadwinning are permitted them by their Christian or Muslim rulers, under special restrictive laws of varying harshness. So Amkha endures almost unchanged—despite ever-recurring expropriations and expulsions, despite the Crusader bloodbaths over two centuries, despite the forced conversions, despite the flames of the Inquisitions, despite the sporadic massacres all over Europe, despite the general immurement in ghettos—despite all, Amkha endures, father teaching son, son filling father's place, the portable civilization proceeding on its eternal way.

This staying power of our scattered forebears through such an aeon must be called a wonder of world history. Swing back that arc of seventeen centuries from the pivot in Yavneh, and one is in the time frame of Abraham; swing it forward from the present day, and the year 4000 is nearly in sight! Who would be bold enough to predict that mankind as a whole, let alone the Jews, will survive to that year? Yet if our people are to fulfill in any modern sense our biblical destiny as a "light to the nations," it is in setting this example of the will to live on, surmounting all odds to survive, and to pass on a heritage. We have been preserving our history and our Godly lore to the present day, as mankind itself is now challenged to preserve this water-girt globe, humanity's precarious little heritage and home, for the generations to come.

Gaonate and Haskalah

One reward of synagogue-going is the people you get to meet. It was how I made friends long ago, for instance, with Israel's shy little Nobel laureate novelist, S. Y. Agnon, who wore a yarmulke, lived in what he called a hovel, and wrote artfully simple tales of deep truth. More recently, I encountered a history professor who sent me a striking essay he has written on a thousand-year period of Jewry, from the Gaonate to the Haskalah. Concerning what other folk would one write a historical essay in a single thousand-year bite? Yet it is a logical bite, for between the Gaonate and the Haskalah—Hebrew for the Enlightenment—there arches our people's immense transit from the fall of Rome to the rise of Hitler.

In classic times a Gaon was the head of an academy in Babylon, and a high arbiter of Jewish law. The office of the Gaonate prevailed well into the Middle Ages, but as Jewry's center of gravity shifted from Babylon westward to North Africa and Europe, the Gaonate slipped into desuetude. The honorific title still persists for rabbis of great learning. In our day an undisputed Gaon was my teacher Moshe Feinstein, a little man of humble lifestyle like Agnon, but otherwise (yarmulkes aside) a different sort of Jew.

In Israel on the street where Agnon lived, municipal signs urged passersby to be quiet, for the great artist was at work. In Moshe Feinstein's small Manhattan flat the foot traffic was incessant, while the sage was writing responses to legal inquiries from all over the world, or answering them on the telephone, or taking ten minutes to eat his dinner. Anybody could come and go—a politician soliciting his favor, a woman whose husband was making bedroom problems, a famed scholar from abroad, a poor father with a daughter to marry off, a student baffled by a knotty Gemara page, a brash novelist seeking Torah—anybody! Such was Reb Moshe Feinstein, a true modern-day Gaon.

I am not sure what Reb Moshe's view of the Haskalah was, the subject never came up in his *shiur* ("seminar") that I attended, but my grandfather's opinion was clear and emphatic. For him, the Haskalah was the ruin of Yiddishkeit.

Excursus: The Return of Paganism

Pagan Hellenism rested on sand, a religion that was charming nonsense. The tide of Christianity came in and swept away, with the sand-sculpture gods, Greek art, science, and philosophy, and most of the voluminous Greek-inspired Roman art and thought as well. Everywhere in the Greco-Roman world works of art of surpassing and irreplaceable beauty were smashed. Temples to the gods became churches or were torn down for paving stones. Greek was almost forgotten in the West, the sensuous and ribald writings of Horace and Catullus were submerged under Church Latin, and philosophy floated on the tide only as the cowed handmaid to theology, always suspect as verging on heresy. That paganism could ever return in Europe seemed beyond possibility; but there are tides in the affairs of men, and here is our friend Matthew Arnold again, in his short poetic masterpiece "Dover Beach":

> The sea of faith was once, too, at the full . . .
> But now I only hear its melancholy, long, withdrawing roar
> . . . down the vast edges drear
> And naked shingles of the world . . .

When Arnold wrote that, the nineteenth-century assault on Christianity was becoming a main theme of serious European thought; like the opening notes of Beethoven's Fifth Symphony, *Fate knocking at the door* of revealed religion. Heaven had been opened up by Copernicus, Galileo, and Newton as a limitless black void, spangled here and there with unimaginably distant gigantic bodies; the new science of geology was asserting that Earth had been laid down in layers over many millions of years; and Charles Darwin was identifying Adam and Eve, at least in the popular view, as hairy primates walking on their knuckles. All this shook up serious men like Matthew Arnold, for whom the Bible was on the one hand sacred, on the other hand apparently hopelessly dated.

What Arnold was discerning and agonizing over was his own uneasy sense that Godly Hebraism was going out, and that pagan Hellenism minus its pantheon was coming back in; a world view contemptuous of all gods and revelations, and confident as Socrates had been in seeking truth with the unaided inquiring human mind. "*Écrasez l'infâme!*" was Voltaire's cry; erase the infamous prison of old superstitions! The Religion of Reason, a new humanism proclaimed by Robespierre and his fellow French revolutionaries, was in the ascendant. This was the Enlightenment, and this was the Haskalah.

Mendelssohn

Moses Mendelssohn, known in Jewry as the Father of the Haskalah, and in Germany as the Jewish Socrates, was a man of weak physique but formidable mind. Mendelssohn still holds a place in German thought as one who influenced Kant's metaphysics and aesthetics. Among his philosophic labors he tried to reconcile Hebraism and the reviving Hellenism—an intellectual feat akin to squaring the circle—with a new-fashioned concept of universalist ethics and religion. To Judaism, working with collaborators, he contributed a German translation of the Torah with his own commentary, all printed in Hebrew characters. For his pains he was subjected to violent abuse by eminent Talmudic rabbis, while his German admirers were hounding him to explain why—since Judaism and Christianity were simply two aspects of one rational universal faith—the Jewish

Socrates did not accept Jesus. His German enemies, on the other hand, made out a nerve-shattering case against him as a crypto-Spinozist. Mendelssohn fought off these challenges throughout his too-short life. His descendants, less heroically disposed, one after another converted to Christianity. The best known of these, his baptized grandson Felix Mendelssohn, composed a violin concerto much favored by virtuosos. "Let's go to Carnegie Hall tonight," your friend may say, "Isaac Stern is doing the Mendelssohn." So the name of the Father of the Haskalah survives outside academe.

My grandfather may never have heard of Moses Mendelssohn. There really were two waves of the Haskalah, the first in western Europe, the second—delayed by almost a hundred years—in the Yiddish-speaking east. Western Jews like Mendelssohn, including my greatly admired Heinrich Graetz, tended to look down on Yiddish as a vulgar jargon, and on the eastern Jews who spoke it as a disheveled low-class branch of our folk. This prejudice among the liberated western Jews against the *Ostjuden* was an ominous hint of things to come in Europe.

Enter Napoleon.

Napoleon's Sanhedrin

"Is it something good for the Jews?" my mother used to ask me about any political development. Napoleon did spread the French Revolution's liberal ideas throughout Europe, albeit with shot and shell, so Mama might well have considered his career good for the Jews. At least nobody can fault Napoleon for not thinking big, whether redrawing the borders of Europe in blood, or sponsoring and enacting the Code Napoleon, or solving the Jewish Question.

With Emancipation in the air of the Enlightenment, and the status of the Jews becoming an anomaly, Napoleon convoked an "Assembly of Jewish Notables" to answer twelve written questions, designed to find out whether Judaism conflicted with patriotism, civil obedience, or public morals. The answers were acceptably bland. He next summoned a "Sanhedrin" to enact these answers into Jewish law. Magnificently staged by the French but meagerly attended by leading Jews, this conclave did what he wanted and then adjourned *sine die* (no date for reconvening), an obscure ineffectual blip in the Jewish tale.

This bizarre Sanhedrin nevertheless epitomized a new time for Europe's Jews. In the wake of Napoleon's meteoric streak through history, they surged into new freedom, prosperity, and prominence almost everywhere in western and central Europe. So far and fast did Emancipation go, that a mere fifty years after Napoleon died on St. Helena, a Jew presided over the British Empire.

Coningsby/Codlingsby

Isaac D'Israeli, the father of Benjamin Disraeli, was a freethinking Sephardic Jew living in London. Irked by a forty-pound fine imposed on him by synagogue elders, he withdrew from the community in a huff, and in time had his children baptized; thereby enabling his son to reach "the top of the greasy pole," as Disraeli once facetiously termed the prime ministry. A commonplace shul squabble thus affected world events, for in those years, Benjamin Disraeli could not otherwise have entered public office. His acquisition of controlling shares in the Suez Canal capped England's ascent to global "*dominion over palm and pine,*" in Kipling's poetic phrase, and the baptized Jew's place in history is secure.

In British eyes and in his own, Disraeli was never anything but a plain Jew. Preeminent in Tory politics, in a perennial seesaw for power with the dour liberal William Gladstone, this flamboyant man also found the time to write very popular novels, to the chagrin of such contemporaries as Trollope and Thackeray. It was as if

Franklin Roosevelt during his presidency had turned out surefire best-sellers like Mr. Tom Clancy. In caricature Disraeli was regularly savaged as a Jew, never more so than in Thackeray's spoof of Disraeli's novel *Coningsby*.

Thackeray called this burlesque *Codlingsby*, a jibe all England could recognize, for in vulgar Yid jokes the Jew always talked through his nose, like a man with a cold. Pitilessly Thackeray carved up the romantic hero Coningsby, modeled on Disraeli himself, as well as an idealized Jew in the story named Sidonia, a noble mastermind of vast wealth, pictured with a big hook nose in Thackeray's own pen-and-ink sketches. I read Disraeli's book and the travesty long ago, and I remember the bestseller as a fustian artifact, while the parody was quite funny, scurrilous artwork and all. Encountering Thackeray afterward in a London club, the great Tory leader publicly cut the novelist dead. Of the two, he probably drew more blood, for Thackeray was abnormally sensitive to social slights. Nevertheless there stands *Codlingsby* in English literature, the red line Emancipation could not cross.

"So what?" the reader may well ask. Thackeray was just a scribbler, after all. Disraeli was occupied in the affairs of a grandiose empire, and caricatures are the gnat bites of the political swamp. Quite so, but able caricature can convey harsh truths or half-truths. In political cartooning the newly freed Jews tended to show up as many prejudiced Europeans still regarded them: sly, grasping, and foreign at best, evil and disgusting at worst. Emerging from the shadows of the ghetto into the light, the Jew was now fair game. Emancipation laws protected him, but they could not alter his image, fixed by the ostracism of centuries, nor could Disraeli by writing *Coningsby*. To unconvinced Europeans the emancipated Jew remained Codlingsby, half a joke and half an unwelcome intruder.

In France, the cradle of Emancipation, the joke ceased to be funny when the intruder, personified in Alfred Dreyfus, had to stand court-martial as a traitor. The national turmoil over the falsely accused army officer is an important motif of Marcel Proust's towering novel *Remembrance of Things Past,* which is nothing like *Coningsby,* except that both books were written by assimilated Jews. The Dreyfus case rose not just out of the social resistance embodied in cartoons and in Proust. Overnight, as it were, a body of new thought about the liberated Hebrews was yeasting in Europe. The outdated Christian doctrine about "the cursed race" was metamorphosing into an inflammatory brew of pseudo-anthropology, popularized by Houston Chamberlain, the British son-in-law of the anti-Semitic Richard Wagner.

According to this view the races of humanity differed in quality, the north Europeans or "Aryans" ranking highest and noblest, the Jew so low and degenerate as to threaten Europe's culture and social fabric. Such were the improvisations of the French Count Gobineau, an eccentric thinker and diplomat, and strangely a friend of Tocqueville. To readers who lived during the Hitler era, or who have waded through *Mein Kampf,* the lucubrations of Chamberlain and Gobineau should sound familiar, for here are the sources of the Fuehrer's racial doctrines. In this regard he made up nothing. He differed in what he did about them.

Uncle Baruch

A modern Hebrew poem I reread often is *Ha'matmid* by Chaim Nakhman Bialik, a sort of Jewish Matthew Arnold, imbued with an old faith yet unable to hold to it, like Arnold, and writing acerbic essays and melancholy poetry on the theme. In this wonderful poem, at once celebratory and elegiac, Bialik buries his own Talmudic youth, and rears over it a lasting work of art as a memorial stone. The title is untranslatable, though a near paraphrase might be *The Driven Talmud Student.* One senses that this must have been Bialik himself. Wearing out his young life over the Gemara, studying dawn to dusk, and then by candlelight half the night, the *matmid* of the poem dreams of becoming an *iluy*, a Talmud prodigy, and one day a Gaon. Such was my own uncle Baruch in his youth. How the Haskalah snared Baruch, I cannot tell. In my novel *Inside, Outside* there is a portrait of Uncle Baruch the Haskalist, or *maskil*, as such departers from the old ways were called. Mama would say of Baruch sadly, "*Er is fun de Haskalah*," ("He is of the Enlightenment") and that was all I ever found out. A Talmud whiz, he evidently discovered Voltaire and Darwin, or possibly even Mendelssohn, and so, farewell, matmid! He rebelled, went to America, and wore out the rest of his life repairing watches in Brooklyn.

In my grandfather's Russian Jewish world, for all its manifold parties and splits within parties, there was one unbridgeable rift: between the *ehrliche Yidden*, "faithful Jews," and the *maskilim* like Uncle Baruch. The religious side was split again between Zaideh's Hasidim and the *Misnagdim*, or Opponents, who resisted the inroads of popular mysticism into their sternly structured Talmudic culture. On the secular side, all was ferment and chaos. While western Jews were pouring into the universities, the professions, business, and art, five million Jews in Russia were hamstrung by restrictive decrees. Helpless against the Czar, the maskilim battled each other in ever-splintering disagreements about how to win political freedom, agreeing only on scorning and badgering the religionists.

Still, these eastern maskilim were different from the assimilating western Jews. Few proposed to become totally Russified in language, dress, and culture, in the hope of achieving universal Mendelssohnian harmony. Even those who most stridently repudiated the yoke of Torah sought some thread of Jewish continuity—the Yiddish language, or a modern revival of Hebrew, or a nationalist return to the Holy Land, or a *bund* of Yiddish-speaking anti-Zionist socialists. In feuilletons and ephemeral magazines, hot Hebrew and Yiddish attacks on the Talmud and on each other's ideas were much in vogue. A rebel like my uncle had a wide choice of camps into which to throw himself.

By the time I knew Uncle Baruch, he was back to keeping Shabbat and going daily to shul, his fiery young manhood far behind, but in those days he probably went in for socialism, the wave of the Russian future which swallowed great numbers of the maskilim. A maskil of remarkable literary and military talent, Lev Bronstein by name, actually became a top leader of the Russian Revolution and Lenin's probable successor, only to end up in exile in Mexico with an ice pick in his brain, courtesy of Stalin. The world knew him as Leon Trotsky. What a leader of the Jewish people Bronstein/Trotsky might have been! Yiddishkeit's worst disaster, before the Nazis came, was probably the massive drain of such brilliant Russian-Jewish freethinkers to the mirage of socialism.

Yet given Czarist repression of the Jews, given ingrained Russian anti-Semitism—both of which socialism promised to abolish—and given the flight from religion, was not the surge of the frustrated rebels into that movement inevitable? Russian Jewish suffering under the Czarist and Soviet governments has been eclipsed in history by the lurid German-inflicted horrors, but the Nazis found precedents in Russia, which they took to maniacal extremes. From the Czarist secret police, they borrowed their policy of official indifference or actual aid to pogroms, as well as the notorious *Protocols of the Learned Elders of Zion.* This propaganda tool, a transparent forgery cribbed from a French political satire, purported to disclose a Jewish conspiracy to rule the world. Discredited beyond dispute, it is on sale to this day in Arab bookstores.* From Lenin and Stalin the Hitler regime also adopted the gulags and the purges, only it carried them the final step further.

---

*The *Encyclopædia Britannica* gives a detailed account of this poisonous rubbish, vol. 9, p. 742, current (15th) edition.

Countersurge

The streaming of Jewry into hitherto barred circles of western European life created a countersurge, not only of specious racial theory but of political action, to which the Jews, beguiled by their new freedom and opportunities, paid small heed. Even while the cloud no bigger than a man's hand was swelling into a thunderhead, they were slower to notice than they might have been.

Dislike of the stranger is as old as tribalism, as old as human society itself. The Greek word *barbaros*, meaning a foreigner, resonates with a sense of unintelligible speech, queer customs, inferiority, and ignorance; it is an onomatopoeic word, suggesting babble that offends the ears. The Mosaic injunction, *"Love the stranger, for you were strangers in Egypt,"* is a uniquely humane Torah precept for a people with a unique history. Jews from the Czarist east—which then embraced Lithuania, the Baltic states, and most of Poland—were trickling westward despite tough border restrictions, strangers irritating to gentiles and embarrassing to the emancipated Jews, what with their old-style religion, shtetl manners, grating quasi-German Yiddish, and outlandish clothes and beards.

The western Jews had been finding their niche, learning to speak excellent French, German, or English, dressing in fashion, and generally blending into the environment. Their religion, when it was not lapsing altogether, was modifying into the modernized Neology or Reform versions, resembling the worship around them; not Christian, to be sure, but hardly halakhic. There was some apostasy as well, for convenience in getting ahead. The unpolished Ostjuden, by their mere arrival, tarred these emancipated Jews with their foreignness, and clouded the rainbow promise of Mendelssohnian harmony.

What was worse, with the shift of Europe's age-old rejection of Jews from the religious to the political sphere, these newcomers supplied damaging ammunition to polemicists and cartoonists. Hook-nosed, blubber-lipped, fur-hatted, and caftan-clad figures grinned evilly on the front pages of the rightist press. Adolf Hitler writes in *Mein Kampf* that, growing up in a small town, he knew no Jews, and thought anti-Semitism an unjust political aberration, until he came to Vienna. When he first saw a Jew on the street— obviously an Ostjude, whom he describes with graphic nastiness— he asked himself, "Is *this* a Jew?" And then, "Is this a *German?*" Thereafter, he declares, he began to grasp the Jewish menace, and came to his absolute lifelong conviction that in fighting the Jewish menace he was doing the Lord's work.

"Anti-Semitism" as a political term first surfaced in slogans of the right-wing press, but the concept was by no means limited to the right. Detestation of the Jew was expounded in leftist thought, with extraordinary viciousness, by none other than Karl Marx himself, descended from a line of rabbis, the baptized son of a baptized Jew. While the racists and royalists were excoriating the Jew as the ultimate socialist enemy of the existing order, Marx was reviling the Jew as the ultimate capitalist whose god was greed, and who had to be extirpated from a just classless society. In the middle class, into whose domain the Jews were in fact moving, the antipathy was not theoretical but visceral, deepening to anger when times were not good. Across the political spectrum, then, the western Jews were in trouble; still rising, however, still prospering, still feeling secure in the legalities of Emancipation.

At the turn of the century Karl Lueger, an anti-Semitic demagogue, was elected mayor of Vienna, the first European politician to ride to real power on this gathering wave of resentment. His speeches, an incoherent populist farrago, assailed Jews as being both the arch-capitalists *and* the arch-communists, a double threat to the stability of Vienna and of all Europe. Scholars of the Hitler era are well aware that the Fuehrer formed his speeches and tactics on the model of Lueger, whose success he had observed while a young drifter in Vienna. The memory of the Viennese themselves seems clouded on that point, since to this day a handsome public square, Karl Lueger Platz, commemorates the pioneer political anti-Semite. Lueger always maintained cordial relations with Jews he found useful, who tended to be flattered and gratified by his patronage. It was Karl Lueger who said, long before Hermann Goering did, "I decide who is a Jew."

The East: Surge and Countersurge

Emancipation came laggardly in the east, for Jewish policy depended there solely on the whims of the Czars. Alexander I, who drove Napoleon out of Russia, had his enlightened side, but like Tolstoy's Pierre Bezukhov, he changed his mind about the Frenchman's liberal notions, possibly about the time Bonaparte left Moscow burning. His heir, Nicholas I, was a benighted autocrat, and only the accession of Alexander II brought a new day, with the freeing of the serfs and a partial relaxing of restrictions on the Jews. A joyful surge of the maskilim into permitted occupations and living spaces quickly ensued, but it did not last long. The countersurge in Russia was swift, violent, and permanent.

To some extent this was bad luck. In 1881, Alexander II was assassinated by a bomb-thrower, and the Czarist police managed to manipulate the tumultuous public wrath so as to pin the terrorist killing on the Jews, whose main hope had been in the slain Czar. Murderous mobs went rioting through the shtetls unhindered by any police action. All the old restrictions were reenacted, and the Russian word *pogrom* entered world languages as early shorthand for the slaughter of Jews, since displaced by *holocaust*. So the year 1881—by a grim coincidence the year Graetz finished his epic work on a note of optimism—became a hinge of modern Jewish history.

For in that year, the movable civilization painfully began to bestir itself. The eastern Jews were learning the hard way what their western cousins did not yet grasp, namely, that after many centuries the modus vivendi with Europe was ending, and that neither assimilation nor Mendelssohnian universal tolerance were real options. Their social and economic hardships were already scarcely endurable. When civil government not only failed to stop hooligans who stormed into Jewish villages, killing, raping, looting, and burning, but sometimes sent its police to join in the game, something irreversible was happening, and it was getting time to move on. Even the Crusader raids had been excesses of troops on the march, not calculated government policy. Nor was this outburst of persecution based on Gobineau's pseudo-scientific, anti-Semitic theories. This was the old nativist Russian hostility, partly Christian and partly nationalistic, breaking forth in red rage. A high official of the Orthodox Church, one Konstantin Pobedonostsev, spoke for the aroused Russian rabble, as well as for the Czarist government, when he expressed the hope that *"One third of the Jews will convert, one third will die, and one third will flee the country."*

Apostasy in eastern Jewry was rare, and the Eternal Wanderer was not about to lie down and die to suit Pobedonostsev, so where was he to flee? Western Europe discouraged Jewish immigration, America was far away, and Palestine was a Turkish province of goat pastures and antique ruins. An Odessa doctor, Leon Pinsker, in his eagerly read pamphlet *Auto-Emancipation*, declared that the Jews could no longer survive in modern times as a "ghost people," that they had to free themselves, either by emigrating to America or by creating a Jewish State. These maskil Zionist abstractions crystallized into the *Hovevei Tziyon*, "Lovers of Zion," an ardent small faction dedicated to pioneering in Palestine, while the movable civilization slowly started to pick up en masse and head for distant America. Millions of Jews made the passage in the ensuing decades before the First World War, my parents among them. Hence these lines.

Personal Note

Many are the books I have planned, and most I have actually written and published, by the good Lord's grace to a very slow worker. In the way of nature, however, I may not get to them all. *Ars longa, vita brevis.*

For twenty years this outline has languished in my files:

> *Requiem for European Jewry.* A short book, pulling together at least Marx, Freud, Einstein, Mahler, and Herzl as personages of world consequence, with those two egregious assimilationists Proust and Trotsky to round out the picture. Just a few, no roster of the famous names going on for pages. The model would be Churchill's *Great Contemporaries;* that is, a few terse essays, a vivid thrust in each case to the heart of the character and the career. In essence the work would be a dirge over that brilliant thousand-year Jewry, a tribute to its splendor, a quiet ironic indictment of the civilization that failed it, and an arrow toward the new dawn in Israel.

I dashed off those words after rereading the diaries of Theodor Herzl, the strange Viennese journalist who almost converted to Christianity. His thoughts turned instead to a revived Jewish homeland, and the Dreyfus case, which he covered in Paris for his newspaper, aroused him to create and lead the Zionist movement, the wellspring of the new Jewish State.

Since scrawling that note, I have learned much Israeli history, mainly in the writing of my novels *The Hope* and *The Glory.* It is clear to me that without the pioneering of the eastern Jews in Palestine, Herzl's electrifying effort would have failed. Moreover, my outline ignores the great eastern Gaonim and Yiddish authors, who to the last sustained and recorded the life and culture of that tenacious doomed Jewry. In what follows, I try for a more balanced précis of my *Requiem for European Jewry,* which will remain unwritten.

Six

THE THIRD DESTRUCTION: II

Requiem West: "We Will Be All Right"

In Vienna at the turn of the century, as the anti-Semitic mayor ful-
minated away, a galaxy of illustrious Jews continued to flourish in
the arts and sciences, in philosophy, in publishing, in finance, even
in popular entertainment. To these notables Karl Lueger must have
seemed a transient political clown, merely playing to the mob by
echoing the lucubrations of Chamberlain and Gobineau. Theodor
Herzl's vision of a deadly crisis brewing for the Jews, and of a
Zionist State in Palestine as the only solution, no doubt struck
them as the crankiness of a lightweight playwright and pamphle-
teer, once talented and charming but now a bit over the edge.

In much the same way, thirty years later, Europe's Jews tended
to look down upon Hitler, as he rose to prominence leading a
"National Socialist Workers' Party," which agitated against Jews in
straight Karl Lueger style. "Handsome Adolf (*der schoene Adolf*)" as
the Germans dubbed him in those early days, probably seemed to
most of the Jews ridiculous rather than menacing, so vulgar and
groundless were his wild diatribes, so overdone his street-agitator
gestures, so comical his Charlie Chaplin mustache. Nor were they
too concerned even when he became the German Chancellor,

though at that point the more prudent ones started to leave the Continent.

Among Germany's Jews who stayed on, comforting bywords were passing, such as, "*It's always hotter cooked than eaten,*" or "*One can live under any law.*" Worsening though conditions were year by year, European life remained pleasantly civilized even in Germany, certainly better than ghetto days, and far better of course than shtetl existence. Ah, how they loved their Berlin, those western Jews, and their Paris, their Munich, their Brussels, their Antwerp, their Marseilles! How they loved the parks, the promenades, the tree-lined boulevards, the concerts, the cafés, the operas, the theaters! And they believed—because they wanted to believe—that in lovely cultured Europe the political monstrosity of an anti-Semitic national government could not long endure. As the storm gathered more and more did leave, some foresighted, some driven out. Jewish scientists, for example, expelled from their academic posts, brought with them to England and America the new nuclear know-how with which Hitler might have won world empire. If the German Jews who by choice stayed on were obtusely optimistic, the rest of Europe's Jews were even more so. Their frame of mind could be summed up thus. "*Hitler won't last. Even if he lasts, there will be no war. Even if there is a war, he will lose. So we will be all right.*"

The rest, in the worn phrase hideous in this context, is history.

Requiem East: The Last Yavneh

Hitler had been in power only three years when the Nuremberg Laws of 1935 served notice on the world that the man meant business about the Jews.

This reversal of a hundred years of Emancipation, reducing the German Jews overnight to virtual enemy aliens, passed easily in a German nation besotted with its Fuehrer. The other nations of

Europe, appalled and cowed by his open rearming and sudden military moves, hardly murmured. Thereafter, though the Kristallnacht outbreak and the shrouded happenings in concentration camps were very ominous, the German Jews, though harshly harassed, were not yet being murdered. It was only in June 1941, when the Wehrmacht plunged eastward through Poland and the Baltic states toward the Soviet Union, that the Third Destruction truly began.

Hard behind Hitler's armies there came the secret *Einsatzgruppen*, roving bands in SS uniform, recruiting local firing squads wherever they went to assist them—as it turned out, all too willingly—in their assigned work of killing Jews. Under these unprovoked fusillades, more than a million stunned bewildered victims perished before the death camps ever came into existence, or any western Jews, including those in Germany, were actually transported to their deaths. That sequence of events is dimming in history, but it should not be forgotten. Screened by the smoke of war, the dagger went for the heart, the shtetl civilization in the east.

Far from being blind to danger, or deluded by Mendelssohnian hopes, those Yiddish-speaking shtetl Jews were by descent wary Darwinian survivors, who through long centuries had evolved ways of coping with the worst that hate could do. Firm in faith, keen in intellect, flexible in policy, this Ashkenazi diaspora had taken up the torch of the splendid Sephardi Jewry of Maimonides, brought down by the forced conversions, the terrors of the Spanish Inquisition, and the expulsion in 1492 of a crushed remnant. Arising mainly in German lands, then spreading eastward into the Slavic world, the canny Yiddish-speaking Ashkenazi Yavneh was equipped by generations of mobile experience to foresee trouble, to bend to passing storms, to overcome adversity, and to endure. How was it, then, that this last Yavneh—for there will never be another—went down and no longer exists? Blaming Hitler and the Germans leaves the question where we find it. We know who the murderers were. The question is about the murdered, and to this question there are some partial answers.

Yavneh Weakens

I well remember how my grandfather arrived in our Bronx flat with a clever daughter in her late teens, wearing a red Young Pioneers scarf and a Lenin cap, and spouting Marx as a yeshiva boy might recite Psalms. To hear this aunt of mine reel off her Soviet catechism, there was of course no God, and religion was the opiate of the masses, a mere device of the bourgeoisie to enslave the toiling proletariat. That gassy communist verbiage, now extinct, was the *Sh'ma Yisroel* of my aunt and countless Russian Jews like her. To begin with, then, the German onslaught struck a Yavneh enfeebled not only by the mass emigration to America but by an endemic desertion to socialism among those who were left, especially the young.

More importantly, Yavneh's long, tenacious hold on the Jewish brain had at last been loosening. Newton published his *Principia Mathematica* in 1684, and the Baal Shem Tov ("Master of the Good Name") was born in a small town in Poland a few years later. Strange juxtaposition; the great thinker of the Enlightenment and the founding saint of Hasidism! Yet it was toward these two magnetic poles that the vital forces of Yavneh had since then been flowing in opposite directions. The maskilim took with them their Talmudic mental energy and rigor, while Amkha was being drawn to the emotional warmth and uplift of mystic Hasidism.

When the maskilim leaped the fence of faith, that was that, they were gone. Hasidism presented a more complex challenge to Yavneh. It was the first major movement inside Orthodoxy since the editing of the Talmud. Its followers were unchallengeably Torah Jews, but the main rabbinic authorities, unable to tolerate their innovations in practice and doctrine, became their Opponents, the *Misnagdim.* The Vilna Gaon, the most brilliant light of eastern Jewry in centuries, fought Hasidism as long as he lived. By the time I was born, that particular tension within Jewry was simmering down, so that my Misnagid father could marry my Hasidic mother. Besides, my parents were among the millions who had left the Yiddish diaspora and its conflicts far behind them.

Such were some elements of the lowered resistance of the last Yavneh, when the Germans came.

"The Third Destruction"

What happened next I have depicted through the kaleidoscope of historical fiction in *The Winds of War* and *War and Remembrance*. For a work of scholarship, none in my view excels Raul Hilberg's classic, *The Destruction of the European Jews*, still the definitive delineation of the Holocaust. This monumental study establishes once for all that the crime was not a passing aberration of a demonic few but the official policy of the legal German government, wielding the nation's entire political and economic machinery, its civil and diplomatic services, its armed forces, and its disciplined and obedient population. The railroads, for example, a crucial element in the carrying out of the massacre, were run not by SS malefactors but by good German citizens, first to last. Not all Germans were involved in the horror, of course; but it is an inescapable and permanent part of Germany's national history. That truth must be grasped.

The French thinker Joseph de Maistre maintained that the world is a slaughterhouse, kept in order only by the hangman, a defensible if morbid way to read human history. In truth, countless mass crimes have been committed since men started keeping chronicles, few probably worse than the recent horrors in Africa and southeast Asia. Yet history not only repeats itself but brings new things. In the Second World War, there were two new things: the successful detonation of uranium, and the secret attempt by a legitimate European government to wipe out the Jewish people. The uranium bomb changed world history in a way not yet measured.

The effect of the colossal German massacre—the Third Destruction—on the remnant of our people, and on the course of all human events, also has yet to be measured.

This wartime act by an advanced western nation was in its very nature so new, so *unbelievable*, that even though it stood revealed at the war's end, it was years penetrating world awareness. What made humankind take notice at last was the capture of Adolf Eichmann by Israeli intelligence agents in Argentina, his subsequent trial in Jerusalem, and his execution. Until Israel beat the white light of justice on Eichmann, the Holocaust story was not well known and this German functionary remained obscure. David Ben-Gurion, to his everlasting credit, authorized the apprehension and trial of Adolf Eichmann as a secret top priority. True, it was Hitler's will that the Jews be destroyed, and it was Goering who issued the orders for a final solution; but it was Adolf Eichmann who obeyed the will, and did what he could to carry out the orders.

"The Banality of Evil"

Covering his trial for a magazine, a writer on philosophy named Hannah Arendt published her articles in a controversial bestselling book, *Eichmann in Jerusalem.* Her main theme, roughly speaking, was that since the *Judenrat,* the submissive Jewish ghetto administrators, had complied on the whole with the instructions of Eichmann and his subordinates, the Jews were themselves more than a little to blame for the massacre and that Eichmann himself was only a sort of ultimate minor bureaucrat, a mere cog in the machine, an ordinary person unfairly burdened with responsibility for the whole vast carnage. Herself a German Jewess who had managed to escape Hitler, Arendt contributed to the subject a phrase that still lingers in popular culture to delineate Eichmann and the entire German crime: "the banality of evil."

In private conversation, a brilliant old friend of mine, another refugee German-Jewish philosopher, whom I frequently consulted on aspects of Nazism, took a position much like Hannah Arendt's. A grim parody of his views appears in my War Books as the writing of a fictitious German military analyst, "General Armin von Roon," who consistently exculpates the Germans, most of all the army, from complicity in what he calls the "regrettable excesses" of the Hitler regime. My imaginary general feels that the Jews more or less brought the Holocaust on themselves. Such an opinion is all very well for an officer in Hitler's headquarters, but it remains passing strange to me that serious German-Jewish thinkers could harbor such notions. Leaning over backward has its limits, I should think, or possibly I lack the detachment of true philosophers.

An Ordinary Person

Adolf Eichmann necessarily plays a major role in *War and Remembrance*, the novel and the serial film. In portraying him, it was my artistic care not to put horns and a tail on a real and important human being, but to bring him to life exactly as people encountered him. He weaves in and out of the thousand pages of my novel, and I cannot duplicate that literary portrait here, but I can offer a bald summary of the facts that matter.

Eichmann was a lieutenant colonel of the SS, in charge of a bureaucratic pigeonhole of the Secret Service, "Section IV b 4," which handled Jewish matters. He showed much hard-nosed skill in dealing with Jews. In Vienna in 1938 after the Anschluss with Germany, he created a "Central Office of Jewish Emigration," where well-to-do Austrian Jews anxious to flee had to sign away all their possessions in various legal documents, emerging stripped naked with a passport and an exit visa. When Hitler seized Czechoslovakia, Eichmann duplicated this process in Prague. At the top-secret Wannsee Conference of January 1942, convened to expedite the Final Solution, the minutes kept by Adolf Eichmann recorded the decision that the Jews should be finished off not by firing squads, as the Einsatzgruppen had been doing—a crude wasteful public procedure which left traces of the deed everywhere—but by herding them to secret camps in the occupied east, working most of them to death, and killing the tough core that would survive. (As Eichmann's minutes phrased it, this core *"would be treated accordingly."*)

And so indeed it was done. Simple soothing hoaxes of "resettlement" and "hygiene" induced the victims by the millions everywhere, east and west, to walk under their own power into the trains and—unless they were fit to be worked some months as slaves—into gas chambers at the destination, labeled *Showers*. In executing this plan, Adolf Eichmann demonstrated that he was not in the least an ordinary low-level person, but an able key administrator of strong willpower and untiring devotion to detail. The organizing of a continent-wide sweep of European Jewry, and the transporting of these millions to gigantic hastily constructed murder camps, presented major challenges, but he was equal to them.

These things having been laid bare by the evidence at his trial, it is hard to understand how the intelligent author of *Eichmann in Jerusalem* could have been taken in. But among his other criminal skills Eichmann was a shifty dissembler. Once caught and put in the dock, his one chance to live was to plead that he was just a small fish, a pallid, banal paper-shuffler in a vast operation beyond his scope. As he sat there in the unbreakable glass box in the Jerusalem court, perpetually and owlishly fussing with papers, he simulated the petty bureaucrat to the life. It was only miming for the credulous. The Israelis had the goods on him, but Eichmann was playing to a world audience. He took his desperate best shot for surviving, as any cornered animal would have. It did not save him, but it furnished Hannah Arendt with her book and her popular phrase.

She was quite right in maintaining that the giant crime could not be blamed on one man. But Eichmann was in charge of carrying out the policy, and he did so indefatigably until the Grand Alliance smashed into the Third Reich and the perpetrators fled for their lives. Most of Eichmann's superiors were caught and hanged, or they committed suicide. Eichmann escaped. Only because the Jews created a new state, and that state reached its long arm into Argentina and brought him to justice, was he hanged.

The dictionary defines banal as ordinary, lacking novelty. "The banality of evil" means—if it means anything at all—that Adolf Eichmann was really like us and that we are like him, except that by chance he fell into an unpleasant job. Happily for the human race, he was unlike us and we are unlike him. He was an extraordinary German hangman of innocent multitudes, a ghoul of the ages, a novelty.

In Memoriam

The question of questions remains: what could the Germans possibly have had in mind in this stupendous annihilation scheme? What were they trying to achieve? How could they have hoped to get away with it in the long run?

Eichmann himself had discovered in Vienna and Prague that he did not have to murder Jews in order to loot them to their skins, except for their gold teeth and their women's hair. The German people, no matter how mesmerized by their Fuehrer, had not metamorphosed into planetary aliens. Those involved directly or indirectly, and they were very numerous, had to realize that by all standards of human society, what they were colluding in was criminal.

One finds the slenderest of clues to this mystery in records of secret Himmler speeches, and in Albert Speer's mock-ups of Hitler's architectural plans for post-war Berlin. According to the higher

Nazi wisdom, the global victory of Germany was absolutely assured, and the Hitler-Speer edifices were therefore conceived to rival the Pyramids in grandeur. As for the Jews, they were a world menace, so once they were gone, as Himmler reassured his murder squads, all humankind would thank the Germans for eliminating them. Afterward, in the glorious era of the Thousand-Year Reich, the entire episode would fade from the memory of man.

For all their weary experience in dealing with hostility to the stranger, the Jews had never encountered anywhere on earth, down all the centuries, such bloodthirsty lunacy. However frightened, however unwilling, they complied with the orders of the authorities to cluster in the ghettos, to mount the trains, and to enter the "showers," scarcely comprehending, almost to the last, that this time the legal government of a mighty modern power simply meant to murder them all.

There were those who did not avert their eyes, who saw through the hoaxes to the truth, and who died resisting the killers. The records of ghetto uprisings, of mutinies in death camps, of Jewish partisan bands in the forests, memorialize the heroic few who caught on well before Eichmann's secret was out, and fell fighting for their lives, without hope but with honor. The over-whelming majority of Europe's Jews believed the Germans, or were terrorized into obeying them; they had no weapons and no options, and died unresisting at their hands.

Afterword

Such was the Third Destruction, insofar as an account pledged to strict brevity can encompass it.

In writing my two novels and the television dramas based on them—the work of nearly twenty years—I have lived twice in imagination through these events, often weeping as I wrung out my few daily pages. Reliving the thing yet again, even in these sketchy paragraphs, has been hard. I cannot match, in eloquence and passion, authors like Primo Levi and Elie Wiesel, who were there. I feel humbled to this day, talking to an aged Jew in the synagogue who rolls up a sleeve to show the camp tattoo. In a note at the end of *War and Remembrance* I wrote, "It is hoped that living survivors of Auschwitz, comparing their recollections with this fictional *Remembrance*, created by one who was not there, will see an honest effort to make the vanished horror live for all the world that was not there." About this thing that befell my Jewish people in my lifetime, I could do no more.

The Accounting

In the long run it will be up to the German people themselves, I believe, to account before the bar of history for the Hitler regime. It is their enigma. The culture that gave the world Goethe, Kant, Hegel, and Nietzsche should be equal, sooner or later, to acknowledging and plumbing to the bottom, the destruction that their nation wreaked on our people and on mankind by the Holocaust. On mankind, I repeat, for among the more than a million incinerated children, who can say what intellect, genius, and religious vision did not go to ash, which might have benefited all humanity?

Today the new Germany, though greatly changed since the Nazi era, seems to be still in a state of shocked denial, not denying that the massacre of the Jews occurred—something that only a few creatures of quasi-Eichmann mentality still try to do—but denying that a further profound accounting is needed, holding rather that the "twelve years of crimes and excesses" are best acknowledged with suitable heartfelt contrition, and then allowed to fade into the past with old plagues and old wars.

But for us Jews what happened will never fade, any more than the fall of two Temples has faded. Our presence on earth will continue to challenge German thought, unless Hitler in his grave is in fact winning his war against the Jews, so that as Eichmann predicted, in time there will be nobody left to remember, no challenging presence, no generation worth mentioning.

Seven

RETROSPECT

W e have traversed three millennia, with hurried glances at eras and events that engross whole academic departments and great libraries, seeking guidance for ourselves, the Jewish remnant after the Third Destruction.

Let me quote here from *This Is My God* one more exchange I had with Ben-Gurion.

> Ben-Gurion said to me—the wise, tough old builder of Israel, with the floating white hair of a dreamer and the hard jaw of an army general—"You Jews in the United States are different from any Jewish community that has ever existed. You are not strangers, or no more strangers than anyone else in your land. America consists of immigrants. You belong like the rest, and you will prosper. But how will you survive as Jews?"
>
> Without thinking I responded, "Through the religion."
>
> The old socialist looked at me aslant with an unfathomable little smile . . .

Across the gap of forty years, I can now fathom that fatherly smile, half amused and half sad, for I would not give that answer today. On the visible present evidence, the religion will not preserve this great but dwindling American diaspora. Behind the old socialist's smile was his vision of a humanist utopia of ingathered New Jews in Israel, living by the social justice of the Prophets, rather than by the Law of Moses. But socialism is as dead as Ben-Gurion, and with it his chimerical vision. Israel is a whole other matter, which we will explore, but it does not answer Ben-Gurion's question.

What then must we do? Ezra and Nehemiah saved exiled Judaea, and five hundred years after that Jochanan ben Zakkai resurrected fallen Jerusalem. But prophecy is no more, Yavneh is no more, and today, in Israel as in America, we are a vortex of contending minorities, with one exception only: the assimilationists. They are everywhere in Jewry. By and large, are they not prevailing, silently or vocally? Even in Hebrew University they sit in professorial chairs, "post-Zionists" repudiating Zionism and Judaism alike, demanding that we drop our struggle of the ages and become like the other nations. Who then can blame the American Jewish boy or girl, compelled to prepare for a bar or bat mitzvah, for snarling at the end of a wearying drill session, "Who needs this stuff?"

Ben-Gurion doubtless anticipated my answer about the religion, knowing that I was observant. I daresay he was smiling at my *galut* ("diaspora") ingenuousness. But how would he have reacted, had I replied instead that we American Jews would survive through "the Jewish Heritage," as the pulpit and lecture talk goes nowadays? I can well imagine him looking startled and then exclaiming, "Heritage? *Mah zeh* [What is this] 'Heritage'? We *fled* from the Heritage!"

Heritage and Humanism

I am a humanist to the bone, shaped by four years of Columbia College, four years as a wartime naval officer, and a lifetime in literature, films, and the theater. It is usually a good idea to define one's terms in a disputed matter, and the clash of humanism and the

Jewish heritage might well be called that. Here then is *Webster's Collegiate* on humanism:

> **humanism.** . . . a philosophy that asserts the dignity and worth of man and his capacity for self-realization through reason, and that often rejects supernaturalism.

Those lexicographers are a careful breed, and through that little qualifier "*often*" the believer can drive, if he chooses as I do, a Merkava tank of religious commitment. In fact, that is what the rest of my book is about. Up to this point, we have been clearing the ground. Now let us have a fresh look at our heritage, and see what we can retrieve from the wreckage of lost Yavneh.

Part II

THE HERITAGE,

OR

THE POWER OF A DREAM

I am not an originator but a transmitter.

—CONFUCIUS

Eight

ZAIDEH AND THE HUMANIST

In the library of my Georgetown home where I started rereading Graetz, I recently came upon two books which have been on the shelf untouched even longer than his *History*, in fact for more than fifty years. They went with me all over the South Pacific during World War II; a scuffed one-volume Hebrew-English Bible, its spine patched with brown paper and Scotch tape, its pages now very yellowed, and a moldering *Critique of Pure Reason*, with a bookmark in it which would have decidedly puzzled Immanuel Kant: a strip of metal foil we then called "window," dropped by a Japanese plane to confuse our radar. So I carried out to sea the Judaism of my father and grandfather, and the humanism I imbibed at Columbia, in good part from Irwin Edman, a philosophy professor.

Even in my raffish bachelor days before the war, writing jokes for radio comedians, I had kept up these two interests. They ran along parallel tracks in my mind, and inconsistencies or contradictions between them did not much trouble me. I would ride the subway to Zaideh's Bronx flat, for instance, reading Nietzsche's abysmally atheistic *Genealogy of Morals,* then spend hours with him, learning some abstruse Talmudic passage about property law or Temple sacrifice. That evening Irwin Edman and I might take in the Philharmonic, or

I might go out on the town with my fellow gagmen and our light-hearted girlfriends. I did not anticipate that the parallel lines would ever meet in a wild shower of sparks of conscience.

That happened when my father died a few months after Pearl Harbor, when I was in a school for "ninety-day wonders," naval reserve officers. I went to see the commandant, told him that I had to go home to sit *shiva*, and that on my return I would remain unshaven for three more weeks. I don't recall hesitating about this, although a week's absence from that high-pressure school was unthinkable, and an unshaven midshipman beyond imagining. The commandant heard me out with raised eyebrows, and by way of assent merely shrugged. I had been leading Friday night services for a handful of midshipmen, and my marks were pretty good, so maybe all that helped.

Anyway, out into the sunshine I walked in uniform, and down the few blocks from Columbia University, where the Navy had taken over a residence hall, to my parents' home on West End Avenue. There, shoeless and in a ripped old jacket, I sat on a low stool day and night, receiving condolences from the visitors who came and went in streams. My father had been active in synagogues, Hebrew schools, temples, business councils, the Masons, and Zionism, and there seemed no end to the strangers who showed up to console the family. It was during that blurry week of grief, home prayers, and endless small talk, that Zaideh and Irwin Edman met and the parallel lines converged.

Professor Edman

Still remembered among academicians, Edman was my mentor at Columbia, and ever after my affectionate friend. My first novel, *Aurora Dawn*, which I began out at sea, is dedicated to him. Irwin had a photographic memory. I sent him my opening chapters, he quoted a few pages verbatim to a New York editor at lunch, and as a result, a few months later, a publisher's contract came in the mail to my minesweeper off Okinawa. I would have dedicated the book to Irwin Edman anyway, for I owed him much more than that contract. His influence on my judgment in the arts and philosophy was inestimable, and it has endured.

At the university, Irwin Edman was what current journalism calls an "icon," revered as a witty yet profound lecturer, a well-known author and editor, and on the lighter side a deft writer of urbane verse for *The New Yorker*. For an endearing touch, he was the absentminded professor personified. A campus legend went that, stopping to talk to a student, he asked which direction he had been coming from, and then said, "Oh, so I've had my lunch." In person he was unforgettable: very short, slightly stooped, an albino with prominent, wavering, pale blue eyes and scanty straight blond hair. Irwin was a Jew, and he taught comparative religion, but he had no Hebrew or Yiddish. When I telephoned him about my father's death, he inquired, "Herman, how will you manage to say, ah, '*kaddish*' in the Navy?" putting heavy quote marks around the word. His special field was aesthetics and his idol was Santayana, in a pantheon that included James, Dewey, Russell, and Whitehead. He was also very good on the Neoplatonists, William of Occam, and St. John of the Cross.

Zaideh

My grandfather was then in his late seventies, a little over six feet tall, holding himself straight as a midshipman on parade. With his full gray beard, broad Russian peasant face, and astute serious eyes, he really looked a lot like the aged Tolstoy, whose work he most certainly had not read. During a lifetime stretching through ninety-four years, Zaideh did not read a novel, hear a symphony, see a play or movie, or look at a painting, classical or modern. Plato and Aristotle were shadowy names, recognizable only because Maimonides mentioned them, figures far more remote to him than the Buddha or Lao-Tzu were to me; a man who without question never heard of Sophocles, Dante, Cervantes, Michelangelo, Galileo, Milton, da Vinci, Fielding, Balzac, Dickens, or Twain. Such was my grandfather, Mendel Leib Levine, a single-minded rabbinic sage of compelling presence, who beyond family cared about and taught me one thing, Yiddishkeit as embodied in Torah and Talmud.

The Meeting

"So this is Haym Zelig's professor!" The tall old rabbi and the little philosopher were shaking hands in the house of mourning. Zaideh never referred to me by anything but my Hebrew name.

Irwin's famed urbanity did not fail him. In slow, careful German he told my grandfather that I was an excellent student, and that he admired my faithfulness to Jewish tradition. Yiddish is based on High German, and Zaideh had no trouble understanding him. His response was noncommittal. Zaideh had small use for philosophers, remembering how our family *filosoffes* had gone off the reservation, and well aware of my own free-style life at the time. A brief halting conversation ensued until Zaideh said something that struck Irwin with its sagacity. "You know, Rabbi Levine," he observed, surprised and impressed, "a great philosopher, Marcus Aurelius, once said much the same thing." Zaideh looked blank, and Irwin persisted, "I mean Marcus Aurelius, the Roman emperor. You know about Rome, of course."

"*Rayme?*" exclaimed Zaideh in his Litvak Yiddish. "*Rayme*? Of course I know about *Rayme*, may its name and memory be blotted out!"

That more or less ended it. Other consolers arrived to talk real

Yiddish to Zaideh, while my mother and sister served tea and cake to my eminent visitor. He and I talked about my grandfather, and I gathered that Irwin found Zaideh charming and full of good sense, if quaint and otherworldly in the extreme. It was an accurate enough Columbia appraisal, but I thought more of Zaideh than that. Over tea and Mama's honey cake, I told Irwin about his tragic life; two wives dying young, three brilliant sons lost in their youth, one after another, to old-country diseases; his surviving son, whom he adored and partly supported, a chucklehead mooning around in Palestine; in short, a much-bereaved scholar eking out an uprooted existence in a decaying South Bronx synagogue, his deep learning known only to a few other scholars who consulted him on divorces and other hard halakhic matters. With all that, I pointed out, he was cheerful, happy, humorous, and indomitably optimistic, beyond anybody I knew.

"Well, Herman," said Irwin Edman kindly, "maybe that only proves the power of a dream."

Those words appear unchanged in the last chapter of my novel *Marjorie Morningstar*.

Pascal and *Marjorie*

Marjorie's former boyish suitor Wally Wronken, now a successful playwright, records in his diary a visit to her when she has become a gray contented suburban mother of three. As they are having drinks on her terrace in a fine summer evening, their talk drifts to religion, and he learns that Marjorie has turned observant, maintains a kosher kitchen, and goes regularly to synagogue. She likens professors of comparative religion to bright kids with clocks. They can take a religion apart and show how it ticks, she says, but they can't put it back together so it will work. Wally mildly suggests that the day may be past when religion can really work for an educated person. She retorts with some heat that she knows better; there have been crushing deaths in her family, and only their religion has kept them going. Wally's diary continues:

> At this point I was probing, perhaps cruelly, to strike bottom. I said, "Well, Margie, maybe that only proves the power of a dream." Like a flash she answered—and her voice sounded just as it did in the old days, full of life and sparkle, "Who isn't dreaming, Wally? You?"

Somewhere in the *Pensées*, Blaise Pascal writes, *"Life is a dream, a little more coherent than most."* That in essence is Marjorie's reply to Wally Wronken, a classic standoff. Great believers like Pascal of course live a life of reason as well as faith, for all the major religions have powerful logical structures. Wise rationalists all the way back to Plato have known that everyday reality is a shadow play, and that from birth to death, on this lost little earth in an incomprehensible universe, human life is at root a phantasmagoria.

Pascal stated the case for believers as well as anyone has since, and "Pascal's wager" is common coin in theological argument. It runs so, very simplified: either God exists, or he does not. The believer, by betting on the Creator's existence, gains in his brief time under the sun a rich tradition and a strong value system, and for all he knows, a reward beyond life. The non-believer, by rejecting the idea of God, is betting on a zero which, in the roulette of human experience, has no payoff here or hereafter. Hence, the smart money bets on God. This argument may not have convinced many humanists to turn pious, and I doubt that it caused the change in Marjorie, but there it is, and Zaideh once said almost the same thing to me. "We can never be sure we are right," he remarked of Torah observance and the hereafter, "but *tommer, tommer* . . . suppose, suppose . . . ?" He had not read Pascal, but he had a way of coming out with these things, as he had hit on the thought of Marcus Aurelius of *Rayme*, in chatting with Edman.

Edman Versus Zaideh: The Maimonidean Controversy

This same standoff sparked a conflict in European Jewry during the Middle Ages, the famous Maimonidean Controversy, never since equaled for virulence and for terrible results.

In essence a showdown to the death between humanism and tradition—between Edman and Zaideh, as it were—the Maimonidean controversy raged over three centuries; raged, subsided, raged again, became quiet, then broke out anew, like a forest fire incompletely controlled. It pitted famous Talmudists against each other, hurling denunciations back and forth until the Church and the Pope himself intervened, and found reason in these internecine Jewish quarrels to ban Maimonides' works and condemn the Talmud to the flames. In Paris alone, in the year 1242, the public executioner incinerated twenty-four wagonloads of the Talmud and its commentaries, a loss and a horror which one stunned rabbinic authority compared to the burning of the Temple, for it occurred long before printing was invented, and every copy was a scribe's handwrought labor.

At the center of this storm was Rabbi Moses ben Maimon, in Hebrew acronym the Rambam, in Christian scholarship Maimonides. Born in Spain early in the twelfth century, driven by persecution and misfortune to sojourn in Europe, Africa, and Asia Minor, he settled at last in Cairo, where he used his knowledge of medicine to become physician to the sultan's harem and to his vizier. He died there and was buried in Tiberias, where tourists today visit his grave. In his seventy years of hard times, illness, and wandering, he performed intellectual labors inconceivable to me as the work of one man, except that they exist and I have studied them. I once heard a rabbi say of him that such a brain appears once in ten thousand years.

The Rambam mastered the entire Talmud, it seems, as a child masters the multiplication table, and rearranged all its laws in one vast clear Code of fourteen books, the *Mishneh Torah* or "Review of the Law," penned in pellucid Hebrew. When the *Mishneh Torah* appeared Jews all over the world took it up, hailing its grand structure and its wonderful fresh light on the Law, while contemporary scholars carped at details, and berated the Rambam's arrogance in offering his own composition as a substitute for the hallowed, thickly forested Talmud.

This, however, was only the start of the Maimonidean Controversy.

The Guide

What really provoked a wild eruption of the poisonous conflict was his second great masterwork, *The Guide of the Perplexed*, written in Arabic. Here on my desk as I write is an excellent new translation in two volumes. It is many years since I have had a real go at the *Guide*, and as I glance through it again I am struck anew by its calculated obscurity and its bedrock medievalism. Zaideh advised me to leave the *Guide* to more advanced scholars, and for many years I did so. Once in my callow youth, when I was up against it at Columbia for a term paper in philosophy, I got hold of an English version, raced through it over a weekend, and batted off the requisite twenty pages on the subject. Irwin Edman was not teaching that course, and I was lucky to receive a charitable barely passing mark, after the professor gave me academic hell in his office, for my airy treatment of this giant monolith of religious thought.

On every page of the *Guide*, for a fact, there is meat enough for a doctoral thesis, but it is tough meat to chew. Maimonides writes:

> These matters are only for a few solitary individuals of a very special sort, not for the multitude. For this reason they should be hidden from the beginner, and he should be prevented from taking them up, just as a small infant is prevented from eating coarse foods and lifting heavy weights. . . .

All too true of the entire *Guide*. At one time, I did give the monolith an earnest try, and at the risk of further excoriation by scholars who make it their lifework, let me briefly describe it, to account for the recurring typhoons of controversy that whirled around the book and its author.

What Maimonides wrote in the *Guide* was nothing less than a sharply reasoned bridging of Aristotle and Torah. He drew on the Arabic sources which had preserved Greek philosophy in paraphrase, and on his own peerless grasp of Bible and Talmud, to construct a reconciliation of Hebraism and Hellenism which, in the view of some sober Jewish thinkers, still holds the field. As his own words above make clear, he was writing not for the public but for a tiny elite equipped to follow his train of thought; and so he cast the work in the strange format of an intimate communication to an adoring pupil, one Joseph Ibn Aknin, setting him straight—if with prudent ambiguity—on questions of faith which had been vexing the medieval mind, Jewish, Christian, and Muslim alike.

Trends in these things can shape whole eras. Problems which he took on about the anthropomorphic passages in Scripture, for example—the eye of God, the hand of God, the throne of God, God's wrath, God's changing his mind—are not of much consequence nowadays in high intellectual circles, but in twelfth-century Europe, where pagan thought was bursting forth from its long sleep under the blanket of Church dogma, perplexities such as God's corporeality greatly mattered. Eminent thinkers found their strong beliefs colliding with their common sense, which told them that the rediscovered Greeks and Romans had something momentous to offer, a different worldview, which, once grasped, could not be ignored except by a deliberate obscuring of the truth.

It required formidable courage and mental force on the part of the Rambam to undertake a resolution of this clash, which the busy heedless "multitude" might ignore, but which was undermining the foundations of the world of the Middle Ages. In the Rambam's ambitious synthesis he took on not only the challenges with which a humanist today would badger a literal defender of Scripture—the account of Creation, the talking snake, animal sacrifice, miracles, dietary laws, Balaam's ass, and so on—but also the apparent gulf between Aristotle's science and the picture of the universe found in the Bible. The *Guide* is so impregnated with the concepts of the Middle Ages precisely because it is a Herculean effort *to break out of them.* Maimonides was no "humanist," the concept itself would not exist for centuries, yet it is neither a disservice nor an exaggeration to describe him as an early modern mind.

He was touching on issues of dangerous voltage, and he knew it. In North Africa, he had once submitted to a forced conversion to Islam, which he shrugged off when he left the jurisdiction. In the same hardheaded way, he composed the *Guide* in an obfuscated style, quite beyond reach not only of the multitude but also of learned opponents who had assaulted his *Mishneh Torah,* and who could be counted on to raise a hue and cry about whatever he wrote. Conveying his most daring ideas in guarded hints and scattered fragments, he relied on his brilliant worshipful pupil and disciples like him to grasp them, while presumably leaving his foes baffled and without ammunition.

And here the great man may have miscalculated. His critics may indeed have failed to understand *The Guide of the Perplexed,* but they got one sure thing out of it, that the author was granting some validity to Greek thought. The controversy broadened to the third-rail issue of the time: whether teaching pagan philosophy was not a heretical breach of halakhah. On this point, in the view of some outstanding conservative Talmudists, the Rambam stood condemned, but his teachings also found strong scholarly defenders. Thus the battle was joined in the mainstream of Jewish life.

When Irwin Edman and my grandfather shook hands in 1942 they were touching gloves, so to speak, to spar yet one more round.

"Let's Look at the Rambam"

This is not to say that their sparring was serious. Today Maimonides holds a place in Torah thought undisputed by the greatest Talmudists and my humble Zaideh alike. A saying of his early admirers stands, "*From Moses to Moses* [Maimonides] *none rose like Moses.*" When I was preparing the day's work in the yeshiva of Rabbi Feinstein, going over the Talmud page with two or three other much younger students, one of us would be bound to say when we struck a snag, "Let's look at the Rambam." The Talmud abounds in intricate, elegant arguments which often leave the outcome open and the halakhah unclear. Maimonides put down the answer to every single unresolved point in those two thousand–odd pages. In consequence, his foes blasted his temerity while he lived, and for seven centuries since then, young students and mature scholars alike have blessed his memory. Each page of the printed Talmud now lists references to his *Mishneh Torah* by chapter and paragraph. Zaideh once put it this way: "Rambam tried to tell us, 'Instead of studying the Talmud, rely on me.' Well, we study Rambam and the Talmud."

A century after the Rambam's death, a master halakhist, the Rashbo, tried to quiet the turmoil by decreeing excommunication for anyone under twenty-five who studied Greek philosophy. The ruling was contested or ignored, for nothing could long halt the advance of Jewish minds into the opening fields of thought. Yet for centuries, the only outside study formally sanctioned by some Talmudic authorities was medicine. In the tales of Shalom Aleichem, as a result, one finds that the most likely *apikoros* in any shtetl was the doctor. With the spread of the printing press, the easy accessibility of the Rambam's work, and the rationalist upheaval of the Enlightenment, the coming of a figure like Spinoza was only a matter of time. The debt of that pivotal apostate to the Rambam as well as to Descartes is unmistakable. Nevertheless, the late Lubavitcher Rebbe—assailed by my secular historian as an arch-obscurantist—himself required his thousands of Chabad followers to take on a regular course of Rambam study in the *Mishneh Torah.*

The prophet Elijah challenges the Israelites, in his famous showdown with Jezebel's legion of pagan prophets, *"How long will you hesitate between two opinions? If the Lord is God, follow him, if Baal, then follow him."* That stark choice, governing life amid the pagans, carried into Talmudic times, when Greek wisdom was entangled with the worship of childish deities. Purged of pagan content in Islamic paraphrase, Attic and Roman thought made it into medieval Europe; whereupon the Rambam took the momentous step of demonstrating that an "Elijah's choice" between Greek and Jewish thought was *no longer mandated.* Inevitably he incurred the savage abuse reserved for a pioneer of jolting new ideas. His shoulders were broad enough to endure the worst his critics could do, and on those shoulders the Rambam carried his people into the modern day. When all is said and done, he accomplished his aim and bridged Zaideh and Edman.

Out Front Alone

Feelings of regret and guilt go with the death of a parent, and I had reason enough to be racked when I lost my father. Beyond that common experience, an unforeseen and special change took place in my spirit. I became harshly aware that while I had been having a good time veering between the parallel tracks at will, he had been carrying on the serious business of life and faith. Now he was gone. I was out front alone, facing the tracks that had briefly met and diverged, and at that point I had to choose a direction.

Irwin Edman died before *This Is My God* appeared. Like his master Santayana, Irwin regarded all religions with tolerant good will as grandiose fairy tales, however freighted with charming poetry and wisdom. Still, he might have given me an A on that simple book, tough marker though he was, for I believe he would have recognized the open-minded tone I learned from him, and the effort at his clear style in treating serious matters. As for the religious content, he would have shrugged it off; that was just Herman Wouk for you. *"The unexamined life is not worth living,"* was his favorite motto from the Greeks, and at least he would have seen that in my book I examined without blinders the tradition I inherited and the direction I chose.

This Is Our Heritage

With these few fragments of autobiography and cultural history as exordium, I proceed to sketch out our Jewish patrimony—what is left in our hands, after the Third Destruction—no doubt a foolhardy undertaking in view of its depth and range. Still, such a spare panorama of surviving Judaica may be of some use, like a navigator's chart of a vast ocean. My Confucian epigraph for this section, *"I am not an originator but a transmitter,"* may seem a humanist lapse, but my knowledge of these folk treasures is no more than that of an unscholarly artist who loves them. If my treatment reawakens interest in them, I will have served only as a transmitter. So I take heart from the fact that Confucius, whose few recorded words shaped China's civilization for millennia, could say that he originated nothing, but was only passing on the heritage of antiquity. Such is the modest aim, at any rate, of the coming pages.

One more word and I begin. From the seventeenth century onward, a body of critical analysis of Scripture has grown up, with some claim to scientific method. This field of thought is earnest, and in its archaeology often illuminating, though an unmistakable vein hostile to Judaism here and there shows through, as in the writings of the German Julius Wellhausen. Among many such works I have slogged through every word of Wellhausen's *Prolegomena*, the dense nineteenth-century polemic of some six hundred pages, now pretty well dated, which launched the "documentary theory" in popular discourse. (Know what to reply to the *apikoros*, said Rabbi Elazar.) Spinoza's *Tractatus*, the fountainhead of the entire enterprise, I have known since Edman's course, and I am familiar with the Anchor Bible series, the voluminous up-to-date repository of academic scholarship in this field. In short, I am neither out of touch nor naive in what I write here about the Bible. It is my informed, honestly digested thought, and it is the truth as I understand it.

In the end, I cannot transcend my limits. "Seventy faces to the Torah," says the Midrash. The face that our Bible presents to the world is in the first instance an epic story about a Creator, a People, and a Land. Storytelling is my bent and my life work, and it is this one face of the seventy that I feel wholly competent to deal with. It lies on the surface, in Hebrew and in translation, accessible to all. One has only to take the Book of Books in hand.

Nine

THE SACRED STORY

A Whiff of Unorthodoxy

The vague label "Orthodox" has been applied to me, but what follows may strike some as more than a shade unorthodox. I take our Scripture, start to finish, as the core of our identity, a study which will never end, a revelation to the Jewish people, and a possession which is our life and the length of our days; yet some of it comes down to us from the Late Bronze Age, with disturbing difficulties and enigmas rendered nearly impenetrable by the passage of time. In half a century of studying the texts with their main commentators, I still encounter mystery, obscurity, or my own incurable obtuseness. Fortunately, Scripture on its face of story is plain to understand, if some antique passages and its ultimate depths are shrouded. Whether one is seeking God, or one's Jewish roots, or only a clue to grasping the current Jewish predicament, the Bible is where one starts, and anyone can start just by looking at the story it tells.

Such a literary approach is natural to me. Now, is it inappropriate or frivolous to discuss Holy Writ as one would novels, plays, or films? Consider that such works without number have been and will be quarried from the Bible, which looms above all these as a granite mountain towers above the stonecutters' hewings at its foot.

That there is more to Scripture than the telling of a story goes without saying. The threefold religious structure of our Bible comprises Law, Prophecy, and Writings—in Hebrew T*orah,* N*'viim,* K*'tuvim*—hence the acronym *Tanakh.* But a sustaining arch of story begins, *"In the beginning God created the heavens and the earth,"* sweeps through aeons of time and all the sacred books, and ends with the return from the Babylonian Exile under Ezra. This preliminary chapter glances at key points along that story arch—Winston Churchill called such historical points "climacterics"—for a crude sense of the whole, before we enter Tanakh's three parts.

In the Beginning

A prime rule of storytelling is swift direction of interest to the protagonist. In its first verse the Bible rivets attention for all time, and eventually in all the languages of earth, on the Lord God, Creator of the universe. This one Supreme Being, Scripture teaches, designated a very minor ancient nation to be a "a kingdom of priests and a holy folk," living by his revealed Law on a certain strip of Mediterranean seacoast territory, with the destiny of bringing the light of the Lord to humankind. That teaching has been a matter of rancorous political controversy in recent decades, but our eye blink of time is passing and the theme will stand.

A counter-theme is equally clear. Canaan was promised to the patriarchs and granted to the nation on the strict terms of a *brit,* an agreement or Covenant. God would protect and preserve Israel in the land, providing they would abide by his Torah; otherwise they would in the end forfeit the shield of Providence and go into exile. Even then, the Creator would not forever abandon them. A Redeemer would come who would restore them to the Promised Land once for all, and bring an era of lasting world peace.

This sacred story, the long saga of a little people and their land, begins when the Lord tells a man named Abram—later called Abraham—to leave his home in Mesopotamia and go to "a land which I will show you, where I will make of you a great nation, and in you all the peoples of the earth will be blessed." This does not happen until the twelfth chapter of Genesis, and the election of Abram is unexplained. True, the *Midrash*, the great repository of ancient rabbinic comment and lore, comes to fill the gap with tales of his remarkable childhood, his pioneer discovery of God, his scorn for the idols that his father manufactures, and his ordeal in a fiery furnace under the pagan King Nimrod. But Holy Writ says not a word about all that. Abram simply obeys the Voice and sets out with his family on the long trek to Canaan. When he arrives the Lord appears to him, saying, "To your descendants I will give this land," and the narrative proper starts.

What, then, of the previous eleven chapters? They seem an anomaly. Only because we are so used to them does the strangeness not trouble us. Who does not know of Adam and Eve, Cain and Abel, the Flood, the Tower of Babel? The images are indelible, the archetypes eternal, but what have they to do with the election of Abram and the saga of his descendants?

The Cosmic Prologue

The great French exegete Rashi zeroes in on this question in his gloss (paraphrased for brevity) to the first verse in Genesis:

> Since the Torah is our Book of Laws, it should have begun with the Passover rules in Chapter 12 of Exodus, the first laws given to Israel. Why then does it start with Creation? Because the nations of the world will one day accuse Israel of brigandage, for invading and seizing the territory of the seven Canaanite nations. Israel will respond, "The earth is the Lord's. He created it, by his

will he gave this land to them, and by his will he took it from them and gave it to us . . ."

Here we have the doctrine, well known to land lawyers, of *eminent domain*. All titles trace back to the Sovereign, who at will can appropriate land for just cause.

Rashi is telling us that the cosmic prologue establishes who the world Sovereign is, as later passages will describe the pagan depravity of the seven nations, which sank as low as burning children to Moloch, causing the Promised Land to "vomit them forth." Before Abram enters the story, we learn in this prologue about the One Creator of all that exists—the earth under our feet, the water that girds the earth, the fathomless starry universe of the night sky, the blazing sun that rises and sets each day—the Spirit who breathed life into man, and who elected Abram and brought his descendants to the Promised Land.

In the Language of Men

Geology, physics, and biology present, of course, a radically different picture of the origins of the earth and of life than these early chapters do, provoking the famous "conflict of science and religion" which boiled up to near-nuclear heat in the nineteenth century. It has since cooled a lot, but is still far from room temperature, so to say; hence the battles to this day over some American public school textbooks.

Oddly, we Jews have had no "monkey trial" and no Creationism controversy, though the Creation account in dispute comes from our own Bible. We have our literalist Jewish readers of the Torah, to be sure, who hold that this account means exactly what it appears to say. As I understand their view, they maintain that the world began less than six thousand years ago, and that in the universal catastrophe at the Flood, nature itself underwent a cataclysmic change; the constants of time, space, and life forms were altered beyond reconstruction, so that inferences from evidence in the present, backward past that barrier in time, have no validity and are irrelevant to their faith.

What prevents a Creationism row in Jewry, all the same, is that such old-time believers educate their children in a system of all-encompassing Yiddishkeit starting virtually in the cradle, and continuing through adolescence. Sooner or later their youth must meet with abrasive contradictions of their upbringing in the dominant culture; but it appears that they mostly weather the encounter, for these communities show much vitality in sustaining themselves and growing. The Nobel physicist Isidor Rabi once told me that he had had such an upbringing, and he talked of it with respect and affection, however far he had departed from it in his work, his beliefs, and the way he lived.

Our broad rabbinic tradition, with its profound arabesques of Midrash, symbol, and allegory, clearly admits of understanding the cosmic prologue as an inspired vision of the human predicament in pre-history. The Torah speaks in the language of men, says the Talmud. All other so-called gods of the ancient world are long since extinct, but the God of Abraham, Isaac, and Jacob remains God today. When a thinker of Nietzsche's pungent power proclaims in *Thus Spake Zarathustra,* "God is dead," everyone knows he means the Jewish God of Holy Writ. Whether his book, written some years before he went mad, makes more sense about God than the Bible does, might be argued; but generally speaking, Genesis has not been superseded by *Thus Spake Zarathustra.*

Joseph: Or, How It All Came to Pass

Another seeming anomaly concludes Genesis. It is certainly the book of the patriarchs, Abraham, Isaac, and Jacob, and my next chapter deals with them. The biggest space in Genesis, however, goes to no patriarch, but to Joseph, Jacob's favorite son. In fourteen chapters, Genesis spins a spellbinding account of the rise of a Hebrew slave to become the grand vizier of Egypt. It is the longest biographical sequence in the Torah. Not even Abraham commands such attention, measuring attention in words. How can this be? No matter how wonderful Joseph's story is, the Torah is not interested in gripping readers, as I must do for my living.

The reason, I suggest, is that the saga of the Jewish people pivots on the Exodus, which in turn pivots on the Joseph story. With the Exodus our national identity begins. To that event we refer at every turn of our liturgy. It is a far-drifted Jew who does not attend a Passover seder to observe the old law, *"Remember your going forth from Egypt all the days of your life."* But how did one nation come to be living within another nation? The story of Joseph answers that precise question in intricate convincing detail, narrated with extraordinary literary brilliance.

The Torah paints such a powerful picture of Joseph's rise, in fact, that we have to look sharp to see what all this is driving at. Step by step, the tale itself is enthralling. His envious brothers sell Joseph into slavery. The lewd wife of his Egyptian master tries to seduce him. Rebuffed, she revenges herself by accusing him of attempted rape. Thrown into prison, he displays a gift for interpreting dreams, which brings him to the attention of Pharaoh. In a stunning yet believable leap, he receives the seal of Egypt's highest office. The upshot is that, after many years, his patriarch father Jacob, also called Israel, descends to Egypt to escape a famine, with his whole household of seventy souls. Anxious as Jacob is to see his long-lost son, whom he had given up for dead, he is so loath to leave the Promised Land that the Lord in a night vision has to order him to obey Joseph's summons.

That is the turn of fate. Once settled in the rich province of Goshen, Jacob's family prospers and grows into the people of Israel, twelve tribes descended from his twelve sons. When Joseph and his generation die out, the ground is laid for the rise of a new Pharaoh, and the historic drama of the Exodus.

The Trap of Human History

Thanks to Hollywood, if not to religious school instruction, the story of Israel's departure from Egypt is common knowledge. Once set free and on their way to the Promised Land, however, what were the Israelites doing, wandering in the desert for forty years? The answer is in the Book of Numbers. Moses sends spies ahead to reconnoiter Canaan. They bring back alarming intelligence about the inhabitants' strength, which stampedes the horde of newly freed slaves into a rebellious panic. Forgotten are all God's wonders of the Exodus—the plagues, the splitting of the sea, the Lord descending on Sinai, the miracle of the manna, the pillars of cloud by day and fire by night. Word blazes through the camp, "Let us appoint a captain and go back to Egypt!"

The display of small faith and weak fiber settles the fate of that generation. God's judgment on them is to keep them in the desert until their children grow up, a new generation of free men, capable of fighting the Canaanites and winning the Land. At the height of the revolt, God speaks to Moses of wiping out this feckless people altogether, and creating a new Abrahamic nation descended from Moses himself; presumably, that is, from his two sons, about whom the Torah says little beyond their birth. If this is a temptation, Moses ignores it, and confronts God with a plea to spare Israel which the Creator appears to find unanswerable:

> Now if you will kill off this people as one man, then the nations which have heard your fame will say, "Because the Lord was not able to bring this people to the land that he swore to give them, therefore he has slain them in the wilderness. . . . Pardon, I pray

you, the iniquity of this people . . . as you have forgiven them from Egypt until now."

Is not this breathtaking stuff? Moses is saying that once God has intervened in the course of human events, he is committed by his own actions to go forward with Israel, because punishing them by putting an end to them—however much they may deserve it—*will be a desecration of his Name.* We can assume that the Almighty has thought of that, and is eliciting this response of Moses for everlasting record in the Torah.

In the Book of Job, we will encounter a variation on this eternal theme. If the Creator truly takes a hand in mankind's history, he must measure up to human standards of conduct for an all-powerful Being. If he does not, *why not?* That challenge is thrown today at Jewish believers, about the horrors of 1940–1945. It has often been thrown at me, and I have no answer, nor has the Voice yet spoken from the whirlwind. Or perhaps it has, and I am deaf as well as stupid.

Moses and David

Once Moses shows up in Exodus, a crying baby boy in a reed basket, direction of interest never leaves him, all through his leadership in the Exodus and the desert wanderings, until he ascends Mount Nebo to view the Promised Land and die. After him only one figure of comparable force appears in the sacred story, several centuries later, David, King of Israel. On these two heroic pillars the arch of Scripture rests. So at least it seems to me.

Few would argue about Moses, but David? From his first appearance, as the shepherd boy who slays Goliath with a slingshot, to his last leonine roar on his deathbed, securing his son Solomon's throne, David holds the Scriptural stage. His weaknesses as the Bible frankly recounts them are so formidable that one may question whether he is

in sum a hero at all, yet as Moses dominates the Torah, so David, alive
or dead, certainly dominates the rest of Holy Writ. His life and poetry,
and the fortunes of his dynasty, occupy a full seven books of
Scripture.* The fate of Jewry turns on the fate of the Davidic monarchy, and in its final collapse, the nation collapses.

But even that is by no means all. *Scripture sees the entire hope for
Israel's future in the restoration of David's line.* Some three thousand
years after David lived, that remains the core of the Jewish
Messianic vision. "David, King of Israel, lives! Lives, and endures!"
So the yeshiva boys sing as they dance with the Torah during the
Rejoicing of the Law. So worshipers turn to each other and say at
the blessing of the new moon, "David, King of Israel, lives and
endures!" The Rambam requires that the Messiah be a descendant
of David. The Gospels are at pains to trace a descent of Jesus from
David. By the phrase, "son of David," we Jews mean nobody but
the long-awaited Redeemer.

In the long perspective of the sacred story, the lawgiver Moses
reaches back to revelation and Creation, and the poet-king David
reaches forward to the vanishing point of the future, the coming of
the Redeemer. This all-embracing perspective shapes our Bible,
start to finish.

Climacteric: Solomon in All His Glory

Of the major climacterics in the story arch, none is more decisive
than a shocking sudden transit in the First Book of Kings.

Following a long account of Solomon's reign as David's heir, we
find him in Chapter 10 at his zenith of royal glory, wealth, power,
and territorial sway; builder of the Temple, beloved of God, ruler of
a united people at peace, the regal marvel of all the known

---

*Samuel I and II, Kings I and II, Chronicles I and II, and Psalms.

world. The Queen of Sheba visits him, is awed by his wisdom and magnificence, lays vast tribute of gold at his feet, and departs declaring his greatness even more wondrous than she had heard rumored. Then Chapter 11 opens so:

> And King Solomon loved many gentile women, and the daughter of Pharaoh . . . and when Solomon was old, his wives led astray his heart after other gods . . . and he did evil in the eyes of the Lord . . . building high places for Chemosh, the idol of Moab, and Moloch, the idol of Ammon. . . .

By the close of that one swift chapter, the country is in revolt, a prophet has promised the rebel leader Jeroboam the kingship, and God appears to Solomon in a vision to castigate him for betraying David's heritage. The kingdom will therefore fall apart at his death, God says, leaving only a rump for his son Rehoboam to rule, to honor the divine pledge to David that the dynasty would endure.

So perishes Solomon the wise. Solomon was the son of Bathsheba, the wife David stole from a loyal military captain, whom he sent to certain death in the front lines. That episode is told unvarnished in the Book of Samuel. Perhaps the fruit of such a union was destined to be shadowed, however glorious.

The Keystone

Reading meanings into Scripture's plain text is the domain of Midrash and Haggada. We have a rich literature created by the ancient titans of such learning. It is also the province of much soporific sermonizing, always a risk. Still, when I perceive a remarkable literary effect in the Bible, or think I do, why not point it out?

Scripture subtly prepares the tragic climax of Solomon's reign, it strikes me, almost from the start. The young king makes a political marriage with Pharaoh's daughter. Before he builds the Temple, he takes part in popular worship at "high places," a pagan practice. The very account of his wealth, magnificence, and military power seems to have something excessive and choking about it. Here is the way the Torah of Moses limited permission to set up a monarch in Israel:

> He shall not multiply horses . . . neither shall he multiply wives, that his heart turn not away . . . nor greatly multiply silver and gold. . . .

And here is how Scripture sums up Solomon's material glory, after the Queen of Sheba departs:

> Now the weight of gold that came to Solomon in one year was six hundred sixty six talents of gold . . . two hundred bucklers of beaten gold . . . three hundred shields of beaten gold . . . and all King Solomon's drinking vessels were of gold. . . . And Solomon had one thousand four hundred chariots and twelve thousand horsemen . . . and the king made silver to be in Jerusalem as stones. . . . And he had seven hundred wives, princesses, and three hundred concubines. . . .

Is Holy Writ here dwelling with naive wide-eyed admiration on the king's grandeur, or is it artfully echoing the "*shall nots*" of Moses in these passages of Solomon's overabundant glitter and opulence, which immediately precede the one shocking chapter of his decline and death?

Chronicles, a sparse retelling of the sacred story, replicates the account of Solomon's reign given in the First Book of Kings with few variations, *but leaves out the entire chapter about Solomon's decline*! This is an omission like cutting the last act of *King Lear*. The author of Chronicles clearly means to celebrate the Davidic dynasty with much light and little shadow. We are fortunate to have the Book of Kings' more candid version of Solomon's triumph and tragedy. For in his reign, the arch of sacred story mounts to Israel's brief moment of high glory in the Promised Land, and slopes sharply downhill toward a far-off doom.

Solomon is the keystone, a complex figure compounded of good and bad as all of us are, with both aspects fabulously magnified. The wisdom in Proverbs and Ecclesiastes, books ascribed to him by tradition, blends the pious, the practical, and the profound. Modernist critics demur at his authorship, but his recorded speeches and actions show him capable of writing those books, and the passion-drenched mystical Song of Songs as well.

Prophecy

After Solomon comes the least predictable and the most *Jewish* development in the sacred story. Other old epics and sagas tell of war and conquest, of temples and deities, of good and bad kings, of the rise and fall of regimes. But our national epic is unique.

As the Ten Tribes under Jeroboam break away from Jerusalem's sovereignty and God's Temple, to drift into idol worship, and as the Davidic dynasty in Judaea gradually degenerates, a new saving force emerges to which ancient literature offers no parallel: the moral phalanx of the great Hebrew prophets. They and they alone save the Jewish people from extinction. The rise of those prophets appears to me as wonderful a Godly miracle as the splitting of the Red Sea, a rescue of the nation against all rational odds, to go marching on through the sea of time to the present hour.

In itself, Hebrew prophecy was not new. Forbidding the pagan practices of necromancy and auguries, Moses says, "The Lord will raise up a prophet like me among you. To him you shall listen." The future is with the Almighty, and if it has to be foretold, Israel will hear it not from sorcerers and astrologers, but from prophets, holy men speaking the inspired word of God himself. Beginning with Samuel, who anoints Saul and then David to the kingship, the prophet becomes much more than a seer. He is a moral force, he is Conscience in the flesh, opposing evil-doing in kings, nobles, and at moments the whole people, with a thundering Mosaic voice. King David, rebuked by the prophets Nathan and Gad, submits and repents, but the later prophets like Elijah and Elisha speak out and act against the kings at the risk of their lives.

After Solomon passes from the scene, the narrative focus shifts sharply to these intrepid figures. As national disaster closes in both north and south, the literary giants appear one by one, pouring out first warnings, then consolations, in poetry of amazingly sustained majesty, beauty, and impact. Isaiah and Jeremiah figure only fitfully in the action, but their books are fiery bursts of tremendous religious force. With Ezekiel, the visionary prophet of the dry bones in the Babylonian Exile, they are the three "Major Prophets." The Bible also preserves the words of twelve "Minor Prophets," briefer books like Amos and Hosea, often of equal power.*

The Prophetic Rescue

Everything found in the Prophets is foreshadowed in the books of Moses. The sacred story is the working out of the tension between the Mosaic moral law and the stuff of history and journalism—politics, amours, feuds, wars, in short, everyday life, the doings of human nature under the stresses of time and chance. This is the content of Greek tragedy as well as Scripture, but Moses introduced into mankind's thought an absolutely new idea, namely, *that the one God loved us, and that we were to love God.* This teaching,

---

* Hosea, Joel, Amos, Obadiah, Jonah, Micah, Nahum, Habakkuk, Zephaniah, Haggai, Zechariah, Malachi.

originating in the Torah, is the eternal light of Hebrew prophecy. Denied or even scorned, as ancient philosophers and some modern thinkers have scorned it, it is the essence of Hebraism, indelibly embedded in world consciousness.

It was this love between God and Israel which struck an answering chord in the Jewish people, as they went down to defeat and exile. That mutual love generated their greatest and most enduring poetry, it awakened hope that has never died, and it has enabled them to hang on to existence. Every day, as I bind on phylacteries, I repeat a few words of Hosea. The strap winds along the left arm and fastens to the hand, weaving through palm and fingers in an intricate pattern, which in black leather spells out "Shaddai," the name of God first revealed to the patriarchs. Here are the words as God speaks them through Hosea:

> And I will bind you to me for ever, and I will bind you to me in righteousness, in justice, in kindness, and in mercy; and I will bind you to me in truth, and you will come to know the Lord.

That is how the Jews survived when the other nations of old disappeared.

End and Beginning: Ezra

The sacred story ends with a beginning, the return of the Remnant to the ravaged Holy Land. Ezra and his co-leader Nehemiah speak no poetry. They act, and their books are found among the Writings, not the Prophets. As the narrative breaks off, the northern kingdom is no more, and Judea has become a minor province of a great empire. Not until the Hasmoneans, and twenty centuries after them the State of Israel, will the Jewish people live again as a free nation in the Promised Land.

Tradition ascribes great things to Ezra: the founding of the Great Assembly, the forming of the Scriptural canon, and the final received text of the Torah: hence he is known as Ezra *Hasofer*, the Scribe. In his book, we see him and Nehemiah contending mightily with rampant intermarriage, widespread loss of faith, political problems with the dominant great power, and guerrilla warfare by hostile inhabitants. Sound familiar?

Nevertheless, with them begins the era of the Second Temple, which stands longer than the first one, nearly six hundred years. Narratives of the Exile like Esther and Daniel are grace notes found, too, in the Writings, but with the Book of Ezra-Nehemiah the sacred story is over in the Bible. In the reality of the Jewish people, it goes on for those who believe.

Such is the main story arch of Tanakh. Let us look now, one by one, at *Law*, *Prophets*, and *Writings*.

Ten

THE FATHERS

In our little Palm Springs synagogue, I sometimes give a *d'var Torah* before Shabbat services, to a handful of early-bird congregants. For ten minutes or so I cite Rashi and the other commentators on the portion of the week, with now and then a literary insight if one occurs to me. What follows here will be only a somewhat longer d'var Torah, for if the Bible is the core of our heritage, the Five Books of Moses are the core of the core, and nothing I write about them can equal the challenge. At best, I offer in these few pages a candle flare that may cast a dim glow here and there, in the vast Mosaic edifice stretching far beyond human sight.

There is a discernible drift among some American Jews back to Torah study, reversing the immigrants' flight from the heritage, and the more frantic flight of their children and grandchildren into deep Yankee Doodledom. Not long ago at a Hebrew University convocation in Jerusalem, for instance, I heard an eminent American executive and philanthropist, in accepting an honorary degree, speak out for a return to Jewish roots. "I'm learning Talmud and Torah now," he said with moving earnestness. Had he said, "I'm learning Talmud and *humesh*," I would have been a bit surprised and yet more moved, for that is the password to old Yiddishkeit.

Humesh is a tough word to transpose into English, because of the guttural first letter. To the unaccustomed English-reading eye, the common "chumash" unhappily comes out "chew mash." Academia favors a dotted *h*, thus: *ḥumash*. In Litvak Yiddish we say HUMesh, throaty *h*, and that is what I will use here, because it is what I've always used. Just the other day I nagged a son of mine about a grandson, "When will you start him on humesh?" The word literally means "a fifth," and each of the Mosaic books is called a humesh, but the word has also come to mean one volume containing all the five books. Nobody calls such a volume a Torah, for that means a scroll in the Holy Ark. The old one-volume Hertz humesh in Hebrew and English is titled The Pentateuch, Greek for "five books." A Christian scholar I have known most of my life casually refers to our Torah as "the Pent." This chapter is not about "the Pent," but about humesh, by which I mean Torah as octogenarians like me and children of five alike study it.

Abraham

One figure dominates the first humesh. "Father of a multitude of nations," the Lord calls Abram, in changing his name to Abraham. Genesis is the Book of Abraham's Covenant. Everything before that event leads up to it, and everything afterward hangs on it. The Covenant—in Hebrew *brit*, Yiddish *bris*—is sealed by the patriarch's circumcision at the age of ninety-nine; hence, our term *brit* or *bris* for that bloody ceremony, when the shaky father says over his eight-day-old son, "Blessed are you, O Lord . . . who have commanded us to bring him into the Covenant of Abraham our father."

"Father of a multitude of nations"? From the viewpoint of the nations, absolutely. The world's Christians look back to Abraham's Covenant as the starting point of their faith, and the world's Muslims even observe circumcision, decreed by Allah to Ibrahim in their Koran. Ours is the senior religion, of that there can be no dispute, and today a reconciliation with the other two may at last lie below the horizon, setting aside age-old clashes of dogma, to recognize the right of Abraham's seed just to live in peace in their miraculously reclaimed strip of Holy Land. Such a peace, not at all a Messianic one, can rest on a simple agreement among the three faiths that the God of Abraham exists and has a primal love for Israel, the original inheritors of Abraham's Covenant; a people called by the Lord my firstborn, and by Moses the smallest among the nations.

Lot

Scripture tends to limn its greatest figures through action. The very first verse about Noah tells us all we have to know of his character— "Noah was a man righteous in his generation, Noah walked with God"—and his role is soon over, but we know nothing about Abram at first. His character unfolds through many chapters deed by deed. Several of these involve his nephew Lot, best known as the man whose wife ended up a pillar of salt. Lot is Scripture's moral counterweight to Abram. He comes to Canaan with his uncle and prospers with him, until their herdsmen start quarreling over pasturage for their large flocks and herds. "Let there be no dispute between us . . . for we are men and brothers," Abram says, magnanimously offering his nephew the choice of grazing land. Lot heads east toward Sodom, at that time green and beautiful as the Nile valley, so Scripture tells us, though notorious for the utter depravity of its inhabitants.

Abram goes the other way. Soon Lot's distress requires action that reveals the patriarch's family loyalty, fighting prowess, and probity. Genesis cuts abruptly to a regional war in which the King of Sodom is defeated, Sodom is sacked, and Lot and his family are carried off captive. At this news, Abram recruits and arms a small force, pursues and routs the plundering horde in a night battle, and returns Lot, his family, and all the city's looted wealth and captured women to Sodom. That grateful king, still tarred from the bitumen pit into which he was chased, offers the booty as a rightful prize to Abram, who declines to take "so much as a shoelace, lest you say 'I enriched Abram.'"

Later mysterious strangers appear out of the desert to the patriarch, who loads them with hospitable largesse. After they depart, God tells him in a vision that he intends to destroy the corrupt cities of the plain. Abraham, as he is now called, does not plead for Lot, but challenges the Creator himself. "Will the Judge of all the earth not do justice?" says Abraham, striking the note that will echo through Holy Writ down to the Book of Job. What, utterly wipe out whole cities? Suppose there are fifty righteous inhabitants, must they die too? God replies that if he finds fifty righteous, he will spare the cities. Abraham persists, "Behold, I dare to address the Lord, and I am dust and ashes. Suppose there are only forty-five? . . . Forty? . . . Thirty? . . . Ten?" Abraham does not push his Maker beyond ten, nor does he mention Lot, but Lot's presence in Sodom underlies the drama, for the strangers are angels sent to wipe out the place and to rescue Lot and his family.

Still a kinsman of Abraham even in Sodom, Lot risks the anger of the Sodomites to take the two strangers into his house for the night, since otherwise they will be raped, robbed, and murdered. And here Rashi quotes a biting Midrash about the salinization of Lot's wife: *She sinned with salt, and with salt she was punished.* At table Lot tells his wife to give the guests salt with their bread, a halakhah he learned from the prophet Abraham, who according to the Midrash, observed in full the yet unwritten Torah. The wife snarls, "What, are you keeping up that ridiculous custom even here?" Assimilation has evidently taken hold on the lady. As they flee, she looks back on burning Sodom not so much out of curiosity, it may be, as with regret and nostalgia. So she is frozen to eternity in that stance, thoroughly salted. Guides will show naive tourists today, down at the Dead Sea, the pillar that is purported to be Lot's wife.

Isaac

Once a visiting rabbi took me aside after services, and said in a confidential tone, "Your d'var Torah was very nice. Now just between us, what can you say about Isaac? I have trouble explaining to some people why he is ranked with Abraham and Jacob. What does he do, compared to them, after all? Very little."

Not a new question. In his big scenes Isaac does appear a more or less passive victim. His aged father all but cuts his throat as a sacrifice. When he is old and blind, his younger son Jacob deceives him and steals the blessing meant for the firstborn Esau. The Midrash and commentators labor mightily to improve Isaac's image, so to speak, with varying scenarios, some very creative, but the plain texts are there, troubling the generations. Flattered to be asked by the rabbi, I responded that of the three, only Isaac never sets foot outside the Holy Land, and the Talmud equates that mitzvah to all the others put together, so in that merit alone Isaac matches in stature the other patriarchs. The rabbi looked disappointed. He knew that one, and was hoping for a literary novelty to fend off his inquiring congregants. I had none to suggest on the spot.

It occurs to me as I write, however, that Isaac exemplifies what Confucius said, *I am not an originator but a transmitter.* The rabbi might not have found this parallel usable, but the master sage of a grand civilization as old as Jewry so defined his own life work. In truth Isaac is the sole second-generation transmitter of Abraham's Covenant. God's blessing of the Father of Nations passes through him and him alone to Jacob, who raises up twelve tribes to create the germ of the eternal people. Isaac spends his years a wandering stranger in the Holy Land, driven here and there by hostile inhabitants, who even stop up the wells his father dug. Via the slender thread of one precarious human life, this patriarch passes on the Godly teachings of Abraham to half of mankind.

The Ashes of Isaac

Yet there is more to it. If one event in Genesis is as awesome and wrapped in mystery as the Creation itself, it is the binding of Isaac, the *Akedah*; not the sacrifice of Isaac, mind you, because the thing never happened, but the readiness of Abraham to do it, and Isaac's unhesitating acceptance of it, right up to the last second, to his father's drawing the knife. In Leningrad's remote Hermitage museum, when I came on Rembrandt's painting of the scene, I was startled to see that he has pictured Abraham holding Isaac exactly as a *shokhet*, a ritual slaughterer, holds a fowl to kill it. Without question, Rembrandt went to a Jewish marketplace, saw it done, and forced that harsh reality into the picture. That is genius. There is genius, too, in the agonized faith that radiates like light from the upraised faces of father and son.

Another vivid non-Jewish portrayal of the Akedah is in a very strange book called *Fear and Trembling* by a Danish thinker, Søren Kierkegaard. For a few years after World War II, when existentialism was the trendy thing in philosophy, there was a to-do among the literati about this nineteenth-century work, a meditation on the binding of Isaac. Fashions fade quickly in that tight little circle, and we do not hear much today about existentialism, nor about Kierkegaard and *Fear and Trembling*, but it is a profound classic by a Christian on the theme of faith. It stunned me when I read it.

The Midrash on the Akedah is copious and enigmatic. One moves from Western rationalism into another dimension in

Midrash of allusive poetry and symbol, presented with deceptively simple surreal clarity. According to the Midrash, on Rosh Hashanah when God metes out the destiny of all for the coming year, the ashes of Isaac lie before him as a remembrance. The *ashes*, mind you. The liturgy of the High Holy Days virtually turns on the Akedah; the *shofar* is a ram's horn, because a ram replaced Isaac as the burnt offering. What then does the Midrash mean, telling us about the "ashes" of Isaac?

Compared to the wild saga of Jacob, which we next glance through, Isaac's is a quiet existence, but that he rates as a patriarch needs no literary sally of mine as proof. Each year as Rosh Hashanah rolls around, I find myself in the synagogue, mulling over the unplumbed enigma of the ashes of Isaac. This past year, as it happens, I was sick, but I dragged myself there to hear every single blast of the shofar. No other ritual of ours so penetrates my soul.

Jacob

At the end of Jacob's saga, when the drama of the confrontation of Joseph and his brothers has been played out, the father comes to Egypt with his family of seventy, and Joseph brings him into Pharaoh's presence. This brief dialogue ensues:

> *Pharaoh: How old are you?* ("How many are the days of the years of your life?")
>
> *Jacob: The days of my sojournings have been a hundred thirty years. Few and wretched have been the days of my life, and they have not attained the days of the years of my fathers' lives . . .*

So saying, the patriarch blesses the Pharaoh and withdraws. Pharaoh's blunt question may be awkward small talk, or the privilege of royalty to speak plain. At any rate, he has sensed in this man, crumpling under the years, an august if stricken personage.

Scripture amply bears out Jacob's melancholy judgment on his life. The birthright he bought from Esau, and the blessing that he stole, bring him no good fortune. He has to flee his brother's wrath, to live twenty years in a foreign land as a bondman. For seven years, he tends his uncle Laban's flocks to earn the hand of Rachel, only to have her sister Leah fobbed off on him on his wedding night. Then Laban gives him Rachel, too, but only on condition that he work for her another seven years. He has to put in yet six more years to earn some property. Laban plays such a shifty game in these dealings that, in the end, Jacob has to decamp in secret with his family and all he has acquired, lest the uncle grab back everything: property, wives, and children.

Returning to Canaan, Jacob sends messengers ahead to sound out his brother. The word comes back that Esau is approaching with four hundred men, more than the force with which Abraham rescued Lot. Blessing or no blessing, Esau has evidently prospered. In the tense encounter, Jacob manages to pacify Esau, but no sooner does he pitch his tents in the Holy Land, than a local prince rapes his daughter Dinah, provoking a sanguinary revenge by her brothers. Then his beloved wife Rachel dies young in childbirth, and his son Reuben, eldest of twelve, commits incest with his concubine, the handmaid of Leah (though the rabbis are at the greatest pains to soften what the plain text says). After this series of shocking calamities, Jacob settles down near his aged father, Isaac, and enjoys an interval of peace, which is shattered when his favorite son Joseph, firstborn of his lost Rachel, disappears, apparently devoured by a wild beast.

This last blow unmans the battered paterfamilias. He refuses all comfort, saying, "I will go down to the grave mourning my son." Twenty-two years pass before he learns of Joseph's survival and amazing rise in Egypt. The news comes too late. Once he is convinced that it is true, he rouses himself to say, "Enough, Joseph is alive? I will go to see him before I die." And so he appears before Pharaoh, a man broken by the years, by terrible turns of fortune, and by decades of inconsolable grief.

What then of the blessing he stole from Esau? Was it nullified? Not at all. When blind Isaac finds out the truth, he tells Esau—knowing in his heart that Jacob was always the destined heir to Abraham's Covenant—"I blessed him, and he will be blessed." It is one of the poignant scenes in Scripture. Whatever Esau's rude ways, the rough, shaggy huntsman loved his father, and Isaac loved him, and perhaps was hoping against hope that the blessing would elevate this man of the field to a man of God. The boyish crying of the disappointed, supplanted Esau compels sympathy, and one commentator even suggests that Jacob paid with his hard life for these tears of Esau. It is one of the darker passages in Holy Writ, this muddled transfer of the Covenant to the third generation through a ruse, but the Torah gives the account raw and straight.

Israel

Jacob has two cardinal religious experiences, his dream of the ladder, and his wrestle with the angel. The dream occurs on the night he flees the Holy Land, the wrestling match happens on the night he returns after twenty years. In other years, God visits him, but these two events bracket his destiny.

In the dream, God appears at the top of a ladder on which angels are passing between heaven and earth, and he confirms the blessing Isaac gave Jacob. The Covenant of Abraham is his, he will inherit the land, and all the world will be blessed through him and his seed. Jacob wakes in the night, gripped by awe. This is his first such vision. The hoax played on his father had been urged on him by his mother Rebecca, sister to the tricky Laban, and here, if only in a dream, comes divine endorsement of Rebecca's trick. Jacob must make his way from now on in a tricky unforgiving world, not in the character that Holy Writ first ascribed to him, "a simple man, dwelling in tents," but by struggle, contrivance, and trouble. Yet it is only a dream. Next day, on awakening, he prays for no more than *bread to eat, clothes to wear, and a return in peace to my father.* If he is granted that much and no more, he will take the dream as fulfilled, worship the God who appeared to him, and pay him tithes.

The wrestle twenty years later is no dream, and as Holy Writ tells it, Jacob's opponent is not an angel, but an unidentified man. The unexplained silent contest goes on all night. Unable to throw the patriarch, the stranger injures Jacob's thigh, but still cannot break loose. As the dawn is coming up, he begs Jacob to let him go. Jacob asks his blessing before releasing him, and the man at last takes on an unearthly aspect to say, *"You will no longer be called Jacob but Israel, for you have struggled with God and man, and have prevailed."* The man refuses to give his name, but he was neither dream nor hallucination, for when the sun rises, Jacob is limping from the thigh injury, memorialized forever in our kashrut laws.

Somewhere in Coleridge's *Table Talk* he remarks, referring to Jacob's displacing Esau and outwitting Laban, "Jacob is a regular Jew." It is the old English view of Jews that created Shylock and Fagin. Yet in a sense is not Jacob the one displaced? Scripture tells us that he is born holding Esau's heel. Destined to inherit the Covenant, barred from it by a minute or two of primogeniture, he seizes a favoring moment to offer to buy the birthright. The impulsive Esau, who comes in ravenous from the risky hunt, mocks at primogeniture—*"I can die anytime, what is the birthright to me?"* He wants a hot meal and he wants it now. Holy Writ then gives us all of Esau in five staccato active Hebrew verbs: *he ate, drank, got up, left,* and *despised* the birthright. Nevertheless, no matter how unworthy Esau was, or how richly he has prospered, what Jacob did to obtain the blind Isaac's blessing halts him at the Jordan, as he is about to reenter the Holy Land. Abraham challenged God, Shall the judge of all the world not do justice? How can Abraham's inheritor face the older twin whom he displaced by a subterfuge?

Here is how Jacob does it. First of all, he prepares to meet the oncoming Esau by sending ahead munificent gifts of flocks and herds, for he has learned the way of the world. Next he divides all he has—wives, children, property, servants—into two camps, so that at least one can escape and survive Esau's onslaught. Then, he prays with all his might to the Lord who appeared to him in the ladder dream. Not enough. He must still wrestle all night with "a man," who the Midrash says is the guardian angel of Esau. The sun rises on a Jacob lamed, changed, and with a new name, Israel. Unlike the irreversible change from Abram to Abraham, Jacob becomes Israel, yet thereafter he is called now Jacob, now Israel all through Scripture. In him, and in us who come after him, the struggle goes on with man and with God.

As for his wronged brother, when he arrives and Jacob prostrates himself seven times in penitence, Esau embraces him and kisses him.

Eleven

THE LAW

Genesis is a family story, a tale of origins, a dramatized genealogy. The story of the Jews as a nation begins in Exodus, and runs through the remaining four books over forty years. Exodus in essence is Moses' book. Leviticus is Aaron's book. Numbers (Hebrew name *Bamidbar*, "In the Desert") takes God's people from Sinai to the Jordan, to the death of Aaron and the last days of Moses. Deuteronomy is Moses' Farewell Address. These four books contain the Torah proper, our religious Law. In *This Is My God* I have already written an account of the religion, sketching the main beliefs, holy days, and disciplines, as clearly as I could. A summary word here then, no more, about each of the last four humashim, to round out this glimpse into the beating heart of our heritage.

Second Humesh: Moses

The second humesh is a many-layered text, composed of the grand drama of the Exodus, a few tight-packed chapters of the Mosaic civil and criminal codes, and a massive account—very hard going except for scholars—of the Tabernacle. The pivot is the Revelation at Sinai, where Abraham's Covenant is renewed between the Creator and all Israel, a commitment that for the faithful among us is binding to this hour.

The statues of the Pharaohs towering in Egypt's deserts, stiff stone giants thousands of years old, project without words the cruel power that Moses had to confront. Joseph's Pharaoh is a cold customer profiting hugely by his Hebrew vizier's farsighted policies, but the Pharaoh of the Exodus is something else. His very entrance is villainous. "And a Pharaoh arose who knew not Joseph"—knew not Joseph, who had acquired all Egypt's arable land for the Pharaohs in perpetuity! This Pharaoh's first act is to enslave Joseph's people, and his second is to try to exterminate them.

My grandfather loved learning this humesh with me. How he savored the flint-hearted arrogant monarch's yielding to Moses, inch by grudging inch, under the lash of the plagues! Zaideh never would have admitted it, but this Pharaoh—in his Litvak Yiddish, *Parreh*—was one of his favorite Scripture characters; as Charles Laughton once said to me, "The villain always has the jammy part." Zaideh never saw a movie, and needed no Hollywood version of this titanic contest of wills. He had the authentic narrative of Holy Writ for his delight, charged with the force of Bible Hebrew, and baroquely embellished by the inexhaustible Midrash. His hero of heroes was of course Moses, *Maysheh Rabbenu*, but his villain of villains was that eternally entertaining black-hat of the second humesh, Parreh.

Zaideh died in Tel Aviv at ninety-four, shortly before the Israelis captured Eichmann and brought him to trial in Jerusalem, when the Holocaust became common knowledge. The grisly parallels between Pharaoh and Hitler might well have made the Exodus story too grim for savoring thereafter. Pharaoh sees in the Jews "*a people more numerous and mighty than we . . . and when war comes they will join our enemies and fight against us,*" Hitler's lunatic rationale for the Nuremberg Laws and the massacre, almost to the letter. Pharaoh enslaves the Jews to work them to death very much on the Wannsee Conference plan,* and orders all male babies immediately drowned at birth. The midwives evade that order, and Pharaoh evidently finds the slaves too useful on his vast building projects simply to kill them outright. There the Germans differed. The Jewish slave labor in factories like I. G. Farben's did hugely contribute to the war effort, and the Germans worked innumerable thousands of them to death, but outright murder took precedence in the end.

The Tabernacle

Newcomers to Torah, however highly motivated, must bog down in the latter part of Exodus when they run into the blueprint of the Tabernacle (*Mishkan*), chapter on chapter about the portable temple of boards and curtains that traveled with the Israelites in the desert. The question arises, why all this huge pile-up of opaque description, putting a dead halt to a wondrous epic narrative?

To traditional Jews that is no question; the Torah is given so, and there an end. I would venture not a d'var Torah, but a mere guess at the reason. There could be disturbing resemblances to pagan worship in any form of temple design, sacrificial ceremonies, or priestly vestments, but the Israelites had this reassuring word-by-word instruction: do it so, because God so commanded Moses. And the Torah reports first the instructions and then their execution, repeated virtually line by line. This Mishkan will be the model for Solomon's Temple and the Second Temple; also the Third Temple to come, "speedily and in our days," as our Chabad rabbi invariably ends every sermon, just as my grandfather did. No detail is too small to be specified, down to the gold or brass hooks for different curtains.

---

*The original Nazi extermination program. See Note, page 290.

Third Humesh: Aaron

Leviticus mostly relates to the Tabernacle. The Lord who descended on Sinai in thunder, flame, and thick cloud has become a Voice from behind a curtain, heard only by Moses. A terrifying practical problem is this *Sh'khinah*, the Presence of the living God amid a people on the march! How deal with it? This is Aaron's domain of service, and so the humesh centers on him. Moses teaches the law as the Voice dictates it. The carrying out is for Aaron and his sons.

The humesh begins with the code of sacrifices, a very high hurdle indeed for the novice in Torah. All of Leviticus, to be plain, is an obstacle course to the uncommitted: dietary laws, marital laws, laws for ritual purity, forbidden sexual unions and practices, priesthood ordinances, and long chapters about a strange affliction, *tzaraat*, inaccurately called leprosy. It is not a humesh for the fainthearted, the hostile, or those inclined to smirk. It is a challenge to the astute inquirer, and—curiously—a traditional study for children, under the rubric, *Let those who are pure come and study the laws of purity.*

Amid these difficult legal passages comes a lurid burst of narrative, on the day of the very first service to the Lord God in his new earthly dwelling. Aaron and his four sons have rehearsed the prescribed ceremonies with Moses for a week. The Tabernacle has been erected, taken down, and put up again, seven times in seven days. The great day dawns, the unforgettable eighth day, and Aaron and his sons, clad in the ordained vestments, commence the service in the presence of assembled Israel. To the mingled awe and joy of the multitude, "fire from the Lord" consumes the first sacrifice ever laid on the altar. With a mighty shout the people prostrate themselves, but their joy turns to disbelieving horror, when almost at once the same fire from the Lord kills Aaron's two older sons stone dead. The cause? They offered "strange" incense, Holy Writ says; that is, incense not authorized by the minutely exact instructions for the service.

In this supreme trial, the iron bearing of Aaron defines him. Scripture tells that, as his sons lie dead at his feet, "Aaron was silent." He proceeds with the service flawlessly to the last detail, even correcting Moses on a recondite point of ceremonial law. The Midrash says that God himself visited Aaron to comfort him. Talmud sages and commentators down the centuries struggle with the bafflement of this gruesome fiasco on an infinitely sacred day. There are many answers. There is no one answer. That is how the Torah tells it. The rest is exegesis and conjecture.

Priest and Prophet

"Be of the disciples of Aaron," says the great Rabbi Hillel, in the Talmud book *Ethics of the Fathers*, "loving peace, pursuing peace, loving the people and bringing them closer to Torah." This Hillel says of Aaron, who was responsible for the Golden Calf, the catastrophic crisis in the Torah where he, so wholly overshadowed by the Lawgiver, briefly takes center stage.

Considering the roles the two brothers played in that crisis, one would think Hillel's model for emulation would be Moses, not Aaron. When Moses has been gone for forty days, the people come protesting to Aaron that "the man Moses" has vanished into the dark cloud on the mountain, and they must have a god to lead them. Aaron does not refuse, he temporizes: *bring me the gold rings in the ears of your wives, sons, and daughters.* The gold is forthcoming at once in heaps, no doubt to his surprise and discomfiture. It goes into the smelter, the calf emerges, and again Aaron stalls: "a feast to the Lord God tomorrow!" Not to the calf of gold, be it noted, but to the Lord God; he is playing for time, confident that Moses will reappear. And Moses does, but only when the sacrilegious orgy is at a roar.

Prophet and priest are different offices. Moses and Aaron are different men. Moses has come out of obscurity at eighty with his mandate from the burning bush. The older Aaron is a familiar figure to the tribes, a senior Levite married into the leading family of Judah. That he can be as strong-minded as Moses, and even more levelheaded, he will demonstrate later, on that terrible eighth day. But the fierceness of the prophet is not in his nature. He loves peace, pursues peace, loves the people, and brings them closer to the Torah. At the Golden Calf that is not enough. The moment calls for a prophet to shatter the tablets, overawe the people, pound their idol to powder, and order execution of the rioters who resist his God-inspired wrath.

The force of a Moses is beyond the likes of us, but the affection of Aaron for his fellow Jews, impelling him to hold contact with them however far they stray, is worth emulating and we can do it, says Hillel. As to showing Aaron's metal in tragedy, we can only pray that we may never be so tested.

Fourth Humesh: Transition

Numbers is a pallid title for this book, a kaleidoscopic forty-year melange of laws, wanderings, miracles, mutinies, plagues, battles, defeats, victories, and leadership crises. The Hebrew name, "In the Desert," is more to the point. Yet the translators, from the Septuagint to the King James Bible, had their reasons for calling it Numbers. The humesh begins with a census of the nation tribe by tribe at Sinai, gives another near the end, and records musters of the tribes on the march, and of the Levites in their Tabernacle tasks. All in all, a lot of numbers.

On the whole, the book is a transition from the exalted visions at Sinai to the dusty jobs of war outside Canaan. Early on, a mutiny against Moses and Aaron is quelled by a fearsome fate for the conspirators; they plummet alive into a fissure that opens in the sands, as by an earthquake on a fault line. That horror past, the Torah does something that still jars me when I go over this humesh. *The narrative skips thirty-eight years without a word about the time lapse.* Chapter 19 ends, Chapter 20 begins, and we are at the death of Miriam, the death of Aaron, and the battles for the territory that today is Jordan. Shakespeare in *The Winter's Tale*, when he leaps sixteen years from one scene to the next, brings on Time as chorus to soliloquize in apology. Our Sacred Narrator does as he pleases, and leaves it to us to "study and earn reward," in the Talmud phrase.

Of the manifold action scenes in Numbers, the story of Balaam and his loquacious donkey tends to overshadow the rest, especially for jokers like the redoubtable Mark Twain. Maimonides convincingly takes this narration as a dream sequence. In any case, what really matters is the singular figure of a heathen prophet, hired by the frightened king of Moab to curse Israel, who cannot help instead blessing them over and over, and prophesying their great future far into a Messianic age.

> Behold, it is a people that will dwell alone, and not be reckoned among the nations . . .
>
> The Lord perceives no iniquity in Jacob, and no offense in Israel, The Lord his God is with him . . .
>
> How goodly are your tents, O Jacob, your tabernacles, O Israel . . .
>
> I see him, but not now; I behold him, but not near; there shall come a star out of Jacob, and a sceptre shall rise out of Israel. . . .

Every morning when we enter the synagogue, the first words we speak on touching the mezuzah are the heathen Balaam's: "How goodly are your tents, O Jacob . . ."

Death of Aaron

In the end, Balaam delivers. He does better than curse Israel, he advises Israel's adversaries instead how to get at them by natural means, to wit, loose women and idolatrous debauchery. At a site of pagan worship called Baal-Peor, a tumultuous replay of the Golden Calf disaster breaks out. By this time, Aaron is dead, and his grandson Pinkhas, leaping into the breach with something like Mosaic rage, halts the revel in as bloody a scene as any in Scripture.

A quietly affecting scene, by contrast, is the passing of Aaron, which has preceded it. The Lord has decreed that both Moses and Aaron must die outside the Promised Land, for an obscure offense which draws copious rabbinic analysis; a slight departure from God's orders, in causing a rock miraculously to gush forth water, to quell a riot over drouth in the camp. When at God's command Aaron's time comes, Moses ascends a mountain with him and Eleazar, his oldest surviving son. At the summit he strips the high priest's garments from Aaron, and before his eyes puts them on Eleazar. Moses and the new high priest descend the mountain together, and Aaron is seen no more. All Israel mourns him for a month, then marches on.

Happy is the father whose last sight on earth is his son filling his place in life.

Fifth Humesh: The Second Torah

Deuteronomy is a book apart. Moses is addressing the new generation about the forty-year epic of wandering that is drawing to a close, and the millennial epic of life in the Land that lies ahead. The prose is of another texture than the rest of the Torah. The sentences are longer, the cadences dithyrambic. The Lawgiver's personal style ranges wide, from plain speaking to soaring poetry, from severe warnings to tender love for the flock he must soon tend no more. There is no action until God orders Moses, in a short passage at the very end, to yield the leadership to Joshua and climb Mount Pisgah alone to die.

The rabbis called this book *Mishneh Torah*, or "Second Law," and the Septuagint Greek title, Deuteronomy, means precisely that. Moses is reviewing the Torah, with some illuminating variations. His version of the Ten Commandments, for instance, differs from the first text, and each minute variant is the subject of massive scholarly comment. He says very little about Genesis and the pre-Sinai part of Exodus. The departing leader is admonishing a new generation about the life-and-death importance of hewing to God's commands, and spelling out the Torah for them anew, in his own voice and words.

The Rav

The peerless philosopher-Talmudist of our time, Joseph Soloveitchik of Yeshiva University, once said that the Talmud, our Oral Law—*Torah Sheh B'aal Peh*—begins in this humesh, an insight like a bolt of forked lightning.

Soloveitchik was known as *the Rav*, "the Teacher." While he lived, those words meant him and him alone. In the Jewish learned world, he remains the Rav still. A slight man with a small beard and singularly powerful eyes, he was as much a savant in Kant as in the remotest reaches of Talmud. When I was a visiting professor of English at the Rav's university—appointed more for my celebrity as a novelist than for my scholarship—I was beguiled into giving a talk in the main auditorium, where there was always standing room only for the Rav's rare public lectures. As I came in and saw a sparse audience barely filling half the rows, I heard one student say to another, "After all, he's not the Rav," which put me neatly in my place in that seat of learning.

The Oral Torah was passed along by word of mouth for many centuries, but this broad corpus of Talmudic law, tradition holds, comes down from Moses on Sinai, no less than the exceedingly terse text of the Torah. The great rabbis who violated the prohibition against writing down the Oral Law in the Talmud based their action on Psalms 119:126, "It is time to act for the Lord; they are traducing the Torah." In a turbulent era they saw knowledge and observance waning, the survival of the faith at stake, so they acted. The Rav, in an annual lecture in his father's memory, explored in his piquant Yiddish a fine Midrash on this theme. Moses in Heaven overhears Rabbi Akiva, down on earth, expounding a razor-sharp Talmudic point in halakhah. "Is that baldhead quoting me?" he exclaims in amazement, and he is told yes, indeed, that point is a tradition from Moses on Sinai. And in that sense, does not the Oral Torah in fact start in the fifth humesh? It is Moses himself who says, *"Hear O Israel, the Lord our God, the Lord is one, and you shall love the Lord your God with all your heart, with all your soul, and with all your might."* According to the Torah, those words, the creed of our people, were not spoken before then by the Voice on the mountain, or in the Holy of Holies. They are the words of the human Lawgiver, making his last farewells.

Learning Humesh

A word to sum up. The Torah for the most part is eminently readable. The world reads it in a hundred languages, but for us it is not reading matter, it is learning matter. One should go slow. A good pace is the weekly *sedra*, which traverses the Five Books in a year. I have been doing that since I came back from my war years at sea, having decided that being Jewish was the key to the life I had laid on the line.

A highly intellectual old friend of mine, now deceased, was a rabid agnostic, and he told me how he got that way. He had a Hebrew tutor who kept shouting at him, "What is Rashi's question? *What is Rashi's question?*" until one day he shouted back, "I don't care what Rashi's question is, I'm not a Jew, I'm an American!" With that he ran out of the house, and declared to his parents afterward that he was through with Hebrew. So he was, more's the pity. He had a good Jewish head, with a broad streak of Jewish stiff neck.

His tale is an epitome of the second-generation flight from Yiddishkeit; on the one hand, old-country teaching by a *melamed* in stumbling English, on the other hand, American kids growing up on movies and Tarzan books, while bringing home from public school the report cards that mattered. That era is long past. The melameds are gone, and day schools offer robust Jewish and general education together. Meanwhile, the catastrophic collapse of Yiddishkeit in the United States has happened. For those of us who want to ensure American Jewish generations worth mentioning, retrieving that heritage is all uphill work. An early stretch of the ascent is learning humesh, and it offers rewarding views as one climbs.

"The Lawgiver"

A scuffed file in my desk drawer labeled *The Lawgiver* contains a few typed yellow pages turning brown with age. When I was writing *The Caine Mutiny*, it occurred to me that there was no greater theme for a novel, if I could rise to it, than the life of Moses. The file dates to that time. The years have rolled over me. I have not quailed at large tasks. World War Two and the wars of Israel were sizable challenges, but I took them on. The Lawgiver remains unwritten. I have never found the way to do it. Other ideas for books I have set aside (no time, no time!), but I still hope against hope for a bolt of lightning, which will yet inspire me to pen my own picture of Maysheh Rabbenu, the Rav of mankind.

Twelve

NAKH: THE PROPHETS
AND THE WRITINGS

The Hexateuch

Old age has its pleasures, exiguous though they may be. Seeing the sweet light every morning is the main thing, and then there is the wry amusement of observing how reputations balloon and collapse, how fashions come and go in ideas as well as in women's hairdos, and how one generation's certainties can become the old-fogy notions of the next. So it has fared with a former finality in Bible study, the Hexateuch.

This notion evidently arose when deconstructing the Bible was a modish game, eighty or ninety years ago. The nub of it was that the Pentateuch as such never existed, that there was a *six-book* history of early Israel, the Five Books of Moses plus the Book of Joshua, hence *Hex*-ateuch. In the Bible article of my old *Encyclopædia Britannica*, dated 1938, the Hexateuch is presented as a matter of fact like the law of gravitation, yet in my current Britannica, it goes unmentioned, even in the index. In half a century the Hexateuch has dropped off the screen of Bible scholarship. How come? Well, almost any professorial speculation can have a good run in academia, if it is speculation à la mode.

The Hexateuch was a chimera from the start, for the Book of Joshua has little in common with the sublime discourses of Moses in Deuteronomy, except that it picks up the story after the Lawgiver dies. The narrative style of Joshua seems to me much more like the rough speedy Hebrew of Judges. Those two books together span several centuries, in a vivid episodic transition from Mosaic to Davidic times, from Deuteronomy to the Books of Samuel. Once the David epic begins there, the narrative pace slows to unfold the grand drama.

Style aside, there is an unbridgeable chasm between the Five Books of Moses and Joshua, indeed between the Five Books and the rest of the Bible. *The Mosaic Books alone contain God's revealed Law; there is not a single law in all of the Prophets and Writings, let alone in Joshua.* How the Hexateuch scholiasts missed this glaringly obvious point is not for me to guess at. One by one, aberrations like the Hexateuch come and go. The adamantine Writ stands.

The First Prophets

When one reads Nakh, especially the history books called in our canon the First Prophets, artistic parallels to works outside Scripture leap to mind. At the moment I am reading again the *Iliad* of Homer, the primal narrative voice of pagan antiquity. In the First Prophets, the scenes and character portrayals march along with Homeric stride—Samuel, first in the line of fierce uncompromising Hebrew prophets; the pathetic King Saul, physically heroic, morally weak; the giant-killing shepherd lad David, anointed to supplant Saul, and forced to flee for his life from the king's murderous envy; the love of Saul's brave self-effacing son Jonathan for David, who is displacing him for the throne; David's amours and wars, worst of all the civil war with his darling son Absalom, the would-be regicide. From an aesthetic viewpoint, just a cool humanist one, surely this is narrative art in the realm of the *Iliad*.

Of course, the bedrock difference is inescapable. Homer passes few moral judgments, and Scripture is all moral judgment. In *Troilus and Cressida,* Shakespeare has the cowardly Thersites say of the *Iliad*'s theme, the nine-year war to recapture Helen of Troy, "The matter is only a cuckold and a whore." The exact detail in the *Iliad,* the poetic sweep, the evocation of nature, the small strokes of character that bring ancient figures to life, can be likened to Scriptural storytelling. Compare, however, Achilles and Samson, both of them flawed supermen.

An angel tells Samson's pregnant mother that her son will judge Israel and deliver the nation from its enemies, and so he does. But a weakness for alien women and a mighty man's will to live as he pleases cause his downfall. "*Oh, God, remember me, and strengthen me only this once, and let my soul perish with the Philistines!*" His prayer granted, the blinded Samson pulls down the temple of Dagon on himself and his pagan tormentors, "*so the dead whom he slew at his death were more than they whom he slew in life.*" By contrast, when Achilles gets over his sulk and roars into battle, he kills Troy's noble hero Hector, and drags his body behind his chariot around the city walls, in full sight of Hector's wife and child. The flaring carnage of the *Iliad* closes with Achilles lording it over the defeated King Priam as he pleads for the broken body of his son. A bitter scene, and cold truth as the Greek spirit sees it.

As for the gods in the *Iliad,* they are amoral whimsical phantasms, who behave on the whole worse than the human players.

The Later Prophets

Comparisons fall away when one comes to the literary prophets, for there is no parallel in other cultures to the intimate if rocky relationship of the Lord God and his people. A recent book, *The Creation of the Sacred,* traces the God-idea to primitive conditions of human society. As conditions improved, the author maintains, the ancient deities became extinct by a sort of cultural natural selection. He does mention in passing the Jewish God as a curious anomaly in the process, an honest scholarly concession. One may not believe that men will ever beat their swords into plowshares and cease to learn war, but Isaiah's prophecy is etched in the stonework outside the United Nations building, as the word of the living God.

In the Later Prophets, one hits boggy passages about ancient public affairs, since they are commenting on the current scene, much as our television savants do nowadays. The words of our talking heads may not survive twenty-five centuries, but in all fairness, they do not pretend to such power and insight; not all of them, anyway. These prophets flourished from about the eighth to the fifth centuries B.C., some three hundred years of blood-soaked troubles swirling around the two small Jewish kingdoms, as Assyria, Babylon, Egypt, and Persia vied for hegemony. The minor rebellions, alliances, and counter-alliances of the time tangle up Israelite history beyond penetration except by lifelong scholars, but it really doesn't matter to the ordinary reader.

Obscured here and there by the fog of old battles and the scuffled dust of old politics, the immortal words shine through, burning with undimmed passion and poetic fire. Isaiah above all has grandeur; Jeremiah, grief-stricken force; Ezekiel, harsh genius of vision. Their oracles are colored not only by their individualities but by the times they were living in. Preaching a century and a half before the end, Isaiah's note is far-seeing and lofty; Jeremiah is present at the Destruction, crushed by woe yet pleading to the last against fatal leadership follies; Ezekiel is a captive in Babylon, addressing his fellow exiles—the dry bones of his vision—in a new vein of consolation. These three very different seers are frozen in painted gigantism on Michelangelo's Sistine Chapel ceiling in the Vatican, far, far above the head of the humble viewer craning his neck. They belong no less in the Jewish reader's hands. If they overawe on the printed page too, it is by what all three have in common, command of language at a far reach of human power.

The Library of Congress has, in its fabulous collections, Bibles in most languages of the earth. I have looked through some of these, and have wondered at what the translators could possibly have made of the tougher passages in our Hebrew prophets. It is a strange feeling to discern in such Bibles, in unfamiliar languages and alphabets, the names of Isaiah, Jeremiah, and Ezekiel.

The Twelve

The Minor Prophets, called in our canon The Twelve, vary in style, from the crystalline Hebrew of Joel and Nahum to the near-opacity of some chapters in Hosea. Those who read the Bible only in English are at an advantage in this respect. One can sit down and read the Book of Hosea in English in an hour, and get a real idea of the book, for the translators have had their go at the obscurities and have ironed them out to readability. A Hebrew scholar who decides to work through Hosea once more in earnest has set himself a tough job.

The Twelve in English offer the reader a kaleidoscopic variety of style, personality, and content, the narrative nugget of Jonah, with his psalm-like prayer in the belly of the fish, contrasting starkly with the exalted social conscience of the mighty Amos. This anthology of prophecies, or fragments of prophecy, is considered in the Hebrew canon as one book, and all The Twelve are contained in a single synagogue scroll.

The Writings: The Book of Job

In the Hebrew Bible, Job stands alone. Ascribed to no Jewish author, void of specific Jewish history, doctrine, or practice, Job deals head-on with the central and ultimate challenge to the Jewish religion: the disparity of things as they ought to be under a just God, and things as they appear to be in Homeric fact. Without this book, Hebrew Scripture would be incomplete. Job balances the Revelation at Sinai. In translation, the book is harrowing enough, but the craggy, sometimes tortured, Hebrew eerily calls up the agony of a just man on the rack of an unjust experiment, performed by Satan with the incomprehensible permission of God.

The King James Version smoothes away the difficulties, and the dithyrambs of Job and his comforters roll along in sonorous Elizabethan prose-poetry, for the translators and Shakespeare were contemporaries. As a Talmud saying goes, "Job was not born and never existed, he was a parable." The story does not purport to take place in real time. A prologue of a debate between the Lord and Satan sets up the frame for the drama, which plays out without any reference to Jewish history, focused sharply on the eternal problem of an omnipotent Creator and a randomly, sometimes horribly, unjust Creation. Our Scripture is a whole work because the Book of Job is there, not comforting, not explaining, "telling it like it is," as we Americans say. Any bland presentation of Judaism is a lie, and the Book of Job gives it the lie. "The Lord God is truth," says Jeremiah. Job is truth. My own small tribute to this anonymous cloud-capped masterwork is in Aaron Jastrow's sermon to the doomed Jews of Theresienstadt, in *War and Remembrance*.

The Five Scrolls

From my desk dictionary: MEGILLAH: *(Yiddish) a long involved story.* Actually "megillah" is old Hebrew, and it means a scroll. Five books called Scrolls are read in the synagogue on different holidays: The Song of Songs, Ruth, Ecclesiastes, Lamentations, and Esther. The Book of Esther is *the* megillah par excellence. The centerpiece of Purim, this book must be chanted in a once-a-year mode from a parchment scroll, and hearing the megillah is obligatory by rabbinic law. An occasion for wassail, gift-giving, mummers, and general merriment, Purim is preceded by a fast day, but the fast tends to be neglected, hence a sharp Yiddish byword for self-indulgence: "with a full stomach to the Megillah."

Esther is a story of Jews in the Persian exile who, faced with a royally decreed holocaust, turn on their would-be slaughterers in a political and military counterblow. Haman, the archetype anti-Semite, is a villain to rival the Pharaoh of Moses. When Julius Streicher, the grossest of the criminal Nazi leaders, was about to be hanged, his last act was to shake his fist and utter a despairing bellow from the gallows: "Purimfest, 1946!" The name of the Lord never appears in the Book of Esther, for the reversal, a masked miracle, happens in an apparently natural way. The queen, a crypto-Jewess, risks death to reveal her identity, turns the king around, and has Haman hanged. Hence, Julius Streicher's apt last words.

The Song of Songs is read on Passover. Its mood fits the springtime, and tradition takes this mysterious sacred text of love lyrics as an allegory of the love between the Lord and the Jewish people. Kabbalah leans heavily on the Song, pious Jews read it every Sabbath eve, and there is no end to its interpretations. Ruth, a pastoral love story about a Moabite widow of a Jewish émigré, who becomes a righteous convert and the great-grandmother of King David, is the megillah of *Shavuot*, read at the start of summer. Ecclesiastes—in Hebrew *Kohelet*—is the long autumnal scroll, read during *Sukkot* (Tabernacles), at the end of harvest time, a philosophical meditation, melancholy, detached, ironic, elegiac, my own favorite book among the Writings.

Lamentations is the scroll of the Temple Destruction, and hearing it read on the Ninth of Av is a religious duty for the observant.

Apocalypse and Common Sense

In two books of the Writings—Daniel and Proverbs—the age-old tension between mysticism and common sense finds its Scriptural place.

Common sense, the sum of experience of human life and the workings of nature, does not vary too widely from culture to culture, from faith to faith. The sun rises and sets on all, the seasons change for all, and all are born to brief life and sure death. The wisdom concerning these things is similar, being anchored in universal fact, and tends to converge in all religions. Mysticism, on the other hand, expresses intuitions of a reality beyond what common sense takes as the real world, and so comes in wildly variant forms, having no limit in the things that can be observed. Judaism has its share of this transcendental vein, notably in Kabbalah.

Holy Writ's handbook of common sense is the Book of Proverbs. My father tried to press Proverbs on me in my youth, but alas, "Seest thou a man wise in his own wisdom? There is more hope for a fool than for him." I imagine that few can read Proverbs in mature life without acrid regret. Proverbs can be as hardheaded as Machiavelli or La Rochefoucauld, but in its Godly essence it parts from those wise cynics. An early verse sets the tone: "Awe of the Lord is the beginning of wisdom." In Bacon's essays, studded with quotes from Proverbs, he puts that thought in his stately English: "A little philosophy turneth a man from religion, but more bringeth him to it again." One is never quite sure, though, whether the wily Bacon is being honest or politic in what he writes.

The Book of Daniel is the mystic locus of Scripture, though a visionary strain runs through the Prophets as well. Daniel abounds in unforgettable images: the handwriting on the wall at Belshazzar's feast (*Mene, mene, tekel, upharsin*),* the saints cool and safe in the

---

*See Notes, page 292.

fiery furnace, and Daniel uneaten in the ravenous lions' den. The book is partly in Hebrew, partly in Aramaic, a puzzlement that leaves scholars at odds. It starts with a simple narrative of a pious young Jewish exile in Babylon, who interprets the king's dreams and is raised to high office with his friends Shadrakh, Mishakh, and Abed-nego. Court intrigue gets the three friends thrown into a furnace, and Daniel fed to the lions. When they emerge unscathed from these ordeals, their accusers are in turn cast into the furnace and thrown to the lions, who *crush their bones before they reach the bottom of the den.*

In a sharp shift to the first person, Daniel himself then recounts his mystic visions of events to come, culminating in the end of history and the awakening of the dead. Angels interpret the bizarre imagery of the visions for him, but the interpretations are not much less ambiguous than the symbols. Powerful rabbinic minds have endlessly explored these mysteries, and no less a gentile genius than Isaac Newton labored over the Book of Daniel, trying to unravel the apocalyptic predictions. His copious writings on the subject are shrugged off as a lapse of bad nerves and old age. Daniel's apocalypse remains a perennial conundrum to scholars, and still awaits a mind greater than Newton's to pierce the veil, and perhaps even figure out just when and what the end of days will be. Meantime the world wags on, as it has in the two thousand and more years since Daniel, and the three-hundred-odd years since Newton.

Psalms: The *T'hillim Yid*

Of all the treasures of our Scriptures that have been taken into world culture, none is more popular than Psalms—in Hebrew *T'hillim*—an anthology of a hundred fifty songs and poems, seventy-three directly ascribed to David. Some Jews recite the whole book or long

sections of it every day. Such a devotee is called a *T'hillim Yid.*
Christianity has appropriated T'hillim whole in the Psalter. In
Islam, the Koran recognizes only two books of our Scripture as
divinely inspired, the Torah and Psalms.

If Job completes our Bible by challenging God, the Psalms
occupy a middle ground between challenged and challenger. A few
Psalms in which the Psalmist cries out from the depths are as
despairing as any passage in Job, but the cry usually ends on a note
of hope. However defeated and crushed, the Psalmist never questions the existence or beneficence of the Lord. The word *tehillah*
itself means praise. The Psalms in sum are an exalted celebration of
life, of nature, and of faith in the Creator.

It is clear from the form of some psalms that they were sung in
temple worship. Some are in our daily and holiday liturgies. When
Menachem Begin signed the Camp David peace treaty on television before the eyes of the world, he put on a skullcap and recited a
psalm. Watchers over the dead read psalms. In the old country,
psalms were hung on the bed of a woman in labor. A wry joke in
Israel tells of a rabbi rushing into a yeshiva at the outbreak of a war.
"The Arabs are attacking. Do something! Read psalms!"

A friend of mine, a Christian Bible scholar, once asked to go
along with me to a morning service. On a weekday we Jews tend to
daven—that is, pray—in a murmured chant at a breakneck pace. I
was not sure what he would get out of it, but I reluctantly agreed.
In the synagogue I discreetly signaled to the rabbi that my guest did
not count for the minyan. This man's specialty, as it happens, is
Psalms; he is a world authority on the text. I could see him look
pained as we davenned through the morning psalms, and afterward
he said to me, "How can they understand a word, rattling off such
marvelous poetry the way they do? And their accents—terrible!" I
recounted this incident to a son of mine. "Go explain to a
Christian about davening," he said.

To an outsider, the Jewish way with Psalms may in truth seem casual, if not rote. More than in any other fashion, it is through Psalms that we talk to our Father in Heaven, or at least try to, not in the sonority of the pulpit, but in our private informal individual voices. Psalms are our open line to the God of Israel, and in that sense every Jew can be a T'hillim Yid, to the extent of his heart's impulse. The Hebrew of these poems varies from simple to extremely difficult. In the King James Psalter, all difficulties are planed down, and one is in the presence of a familiar classic of the English-speaking peoples. "The Lord is my shepherd, I shall not want . . ." is well known beyond the circles of the T'hillim Yid.

Nakh: Summary

I have raced through Nakh like a davener on a busy weekday, pledged as I am to sketch the Heritage so that "he who runs may read," and at least glimpse the rich patrimony that is there to be claimed. The Writings are the Scripture books most accessible to the questing mind. The histories can get complicated, the Prophets can seem in parts remote and obscure, the Torah is daunting in its Mosaic awesomeness. But the Books of Ruth and Esther are perfectly constructed short literary gems, Ecclesiastes is Montaigne and Marcus Aurelius in a small Godly compass, and the T'hillim are the hymnal of the world to the Creator. The peoples sing the hymns, but they are ours.

Thirteen

THE TALMUD AND I

"Laig Tzu Kop"

For readability the Talmud is a different literary landscape than the Bible. After half a lifetime of almost daily study, I can open a Talmud tractate to a random page and at first not make head nor tail of it. Much of the Talmud is in Aramaic, but that is not the problem; I have learned to handle Aramaic. The problem is in the compression, the speed, the multiple recondite allusions, the assumption that you are equal to this fast-paced game, for if not, what are you doing poking your nose into the Talmud? And sure enough, once I "lay head to it" ("*Laig tzu kop!*" Grandpa would say), the page begins to come alive with the elegant music of the mind which restores a Jewish soul, and peculiarly appeals to a Jewish head.

This Is My God contains a detailed account of the Talmud which needs no updating, as the subject is changeless. Here is a much abridged extract:

> To begin with, the Talmud is not one book, but two books run together. They are the *Mishna* and the *Gemara,* a pair of very old classics of Jewish law. . . . The Mishna states the legal decisions of a line of analysts and judges, the *Tanna'im,* or Teachers, stretching over some four hundred years . . . two centuries before

and two after the start of the Christian era. Rabbi Judah the Prince compiled the Mishna (the Review) in Palestine about the year 200. . . . A second great line of sages, the *Amora'im,* or Commenters, explored Rabbi Judah's work for three more centuries, debating it line by line and between the academies of Palestine and Babylon. . . . That is how the Talmud came to take its present form. We have four or five sentences of Mishna, laying down the law . . . followed by a page or twenty pages of close legal analysis, in Hebrew and Aramaic, which can branch off into tales, poems, prayers, history, reminiscence, science, or table talk. This is the Gemara, the Completion. . . .

Such are the bare facts about the Babylonian Talmud. Mishna is the legal core. Gemara is the game. Gemara arguments can strike fire from a Jewish head, as a safety match does from its folded cover. Strike the match on stone and nothing happens; strike it on the cover and it flames. I ask the reader to *laig tzu kop,* believe me that the scary Talmud can be accessible, and come along on a brief guided tour. The paradox of all this is that at any age, and on any page, one can start learning Talmud and—with a teacher who knows something—be rewarded at once, and perhaps caught for life. I can prove it. I have seen it happen.

Digression: The Jewish Head

Let me be clear. Anyone who thinks that there really is such a thing as a *Yiddisheh kop,* Jewish head, and that it is not just a figure of speech, is being elitist, unscientific, and politically incorrect to a tar-and-feathering degree. I got the intellectual dressing-down of my life from a famed microbiologist, for suggesting that Talmudic acumen might pass down by inheritance, as certain ailments do among ethnic groups, Jews included. I was crushed to a bloody mental pulp. Such diseases are due to *defects* in genes, I was reminded, likely to recur in small inbred populations; but as for an "acumen gene" or balance of genes, all people inherit the same human genome. The central dogma of genetics, I was further harshly admonished, is that information goes one way, from the genes to the individual. To suggest that an individual's acumen can somehow be captured in his or her germ plasm and passed on is a heresy of bigoted Lamarckian ignorance. I humbly agreed and submitted. Perhaps I barely muttered under my breath, "Nevertheless, it moves."

> *A man convinced against his will*
> *Is of the same opinion still.*

Open and Hidden: Talmud and Kabbalah

For reasons outside the scope of this book, I was self-marooned with my family for years on St. Thomas, Virgin Islands, a bustling green rock in the azure sea, where a Hasidic rabbi on a fund-raising swing through the Caribbean once paid me a visit. Pathetically glad to hear a Yiddish word, I made him very welcome. "What are you learning?" he asked almost at once, for that is how old-time Jews greet each other. I mentioned the Talmud tractate on property law, *Baba Basra*. "Oh, that's *Nigleh*," he said with a dismissive hand wave. "What about *Nistor*?" Nigleh means *open, clear*. Nistor means esoteric, hidden. He was referring to Kabbalah. I admitted I was not much up on Nistor, and though my donation pleased him, I obviously sank in his regard.

The difference between Talmud and Kabbalah is not too unlike that between Proverbs and Daniel, between pragmatic wisdom and transcendental visions, although to be sure the Talmud has its mystical passages, and Kabbalah its inner logical coherence. At any rate, my visitor was reacting in character, for modern Hasidism starts with a revealing of the "hidden" by the eighteenth-century saints of the movement, primarily the Master of the Good Name, the Baal Shem Tov. (More about that in the chapter that follows.) Kabbalah is today an open study among Hasidim, called "Nistor" mainly to set it off from Talmud, "Nigleh." My grandfather told me to let Kabbalah alone until I was forty, and concentrate on Talmud. So I did. Since my Caribbean years I have learned something about Kabbalah, an undeniably powerful element of the Heritage, which I treat later in this book.

Daf Yomi: The Daily Page

In Venice in 1523, a Christian publisher named Daniel Bomberg put out the first printed Talmud, and remarkably enough, no matter where or by whom published, *the Talmud has never since gone to press in any other page-by-page format.* The way Bomberg's Jewish typographers set up the text and main commentaries is exactly the way it appears at the present moment, everywhere in the world. The pagination never varies one iota. Wherever one picks up a Talmud today—Jerusalem, Sydney, Hong Kong, Buenos Aires, Palm Springs, Anchorage—the printing date may be 1876 or 1997, the paper may be excellent or flimsy, the binding gorgeous leather or cheap cardboard, the text may be sharp print or fuzzy photostat, but there is, and for over four hundred years there has been, only one physical layout of the Talmud.*

This unique uniformity enabled a Polish rabbi, Meir Shapira, to propose in 1923 that all interested Jews commence learning one page every day, *the same page,* thereby going through the entire Talmud in a worldwide body in seven years. The idea caught on. By the time I entered the scene, my grandfather was sedulously

*See Notes, page 292.

doing *daf yomi,* the daily page. When I asked him about it he explained, "The whole world learns *daf yomi.*" That was his way. When I would query him about a tough Gemara point, he would say, "The whole world asks that question." That I might enter that "whole world" of his never occurred to me. That I would ever do *daf yomi* was utterly inconceivable.

In my teens I put up with Talmud study for two reasons, really. My grandfather charmed me, and my father cared about it. When I came back from the war with a settled intent to live a Jewish life, I sought out available young rabbis and did serious if sporadic Talmud learning with them. And so, I was able to go it alone in my six-year Caribbean exile. On my return to the States, I landed in Washington, D.C., as the best place to start my War Books, and I also started daf yomi, jumping aboard as it was moving along at a page a day.

Why?

My motive was neither pious nor scholarly, but personal. A dear Israeli friend suddenly and tragically died at fifty, and I determined to try to learn daf yomi in his memory.

Yaakov Herzog managed the Prime Minister's office from Ben-Gurion's time through Golda Meir's. A brilliant diplomatic career followed, during which he once bested Arnold Toynbee in a memorable debate over Toynbee's characterization of Judaism as a "fossil religion." The son of the first Chief Rabbi of Israel, and himself a noted Talmudist, Yaakov's daily radio broadcast of Mishna study had a worldwide audience. He was a rarity among us, and a terrible untimely loss. In the first chapter of this book, my words "I am a Jew of the Talmud" stem from that decision to attempt daf yomi as my private memorial to Yaakov. The learning I had done until then made the effort possible.

What follows is a purely personal account of an unlikely try by an American novelist, while working on an immense World War Two panorama, to learn daf yomi. Facts about the Talmud are available in English nowadays, in encyclopedias and scholarly works, to any depth desired, something that was not true when I wrote *This Is My God*. Nor at that time would I have called myself a Jew of the Talmud. I offer here to share with the reader my seven-year ride on that rocket I caught.

The first thing I found out is that the daily pace is killing. I asked a pious dermatologist I knew, who went into skin diseases because emergencies on Shabbat were unlikely, how much time I should allot to daf yomi. "A half hour a day," he said. I started at two hours, never got below an hour, and at that fell behind time and again. In the daf yomi circles that have sprung up over the years, I daresay the members strive to stay current so as to avoid losing face, but even among them some discreet skimming must go on, every now and then. After all, the world is always with us. Business, flu, travel, holidays, celebrations, deaths, births, marriages all break into that remorseless day by day requirement of learning a page; both sides, by the way, for a daf means a leaf.

The Pilot

Bomberg's learned Jewish typesetters made one inspired decision. Of all the commentaries that had accumulated in manuscript, in the thousand years from the close of the Talmud to the invention of printing, they chose one and only one running guide to the text: *Rashi*, an acronym for Rabbi Shlomo Itzhaki, the eleventh-century French Torah giant.

For many Jews Rashi is the plain-spoken childhood teacher of "*humesh and Rashi*," the Torah text with his short clear comments printed in special "Rashi type," and replete with vivid Midrash.

The Rashi of the Talmud is another man. Only the type is the same. In this work Rashi set himself the giant task of walking Jewry through the whole Talmud, the baffling heritage passed down from Babylon hand to hand in manuscript, reaching his hand after five hundred years. Without his column beside the text, I believe the Talmud would belong today not to all Jews who want to learn, but to a very restricted cadre of scholars. He mastered the vast Talmud as thoroughly as Maimonides would do a hundred years later. With self-effacement rare in genius, he contented himself with line-by-line elucidation for every Jew who could barely learn, like me. Since the Talmud is so interwoven with all halakhah, the threads reappearing sometimes in the least likely contexts, he had to be a Talmudist on the level of an *Amora,* a Commenter, with the same encyclopedic memory and total grasp, to bring the thing off.

There is nothing in the least elementary about his comments. On the contrary, they are as profound as they are understandable. Rashi holds place as one of our mightiest legal authorities. Intellectual power aside, he is a master stylist, so plain and clear that he seems to have no style at all, just to be talking to you. His style flows like a mountain stream, only not icy but warm. I have to add that he writes in rabbinic Hebrew, which with its admixture of Talmudic Aramaic takes a lot of knowing. It is not the Hebrew of an Israeli newspaper. I owe my knowledge of rabbinic Hebrew to Zaideh, bless his memory.

In my humanist way, I cannot help mentioning Shakespeare at this point—"*L'havdil,*" as my learned friends would hastily exclaim, meaning "Distinguish between mundane and holy!"—but I mean this comparison only in the matter of Rashi's self-effacement. I have always been awed at Shakespeare's apparent disregard of what would become of his inhumanly great works. A printer collected up prompters' copies of the plays for the first edition, and it is not known that Shakespeare took any interest in the process. How could this be? Did he know that he was *Shakespeare,* and that therefore humanity would find a way to preserve his plays?

Maimonides belongs to the world, but Rashi belongs only to us. I was into daf yomi for a year or so before his meek greatness began to dawn on me. He was always there at my elbow in my solitary studies, anticipating what Aramaic words I would miss, what sharp subtleties would escape me, and always, *always* pointing me to the hard sense on the page. If daf yomi was a rocket ride, Rashi was the pilot. Every Jew who learns Talmud till time ends will have this immortal spirit beside him like a grandfather, conjuring from the laconic difficult words the polyphonic Jewish marching music of the centuries.

The Space-Time Voyage

Nowadays the end of a daf yomi cycle is a global event. Devotees everywhere gather in venues like Madison Square Garden to learn the last page together by the tens of thousands, to join in the special *hadrans* (completion prayers), and to daven with ecstatic joy. Rabbi Meir Shapira really started something.

As for me, having caught the rocket in mid-flight, I was only half through my seven years when the next completion celebration came along, so I took no part in it. Anyway, I am a daf yomi loner. Of course the Talmud is the main thing, and it can be learned in endless depth of commentary if one has the time, but my dermatologist friend correctly assumed that I would do mainly text and Rashi. The quiet grandeur of Rashi remains for me the most prized discovery of those seven years. Another flanking column on each page, *Tosafot* (Additions), includes Rashi's grandsons among scores of later commentators, often opposing Rashi in ultrasubtle analysis. I learned enough Tosafot to perceive that I had better stick to the text and the grandfather, if I wanted to make it through the seven years.

I did make it through. The Talmud was rocketing along in space-time (as I thought of it) with me aboard, in daily morning hours of exalting challenge. I have no idea what the four-dimensional "space-time" of the physicists really means, but the compound word perfectly describes my excited sense of exploring the Talmudic universe of discourse with the quiet expert piloting of Rashi. As my watch crawled through the minutes, my mind was flying among the millennia, among generations of Talmud Jews, from the Second Temple era through Rashi's time to my own day, when throngs of black-hatted, black-coated, mostly bearded daf yomi learners assemble every seven years all over the world to celebrate a *siyum,* a completion, each of them in lifelong debt to an eleventh-century Frenchman, Rabbi Shlomo Itzhaki.

Aspen

In 1973, I spent a summer doing daf yomi in Aspen, Colorado. Aspen was not then a jazzy resort for celebrities, but a quiet mountain retreat and ski place, half hippie and half highbrow. Nowadays the intellectual part is still going, I understand, if somewhat submerged by the beautiful people, but the hippies have long since given way to the well-heeled. The Aspen Institute where I spent two summers as a scholar-in-residence was a solemn enterprise. Business leaders and eminent thinkers met in seminars based on demanding reading lists, to grapple for a couple of weeks with great matters like political governance and eastern religions. The businessmen footed much of the bill, the scholars—we were designated "sources"—lived there free in luxury. Aspen also had a music institute and a physics institute, all in all, a remarkable ephemeral summertime Athens at eight thousand feet.

It was there that Saul Bellow and I climbed the trails talking Yiddish, and there that I encountered Richard Feynman again, having bothered him years earlier during my research on the atomic bomb. He and I took to lunching together. With considerable nerve, I asked him his opinion of a book by Karl Popper that I was reading, on the philosophy of science. (I found out only months later that Feynman had the most rabid contempt for philosophy and philosophers.) He took the book, and a couple of days later brought it back. "This man is like a foreigner watching a tennis match for the first time," I recall him saying, "studying the game intently, and declaring that the key to the game of tennis lies in the tightness of the racket strings."

I mention this short way Feynman had with what struck him—rightly or wrongly—as foolishness, because I tried a complicated daf yomi problem on him, to see how he would react. Feynman was Jewish, without an atom of interest in Yiddishkeit, yet he lit up when I said I was studying Talmud and would like to put a problem to him. It was highly abstract, but for the curious reader, here is the gist of the passage, with the problem and the answer.

(a) A draconic Torah law provides that if a town in the Holy Land is found by the Sanhedrin to be given over to idol worship, the inhabitants are put to the sword, the town with its property becomes *herem*, "banned" from all use or benefit, and everything therein is burned to ashes. (The Talmud remarks that such a town, called *ir ha'nidahat*, in fact never existed or was likely to exist. Then why this extreme theoretical punishment? "Study, and receive reward.")

(b) When a fowl is ritually slaughtered, the Torah orders its blood covered with earth or the like.

(c) Can the ashes of a "banned city" be used for this purpose?

(d) On the one hand, the ash heap presumably comes under the ban against "use or benefit." On the other hand, the ban conflicts with the *mitzvah* (commandment) of covering the blood. Which prevails, the ban or the mitzvah?

(e) The point of this abstract discussion is to shed light on a key issue of Talmudic thought: are the Torah commandments given for man's use or benefit, or are they fiats from on High, to be performed to obey our Maker? [Of course I did not disclose this issue to Feynman, this was the test of his grasp.]

(f) The upshot of the passage: the mitzvot are fiats of the Creator, not necessarily given for use or benefit.

(g) Therefore the ashes of the banned city could be used to cover the blood.

You might think that a Jewish Nobel physicist, wholly secular in outlook, would be condescending or dismissive about such ancient notions and practices. Not a bit of it. Feynman listened carefully, then rapped out, "It would depend on whether or not performing commandments comes under the heading of 'use or benefit.'" I had needed a half-column of Rashi to help me get the point.

Feynman's quickness did not surprise me, but his acceptance of the Talmudic frame of thought did. He made no objection that the idea of a condemned city was barbaric or silly, or that covering a kosher-slaughtered chicken's blood with ashes made no sense and was utterly primitive and trivial. Instant grasp, acceptance of the premises, straight to the point, that was Feynman on Talmud. He showed the same pleasure in getting the thing right that a bright yeshiva boy would have. My lunches and long walks with Feynman in Aspen remain a treasured memory. If time and chance allow me to write a memoir of my days, that will be an experience I'll enjoy recounting.

Altogether, that was quite a summer. I was then writing my Battle of Midway sequence in *War and Remembrance*, swinging back and forth daily between the subtleties of the Talmud and the intricacies of naval strategy and aircraft carrier combat. For relaxation, there was the convivial company of heavyweight scholars, among them Alan Bullock, Lionel Trilling, and the Nobel laureate in genetics, Sir Peter Medawar. Medawar and I discovered a shared admiration for Trollope's novels, and we struck up a friendship that lasted until he died, visiting each other every year or so in London or Washington. I once tried a daf yomi tough nut on him, as I had on Feynman. His reaction was the same: immediate lively interest, acceptance of the Talmudic world of thought, and a quick stab at the correct answer, much to his own satisfaction.

The *Sugya*

Yet how could an isolated stretch of Gemara be communicated intelligibly even to a Nobel laureate? One cannot plunge into Descartes's *On Method* or Plato's *Republic* and make much sense of a single passage, without substantial grounding in what has gone before. The peculiar nature of Gemara is the reason. In passing from the orderly Mishna code to Gemara, one leaps into a free-form compilation of relatively short give-and-take dialogues, each one coming to a sharp point and standing by itself, with some general bearing on the subject at hand. Such a dialogue, called a *sugya*, can be half a page or a couple of pages long. Here one finds the pearls of gleaming logic that gave pleasure to Feynman and Medawar.

These sugyas (modern Hebrew, *sugyot*) were Zaideh's meat and drink. We would grind down the page alternating Rashi and text, and, because I was a good boy, I droned along as best I could. When we finished a sugya he would exclaim, his eyes sparkling, "Do you understand?" I would answer a shade wearily, "Yes, Zaideh."—"Yes? Yes? *You should spring to the ceiling!*" From time to time, I did catch on, and expounded the pearl to his satisfaction. Then it was he who jumped to the ceiling. All this perhaps makes clear why—as I asserted at the start—anybody can begin learning the Talmud on any page, at any age, with a teacher who understands a sugya and can convey its elegance. As I presented the condemned city problem to a man who, however sharp-witted, had zero grounding in Jewishness, so it can be done and is being done here and there in Jewry today.

There is a muted turn to Talmud going on, at the other end of the Jewish spectrum from the daf yomi devotees. The philanthropist who announced he was learning Talmud was a striking instance, and here is another. Once my wife and I were invited to lunch by the President of Israel, the late Chaim Herzog, Yaakov's older brother, a former diplomat, army general, and military historian, truly a great Israeli. Next to me sat a handsome young American woman who told me she had been teaching literature at Yale before making aliya with her lawyer husband. "You know, I had a lot of fun learning Talmud this past summer," she remarked.

"You did? What tractate?"

"*Hullin.*"

This really startled me. Hullin contains the kashrut (dietary) laws, and there is hardly a bumpier stretch in the Gemara. The note of warm pleasure in her voice told me she had learned and grasped some delectable sugyas.

Cavils

Yet one can never forget that we are exploring a long-gone Jewish world, and that even our greatest interpreters like Rashi and Rambam lived almost a millennium ago, in a time called the Middle Ages. When my uncle Baruch rebelled and left the old-country yeshiva, the Talmud had become for him a prison, taught as the sum of all truth and authority, to be studied and never questioned, except in the approved give-and-take of Gemara. How the lovely lady who enjoyed Hullin handled the Talmudic treatment of women, I do not know. "*Nashim da'atan kalot,*" a Talmudic saying goes, which can be translated, "Women have quick minds," or

"Women have light minds." She was a quick one, no mistake, but she had certainly run into the other view.

For fifty-odd years, I have been married to a woman more quick-witted and hardheaded than I am, and I do not agree with the derogatory translation. Nor do I have to. We were wed and have lived by the halakhah, and my judgment on women is my own. When disputes arise about the ancient status of women, apologists can cite abundant passages in praise of them in the Gemara, but I am not about to apologize for a two-thousand-year gap in some aspects of world culture.

There are two recensions of the Talmud, the Babylonian and the Jerusalem (Palestinian) Talmud, the latter a province of specialists and lifelong scholars. Our Babylonian Talmud contains some jarring superstitions and outmoded science, reflecting its environment, though the anatomy and astronomy are at a high level for the era. Uncle Baruch might have been reproved or slapped for questioning some farfetched parable, metaphor, or Babylonian demonology in the text. Who can say?

The Talmud can be culled by its opponents for objectionable patches, which can be assembled into one long cavil to the affectionate portrait I have drawn here. In medieval times, apostate Jews who were Talmudists had no trouble digging out, for their Jew-hating bosses, passages to be used for baiting the faithful at forced public disputations, thereby putting former Talmud colleagues in peril of their lives, and perhaps provoking the periodic burnings of the Talmud. In our own day, we do not lack scoffers and negativists, some showily talented, but they seem to know little or nothing about Talmud or Yiddishkeit, which is probably a good thing, since they, like those medieval apostates, would no doubt just root for damaging dirt.

The View from Daf Yomi

Such has been my adventure with Talmud and with daf yomi, which I still keep up; not with anything like the zest of my first flight, but I do my best to stay with it. In traversing the tractates again, I come on pencil strokes marking my dogged daily push through the pages in former years, and my own marginal notes, which at first puzzle me like the text. Always accessible, never easy, that is Talmud. You have to *laig tzu kop*.

The great thing about daf yomi was that by going through all the Mishna and all the Gemara, however hurriedly and cursorily, I at last captured a perception of the whole. To return to my rocket metaphor, all the laws and all the sugyas in the end pulled together, like the seas and the continents to the view of an astronaut, and the entire planet of Torah law, the magnificent structure of our halakhic heritage, came into view, rounding on itself in those two thousand pages as a single great Whole. This vision, once perceived, is there in mind and heart forever.

Fourteen

KABBALAH

A living Talmudist of note has said ruefully of Kabbalah, quoting Genesis 49:6, *"My soul enters not into their secret counsels."* Nor does mine, alas. To all mysticism I am, and have always been, tone-deaf and color-blind, so my writing about Kabbalah is a bit like a sightless man trying to describe a rainbow. I have read much mystical literature, including translated Hindu and Chinese classics as well as Kabbalah in the original Aramaic, trying to get the hang of this ancient and perennial vein of religious experience. I understand the words and the imagery, but there my mind stops. Good books on Kabbalah exist in English nowadays, some by committed Kabbalists, others by critical scholars, but among Kabbalists writings by outsiders are considered obtuse and worthless, and my very brief account here may also be so regarded. Nevertheless I take up this weighty part of our Heritage, so sacred to its devotees, with due respect.

I first encountered mysticism in Irwin Edman's philosophy courses. Irwin had no patience with mysticism in any form, considering it all a lot of complicated cloudy nonsense, but he taught Neoplatonism and the Christian mystics with a straight face, and you had to answer his exam questions with the same straight face. It would not have done to write, "Sir, I have carefully read the assignments in Plotinus and St. John of the Cross, and they are too ridiculous to be discussed." The professor might agree, but you would flunk. As for Jewish mysticism, Edman never even mentioned it. At that time, Kabbalah was not taken seriously in academia, and available reading matter in English was scanty, mostly third-hand stuff in encyclopedias, culled from obscure Christian scholarship.

The prevailing view on Kabbalah, therefore, among uninitiated Jews like me, derived largely from Graetz. Whatever Heinrich Graetz did in his epic work he did con brio, and here is his haymaker on the rise of Kabbalah in the thirteenth century:

> . . . Through the rupture that arose from the conflict for and against Maimonides, there insinuated itself into the general life of the Jews a false doctrine which, although new, styled itself a primitive inspiration; although un-Jewish, called itself a genuine teaching of Israel; and although springing from error, entitled itself the only truth. The rise of this secret lore, which was called Kabbalah (tradition), coincides with the time of the Maimonidean Controversy, through which it was launched into existence. Discord was the mother of this monstrosity, which has ever been the cause of schism. . . .

When I first read Graetz, I took this severe verdict at face value. I have since come to understand that on some matters, in the way of most great historians, he held partial and time-bound views. My old 1936 *Britannica* offers a meager column on Kabbalah, in which the anonymous contributor is already backing away from Graetz:

> In the Kabbalah, as in all mystic systems, excesses and extravagances sometimes arose. Hence modern scholars such as Graetz, influenced ultimately by the rationalism of Maimonides . . . have looked askance at Kabbalah and decried it. The trend of the last century was almost unmitigated disapproval. But latterly a more temperate verdict has succeeded to the one-sided judgment of

the past. The Kabbalah is being studied instead of being condemned. . . . The reader is cautioned against accepting many of the categorical statements of the past century without reference to present-day views.

Since then the pendulum has swung so far the other way, that the current *Britannica* devotes twenty columns of dense print to Kabbalah, and the *Encyclopedia Judaica* gives it no less than *one hundred sixty double-columned pages.* That entry has been published as a separate book, *Kabbalah,* by the Israeli Gershom Scholem, an academic pioneer in exploring Jewish mysticism. Scholem's extensive studies are far from the last word, but he has cast welcome light for the modern reader on this grandiose body of Jewish teachings, obscured for centuries in the dusk of esoteric secrecy. A true Kabbalist would advise the inquiring Jew, "Listen, dear friend, forget those university professors, let's just sit down and learn a little Kabbalah," and that advice would be sound enough, for one who wants to hear the real thing straight.

What Is Kabbalah?

Kabbalah is a visionary superstructure reared on a deep base of Tanakh, Talmud, Midrash, and strict Orthodoxy. The *Zohar* ("Radiance"), its central holy book, takes the form of a free-ranging commentary on the Pentateuch, disclosing high secrets of ancient wisdom about the nature of the Almighty, the origin of the Creation, and the destiny of mankind. These secrets were first revealed—so Kabbalah doctrine teaches—by a wonder-working Talmud sage of the second century, Rabbi Shimon bar Yokhai, and they have passed down the generations within a tiny circle of the elect, the *Mekubalim,* "Receivers of the Tradition." Here and there in the Talmud are veiled passages about dangerous mysteries called *Maaseh Merkava,* "The

Work of the Chariot," and these mysteries are at the core of Kabbalah and the Zohar. The "Chariot" is God's throne, as depicted in the awesome vision that opens the Book of Ezekiel.

Here on my desk is a volume of the Zohar in the original Aramaic, from a handsome blue-bound edition of twenty-four volumes, published in 1991 in the Old City of Jerusalem. An exhaustive commentary in Hebrew, "The Ladder," makes the difficult text more accessible. The title page reads:

> The Book of the Zohar
> on the Five Books of Moses
> by the Divine Tanna
> Rabbi Shimon bar Yokhai
> published by The Voice of Judah Yeshiva Press,
> for the Dissemination of the Study of Kabbalah.

Dipping into these pages, I am at once caught as usual by the apt colorful Midrashic imagery, but soon—as usual—left behind as the text soars into the empyrean of allegory and symbol. The history of this text is a matter of controversy. The Talmud, in both Babylonian and Jerusalem recensions, has a clear historical and literary pedigree, as to its authors, their sources, and the authenticity of the text. Not so *Nistor,* (the "hidden learning") and not so the Zohar.

To the Mekubalim, ascription of the Zohar to any author other than Shimon bar Yokhai is obviously sacrilegious. Graetz's view, supported by some contemporary scholars who unlike him admire the Zohar, is very different. The modern consensus is that the Zohar appeared in Spain late in the thirteenth century at a time of widespread Kabbalistic study, and that the work is not like the Talmud, a compilation of ancient material accumulated over centuries, but an original book written by a prolific author of the period, the Castilian Jew Moses de Leon. There may be small later additions by other hands, but the body of the work is said to be his, and why he chose to mask his presumed authorship remains in debate. At any rate, critical academia now tends to credit the most influential Jewish work since the close of the Talmud to this one medieval writer, a remarkable conclusion indeed.

The most influential, I say, but what about the mighty Maimonides, who flourished a century earlier? True, Maimonides spoke to all Jews, not just to a closed circle of devotees. On the other hand, he did not, like the reputed author of the Zohar, give enduring voice to a radical new vein of Judaism. Rather, Maimonides articulated the old mainstream faith once for all in terms viable for the modern world. It is known that Moses de Leon studied his *Guide to the Perplexed.* Though Graetz's violent diatribe is out of fashion at the moment, his linking of the rise of Kabbalah to the Maimonidean controversy remains a penetrating insight.

In Moses de Leon's time Jewry was being increasingly confronted by formidable philosophical challenges from both Islam and Christianity, as well as by the revival of ancient Greek and Roman thought. Maimonides had elected to grasp the nettle by codifying and reformulating Talmudic Judaism, so as to withstand assault by all comers for all time. Kabbalah handled the confrontation the opposite way, by withdrawing into the shadows of the occult, and creating a hedged-off spiritual preserve, in which the antique faith could survive philosophical challenges by ignoring them.

Excursus: The Dime

A personal anecdote, more or less to the point, comes to mind. Emerging from midshipman school a newly minted ensign in blue and gold, I was prevailed upon by my widowed mother to come with her to the Lubavitcher Rebbe. I was not going in harm's way as yet, just to communications school in Annapolis, but I did not argue. The Rebbe was a gentle personage of imposing presence, recently escaped from Nazi-ruled Europe after a harrowing ordeal of Soviet imprisonment. He knew of my grandfather as a profoundly learned follower, he received us with grace, and we conversed in Yiddish, his voice weakened by asthma to a near-whisper. As I left, he gave me his blessing, and with it a dime. His successor, the late famous Rebbe Menachem Mendel Schneerson, gave dollars. Inflation does not spare amulets. The dime went with me to sea as did my phylacteries, which I would strap on each day in moments snatched from ship routine.

A month or so after the war ended, a typhoon swept over Okinawa, damaging or beaching more than a hundred vessels with some loss of life. My destroyer-minesweeper was thrown up on the rocks, pounding and grinding through a grim howling night. Next day, when all hands had been safely taken ashore, I observed a new warm respect toward me in the crew. As the executive officer, the captain's enforcer, I was not loved. During the storm I had done nothing but hang on like everybody else. I asked an old chief what this was all about, and he told me that the sailors were convinced they had been saved by "Lieutenant Wouk's black boxes."

I don't remember why I carried the Rebbe's dime to the South Pacific, Edman-trained rationalist though I was; probably on the disreputable notion that it couldn't hurt. There are no atheists in foxholes, people say, and I have heard that there are few atheists among American and Israeli fighter pilots. In war and in training for war, the unknown lurks just ahead, all too close and menacing. Hence amulets, and hence I guess my crew's belief in the thaumaturgy of black boxes. Agnostics tend to ascribe religion to fear of the unknown, and ritual to mumbo-jumbo propitiation of the unknown. There may be something in that, but not everything. I have a teaching from my fathers, *Bind these words on your arm, and let them be as frontlets between your eyes.* That is why I tied on the black boxes in the South Pacific as I do today.

"But what did you get out of tying them on out there?" the agnostic may persist. "Did this obsessive business with leather straps, and Bible quotes inside black boxes, really bring you any closer to your God? Be honest. What was the difference in that, if any, from the Rebbe's dime?" Fair question. Putting the best face on the conduct of the young man I was so very long ago, it was the difference between halakhah and Kabbalah.

"The Perennial Philosophy": Mysticism

Let us take the plunge, and glance over the general field of mysticism, then see where Jewish mysticism differs.

Mysticism offers, by means of various esoteric doctrines and disciplines, a way to transcendental knowledge of the Unknowable. If that strikes you as a paradox, the smiling mystic is likely to agree that *of course* it is a paradox, and offer to explain. If you think it plain nonsense, you are in Edman territory, and you can read all the books and even—if you are an academic—lecture on them, but Irwin's biting irony will tinge your voice. Aldous Huxley, the amoral, cynically witty novelist of *Point Counter Point* and *Brave New World* fame, had a total change of heart, experienced transcendental enlightenment, and became the most articulate of British literary mystics. Here are some opening words of Huxley on mysticism, in his grave book, *The Perennial Philosophy*:

> ... Rudiments of the Perennial Philosophy may be found among primitive peoples in every region of the world, and it has its place in every one of the higher religions. A version was first committed to writing more than twenty-five centuries ago, and since that time the inexhaustible theme has been treated from the standpoint of every religious tradition, and in all the principal languages of Asia and Europe ...

Huxley's book is as clear as any I have come upon in this tenebrous field. He backs up his own searching treatment with mystical writings from a wide range of sources, including the Alexandrian Jew Philo. Quite early in his book he confronts the reader with the essence of mysticism as he sees it:

> Going back further into the past, we find in one of the earliest Upanishads the classical description of the Absolute One as a Super-Essential No-Thing.
> *"The significance of Brahman is expressed by* neti neti *(not so, not so); for beyond this, that you say it is not so, there is nothing further. Its name, however, is 'the Reality of reality.' That is to say, the senses are real, and the Brahman is their Reality."*
> —BRHADARANYAKA UPANISHAD

And so on. Not exactly your sprightly author of *Antic Hay*, this later Aldous Huxley. Still, the skeptical reader, though perhaps disagreeing page by page, will find in his book an earnest quest for religious light.

Professor Edman, introducing the subject to bemused sophomores, was easier on them. He would quote from *Adonais*, Shelley's elegy on the death of Keats:

> *The One remains, the many change and pass*
> *Heaven's light forever shines, earth's shadows fly;*
> *Life, like a dome of many-colored glass*
> *Stains the white radiance of eternity.*

A great poet can say much in few words. All Huxley's cited sources converge on that single image. To paraphrase Shelley's luminous lines in mundane prose: *ultimate reality, in all forms of mysticism, is Unity.* It is God, or Brahma, or the Absolute, or the One, or the Clear Light of the Void, or the Tao. Huxley calls it the Divine Ground. In Kabbalah this ineffable Unity is the *En Sof,* the Endless. All mysticism teaches that the enlightened human spirit yearns toward an exalted state of unity with the Divine, and (as I understand it) Kabbalah calls that state *Dvekut* (Yiddish, *dvekus*) meaning union, oneness.

When the first atom bomb went off in the New Mexico test, and the coruscating cloud of fire climbed skyward, the Jewish physicist in charge, Robert Oppenheimer, was reminded of a passage in the *Bhagavad-Gita*: I AM BECOME DEATH, THE DESTROYER OF WORLDS. A man of parts, Oppenheimer had taught himself Sanskrit so as to read the classics of Eastern mysticism in the original. Years later, during a congressional hearing on Soviet spying, he took an arrogant tone, made mistakes he himself admitted were idiotic, and half-wrecked an illustrious career. He never won a Nobel Prize, and his colleague, Isidor Rabi, who did, said sadly of him, "Instead of Sanskrit, Robert should have studied the Talmud."

That is not too far from what my grandfather said to me seventy years ago: "Never mind Kabbalah, study the Talmud." The inescapable fact is that since my grandfather's time, popular interest in Jewish mysticism has exploded. Hollywood stars are learning Kabbalah today, or at least they believe they are, though it may be that, in the jocose Israeli idiom, they are being sold noodles.

Where Kabbalah Differs

A most unlikely source for light on Kabbalah is the dour German pessimist, Schopenhauer, no friend of Jews or Judaism, and here is what he has to say:

> The basic character of Judaism is realism and optimism, which are closely related and the preconditions of actual theism, since they consider the material world absolutely real and life as a pleasing gift made expressly for us. The basic character of Brahminism and Buddhism, on the contrary, is idealism and pes-

simism, since they allow the world only a dreamlike existence, and regard life as the consequence of our sins . . .

Schopenhauer could hardly have known much about Kabbalah, but that is an insightful shot. The Zohar vision virtually stands the Perennial Philosophy on its head.

My resistance to Kabbalah was shaken by my discovery that the great sixteenth-century Talmudist Joseph Caro was also a fiery Kabbalist. I found this out only by happening on his biography, which interested me because he was the author of our definitive legal code, the *Shulkhan Arukh* ("Ready Table"), a bone-dry digest of halakhah. The Ready Table is to this day the focus of yeshiva legal studies, the rule book of Orthodox observance. I was stunned to learn that this same Joseph Caro, the aridly rational halakhic master, had Kabbalistic visitations by a *maggid,* a spectral voice issuing from his own mouth in company of others, which identified itself *as the Mishna!* There is no doubt about it. An authenticated diary kept by Caro documents his mystic experiences.

This astonishing Spanish Jew lived to be eighty-seven. After the expulsion in 1492, he spent the latter part of his life in Safed, a center of Jewish learning in Palestine, which then overshadowed the circle of scholars in Jerusalem. There he encountered Isaac Luria, who in his short span of thirty-eight years became the great light of modern Kabbalah. Unlike Caro, who was a voluminous author, Luria wrote almost nothing; yet in his oral teachings, recorded by his followers, he voiced a new vision of the Zohar addressed not just to the Mekubalim, but to all Jews willing to give ear.

How did Luria's Kabbalah spread beyond the hedged sanctuary of the illuminati to the Jewish masses? For one thing, printing had recently been invented. Until the Zohar went to press, the hidden lore remained sequestered, and then—whether or not it was cause and effect—a new era in Kabbalah began, the Lurianic era, which still continues. Hasidic tradition holds that Luria himself had felt the time was at hand, because of the weakening of the faith, to reveal the esoteric learning to *Amkha*, "Your people," the common folk. The revelation was primarily accomplished, according to Hasidic lore, by their widely venerated eighteenth-century saint, the Baal Shem Tov. I have more or less puzzled through the main doctrines of the Kabbalah of Luria, if perhaps only like Feynman's foreigner watching the tennis match. Herewith then, is an outsider's sketch of that doctrine, as taught today in Jerusalem and Beverly Hills.

Repairing the Universe

Between Huxley's battery of mystics and Isaac Luria's Kabbalah, there is a red line. Other mystics tend to devalue the individual in relation to the One, whereas for Luria the individual is central.

In my morning mail the other day came a notice from the local United Jewish Appeal, an invitation to dessert, coffee, and fundraising:

Tikkun Olam Event
at The Club at Morningside

Tikkun Olam is the Kabbalistic principle meaning "Repair of the Universe." So far down in Jewry has Luria's thought trickled! To his followers he is the Ari-zal, The Lion of Blessed Memory, a play on the Hebrew initials of his title, "The Divine Rabbi Isaac." Four centuries after his brief time on earth, the Arizal's teachings are becoming common coin in Jewish discourse. The reader new to all this may wonder how a contribution to the Palm Springs Federation can help repair the universe, or indeed why it needs repair. I will venture a description of this one aspect of the Lurianic system, Tikkun Olam.

There is a flaw in the universe, the Arizal teaches, traceable to the event of Creation itself, and this imperfection is the cause of all we know as evil. How such a flaw could come to be, in a universe created by an omnipotent En Sof, merges into the age-old problem of evil, which traditional Judaism plumbs in the Book of Job and leaves open. The Lurianic system sets out to cope with evil in a fantastically complex body of thought about Creation. We are taught that the flaw exists, that it is reparable, and that the destiny of man is to repair it, so that the Messiah can come to establish the everlasting peace of God.

The Torah is the point of departure in this system, for as one bold Midrash declares, it is the blueprint of Creation. Mysticism in other forms tends to be a pantheistic submerging of this world in a Divine Unity that encompasses all. But the Jews have been in direct dialogue with that Divine Unity through the Torah since Sinai, and their responses to God's commands, according to Kabbalah, reverberate through Creation. The faithful Jew does not lose himself in the Divine Ground, he reaches toward the En Sof with deeds of obedience and love; and each performed mitzvah, in a way unmeasurable but real, is a tiny step of Tikkun Olam, the great Repair of the Universe.

Nor is mundane reality an illusion, as the Perennial Philosophy would have it. Kabbalah takes the world we know as the place, in the Psalmist's phrase, to serve the Lord with joy, the stage of the grand drama called Tikkun Olam, in which every Jew has a vital part to play. The optimism that Schopenhauer decried stems from the Kabbalah view that human existence, which he himself regarded as a vale of delusion and gloom, will be transformed by a Messiah, in the fullness of time, to a felicitous world for all humanity here on earth.

Most Jewish of all is the theme that Israel, as a nation of priests and a holy people, is charged with the special mission of Tikkun Olam, and that therefore all Jews are bound together by the love of comrades in arms. So on the whole, Lurianic Kabbalah differs from other mystic systems, almost as the Tanakh differs from the Upanishads. About that, Schopenhauer was also right. To an outsider's understanding, the system is a sweeping poetic metaphor of a link between the human and the Godly, but as doctrine, not mere metaphor, it touches the lives of Jews, followers of the Arizal or not, more than is generally perceived.

Forty years ago, when I was writing *This Is My God,* I included just a short note on Kabbalah, acknowledging my ignorance. Gershom Scholem's studies, then available mostly in Hebrew, were unknown to me, and my Aramaic was minimal. The fact that the Vilna Gaon, the great Talmud master of the modern era, had fought Luria-based Hasidism all his life turned me off from delving further into what seemed a sterile area. Graetz did mention that the Gaon was a committed Kabbalist, expert in both streams of Jewish holy literature, but this did not sink in, so I failed to grasp the real reason for his unrelenting war on Hasidism. It was rooted, I now surmise, at least partly in the debacle that befell Jewry late in the seventeenth century, when Lurianic Kabbalah escaped from the secrecy of the illuminati and swept the Jewish masses.

The Two Apostates: Spinoza and Shabbetai Zevi

Only Graetz, my mentor throughout this effort, would have thought of bracketing the philosopher who blazed the way out of medievalism into modern times, with a dreamy false Messiah who caused a brief mass hysteria in Jewry and faded to a disgraceful memory. The chapter in his history entitled "Spinoza and Shabbetai Zevi" is one of his finest. The two men were contemporaries, though living worlds apart, in Christian Holland and Muslim Turkey. Graetz's astute linkage unlocks the modern history of the Jews, at least for me, giving it coherence and suggesting its dynamics. Graetz traces the course of

Spinoza's apostasy, and his expulsion by rabbis painfully reluctant to lose him from the fold. He points out the tragic mistakes on both sides, and gives a singularly deep, clear, and fair appraisal of Spinoza, both the good and the bad of him. To Shabbetai Zevi he devotes far more space, of course. Dramatic history on the operatic scale is his specialty.

What these two apostates had in common was only Spanish Jewish ancestry, and the intellect in youth to absorb Talmud and Kabbalah. There all resemblance ends. Spinoza changed the way the world thinks. Great modern minds, including Goethe and Coleridge, have been to an extent Spinozists. By contrast, Shabbetai Zevi sparked a short-lived frenzied worship by the Jewish masses, then fell into ignominy. Those who called themselves Shabbateans after that had to do so in secrecy, confusion, and shame.

The False Messiah

Shabbetai Zevi, born in the west Turkish port of Smyrna, seems to have been driven out of his mind by preoccupation with Kabbalah. That may seem a harsh reflection on the Arizal's teachings, but no more than the facts appear to show, not only as Graetz marshaled them more than a hundred years ago, but as modern scholarship has done with far better research resources. Moreover, the flash-fire acceptance of the pretender among ecstatic Jewish masses—one of the saddest episodes of our long history—would appear to have fed on the rapid spread of the secret learning among the common people. Luria's exceedingly difficult system was simplified, in the popular version, to the only point the Jews wanted to hear and believe in a time of war, riot, and massacre: the Messiah was at hand!

Some Kabbalists claimed to find in the Zohar that the Redeemer was due in the year 1648. In that year, Shabbetai Zevi confided to a few friends that he was indeed the predicted Messiah. In that year too, the fearsome Chmielnicki massacres broke out in the Ukraine, the goriest slaughter of Jews since the Crusades; actually called by a contemporary rabbinic author *The Third Destruction*, as though nothing more catastrophic to Jewry could ever happen thereafter. The victims numbered in the many thousands—some say, hundreds of thousands—and *Chmielnicki* became a byword in Jewish discourse for mass destruction, until Auschwitz supplanted it.*

Amid Jews demoralized by these horrors and newly seized by Kabbalistic fever, the word about the great news rapidly spread. When Shabbetai Zevi came out publicly as the Messiah in 1665, he was widely believed, traveling throughout Jewry in eastern Europe and Asia Minor in tumultuous triumph. But the brief madness came to an abrupt end. His incautious adorers announced, among other incredibly wild extravagances, that the Messiah was going to seize the Sultan's throne. That got the attention of the Turkish authorities. In 1666 he was arrested and given the choice of death or conversion to Islam. He converted, and lived out a queer deflated existence as a minor courtier to the Sultan. The Messianic movement fell apart in pathetic fragments. Graetz's magnificent account is crammed with startling detail—the dissolute wife this false Messiah took, his changing of fast days to feasts in his honor, and so on—not sparing the grotesque forms in which the shattered illusion persisted among a deluded few.

Born not long afterward, Elijah of Vilna must have grown up well aware of the devastation wrought in Jewry by Zohar learning let loose among the unlettered. Between the devil-dance of the false Messiah and the Baal Shem Tov's revelations, he evidently drew no distinction, seeing mainly the danger of misunderstood Kabbalism breaking out again in catastrophe. In fact, Hasidism differed from the ephemeral craze over an impostor, no less than the modest Israel Baal Shem Tov did from the imperious Shabbetai Zevi. The

---

*See Note, page 294.

rise of Hasidism was unstoppable, and the Talmudic authorities who rallied against it became in popular speech *Misnagdim* (Hebrew, *Mitnagdim*)—opponents, naysayers, "againsters." By what they tried in vain to stop, they were defined.

Afterword: Dialogue of Two Misnagdim

Recently I told a friend of mine here in Palm Springs, a truly hard-bitten Misnaged, that I was writing something on Kabbalah. "Don't be nice about it," he snapped. "I know you! Don't be mild, don't be tolerant, and don't pull your punches. All the wrong people believe in it."

Forty years ago I might have agreed with him, but I have come quite a way since then, as have the editors of the encyclopedias. I tried to point out some positive aspects, but that only put his back up. "I didn't say it wasn't spreading. Disasters spread, too. How about that Chabad synagogue of yours? Pictures of the Rebbe wherever you turn. Posters all over the walls, *'We want Moshiakh now!'* I even heard kids singing a song about that. Back to Shabbetai Zevi, hey?"

He comes there now and then for a holiday or a *yahrtzeit* (anniversary of a parent's death), doesn't drive on Shabbat, and eats kosher, but he gets testy about fur hats and long black coats. They make him uncomfortable, I guess, about being observant, and therefore being mistaken for one of *them*.

"Those kids were probably the rabbi's," I replied with my accustomed mildness. "He has twelve, and they're all very bright."

"Bright sociopaths, you mean. A pity! Totally unable to function in the modern world."

There is no moving a Jew who sees red when he sees a fur hat. "We won't agree," I said, a shade less mildly. "They function well enough, from what I've seen, and they're growing up knowing a lot of halakhah. Moreover, they speak flawless Yiddish."

"So what?" he retorted. "Yiddish is dead."

"You don't say!" I lost patience. "*Webster's Unabridged Dictionary* has a section that renders basic English words into six important world languages. One of those is Yiddish."

"Leave it to the bookworms who write dictionaries," said this stiff-necked Jew, "not to get the word."

Many aspects of the Kabbalah and the Hasidim remain controversial; especially, as I write, the appalling dispute within Chabad since the recent death of their Rebbe, on the issue of his Messianic status. I pass over that, Misnaged that I am, in silence. The Hasidim have a rich lore of the tales, parables, and Torah teachings of the Rebbes. My grandfather passed much of this lore on to me. In their warm, consistent, and coherent way of life, they have certainly clung to the Yiddish language, and preserved it for their children, out of the wreckage of eastern Jewry. For that I unreservedly honor them. Yiddish is a dust-caked jewel of the Heritage. Jewels last. The dust can be blown off.

Fifteen

YIDDISH AND YIDDISHKEIT

In the early roseate glow of a love match, I once decided to learn how to slaughter chickens. My bride and I had set up house far out on Long Island, in bucolic peace where I meant to write great things, but where there was no kosher butcher. The nearest one was in a distant suburb, a kindly *shokhet* ("slaughterer") of the old school, complete with big round black yarmulke, bloody apron, grizzly three-day beard, and piquant Yiddish talk. He willingly loaned me his Hebrew manual on slaughtering, and for starters he drilled me on sharpening a *halef*, the ritual knife. That was about as far as I got. Running a thumbnail along the edge, to detect nicks which render a fowl unkosher, I repeatedly failed this elementary test. On the whole I was relieved. Not my thing, after all, killing meat for my table in cold blood.

"Tell me something," he remarked one day, as I was fumbling with the knife and the whetstone. "We have here a temple, where the rabbi talks all the time about something he calls '*Jeedaism*.' Jeedaism, with a *Jee. Nu,* so what exactly is this Jeedaism?" It was a rhetorical question, for he excitedly went on, "Jeedaism! Why that *Jee*? Why *Jeedaism*?" He shook both hairy fists in the air and shouted to the skies, "Yiddishkeit!"

The love match is now well past the half-century mark, and that cry to Heaven of the old shokhet has stayed with me.

The Origin of Yiddish

Not everybody knows that Yiddish and Hebrew are different languages. Hebrew is a Semitic tongue thousands of years old, whereas until the nineteenth century Yiddish was not considered a language at all, but a sort of pidgin German laced with Hebrew loan-words. Jews themselves called it "*jargon*," to distinguish it from the holy tongue. Graetz scorned it. His purist historian's soul could not abide this grating German dialect, written backward in the Hebrew alphabet, with copious Slavonic barbarisms and incongruous snatches of Talmud and Bible. The Yiddish works of his contemporary, Mendele the Bookseller, had not come his way; or if they had, he had missed the genius under the surface of what he regarded as crude marketplace babble.

The history of Yiddish is complicated. We know it arose in the Middle Ages amid the populous Ashkenazic Jews of Germany and France, steeped in Talmud and rigorous in observance. In time this Jewry migrated eastward, bringing to Slavic lands their Germanic lingua franca, known as *Jüdisch-Deutsch*. This transplanted dialect, its name shortened to Jüdisch (Yiddish), came to be pronounced a bit differently in different countries—Poland, Lithuania, Hungary, Russia—but it remained a mamma-loshon, "mother tongue," cutting across many borders. For the common people it was the language of everyday life. Hebrew was for praying. The learned elite also expounded the Talmud in "jargon" and used it in business, yet continued to look down on it, for Hebrew was the noble tongue, the true Jewish tongue. The Haskalists tended to be hostile to Yiddish, and to write their early secular belles lettres in modern Hebrew, called *Ivrit*. But I would guess that when lecturing to popular audiences, or arguing among themselves, they often lapsed into effortless Yiddish. A story goes that the great Hebraist Bialik came into a bookstore and inquired in Yiddish about some book he wanted. The shocked proprietor remarked, "You, Bialik, talking *Yiddish?*" To which the old author replied, "Sorry, I thought you too were tired."

Certainly Yiddish was effortless for me to learn. I have no recollection of ever being taught a word of it. It was just there, like street English, when I began to use language. A saying among the immigrant Jews went, "Hebrew one has to learn. Yiddish talks itself." And so it was. I did not read Yiddish. There seemed no point. I could speak it, and even when we went to the Yiddish theater, I had no trouble understanding it, and that sufficed. Theater parties were a staple of synagogue fund-raising, and Mama was the perpetual theater chairlady—chairperson, as we say nowadays, which would have made her giggle. In high school and college days I was still enjoying Mama's forays to "Second Avenue," the generic name for Yiddish theater.

I have never laughed harder in my life, in fact, than at a Yiddish musical comedy about an immigrant couple trying to keep up with their collegiate children. Jitterbugging was the dance craze then, and the parents sang and danced a number called "*Du Muzt Zein a Jeeter Boog.*" I tell you, those two old cut-ups, veteran comic stars, did the damnedest monkeyshines I ever saw. I all but died laughing. I howled, tears ran down my face, and I slid down out of my theater chair in hysterics. Painful incongruity is at the heart of much comedy, and in that Second Avenue parody of the dance we were all doing uptown at Columbia, the tension between my Edman-inspired skepticism and my troubled Yiddishkeit exploded into relieving guffaws.

During all those years, I have no recollection of trying to read and write the language. I was a functional illiterate in Yiddish, and it never bothered me a bit. Yet when I first went to Hollywood, a year or so out of college, as a staff joke writer for a radio comedian, I took along Shalom Aleichem's novel *Menachem Mendel,* which my father had once read to us; that was his custom, Yiddish reading on Friday nights, and we kids had imbibed a lot of the literature that way. It would be romantic and pretentious to claim that I was clinging to my Yiddishkeit with that volume. I also took along Marx's *Das Kapital.* I was only twenty-one, and still trying to figure myself out.

So there I was in fabled Hollywood, living la dolce vita in a garden villa, concocting laughs for the famous Fred Allen, and spelling my way through *Menachem Mendel.* Since I knew the alphabet and the language, I mainly had to gain ease and speed. I learned to write only much later, when my grandfather made aliya, and that was how we communicated. My written Yiddish remains a sometime thing, but since *Menachem Mendel* I have read widely in Yiddish classics, and I still discover authors new to me.

The Dwindling of Yiddish

Second Avenue put up the final closing notice decades ago. Yiddishisms have entered the American language—*mentsh, hutzpah, shlemiehl*—while Yiddish has been leaving American life. The radical newspaper *Freiheit* ("*Freedom*"), Zaideh's religious *Morning Journal,* and a host of smaller publications—gone, all gone. The waning of Yiddish in the Melting Pot has been inexorable. What has happened to this lively language? Prosperity has happened, college has happened, dispersion from New York to California, from Illinois to Texas has happened. Above all, the Holocaust happened, and our Yiddish-speaking reserves in eastern Europe were wiped out. By murdering them, Eichmann believed he had doomed the rest of us to extinction. That question stands open.

In Russia a couple of million Yiddish-speakers did survive the

Nazi scythe, but when the senile Stalin sank into Jew-hatred rivaling Hitler's, the Jewish intelligentsia was liquidated on his orders. After he died, the Soviet system all but finished the job of stamping out Yiddishkeit. Most Russian immigrants arriving in Israel today know little more of their origins than the notation *Yevrai* (Jewish) in their papers. To the deluded Jewish socialists, Karl Marx had been the Shabbetai Zevi of a new and deadlier Messianic folly, the dictatorship of the proletariat, which for them, in the end, only dictated their doom for being Jews.

Those who had emigrated early to America poured their Yiddish culture into the labor movement, remaining hostile by socialist dogma to religion, "the opiate of the masses." My parents would buy tickets for any Yiddish show, and on Second Avenue we saw much mockery of the faith. My father, who had had a fling with socialism in his youth in Minsk, would shrug off the irreverence with a smile. "They go a little too far," he would say.

With the success of the labor movement, the crusading steam went out of the Yiddish socialists, and there was no sufficient reason to pass on the language to children and grandchildren. As the newspapers and Second Avenue withered, awareness of Yiddish in the next generation faded to amused nostalgia at best, ignorant jeering at worst, and generally to bland indifference. There were earnest efforts to preserve the language for its cultural value, but they beat against a tide going out.

The Unsinkable Jargon

This sad picture is parochial to the United States, and far from the whole story. Any Jewish traveler who knows Yiddish will tell you that the old lingua franca, though much weakened, is hanging on. If Americans are letting it languish, the rest of the world is no melting pot, and *mamma-loshon,* the mother language, appears to be surviving on strict Darwinian terms, as a selective advantage for commerce and cohesion.

The first time I set foot on foreign soil in a foray from Hollywood to Tijuana, I heard shopkeepers speaking Yiddish, and ever since I have been encountering it worldwide. In the Soviet Union, in the darkest Brezhnev days, I came upon Jews in Rostov doggedly and illegally repairing a decaying synagogue. They had bribed the authorities, they told me in Yiddish. In Sweden, in Hong Kong, in Cape Town, in Iran, find Jews, and you hear Yiddish spoken. I have yet to visit South America, where I understand intermarriage is rampant, yet a Yiddish press exists there which has published my work. None of this suggests that Yiddish stands a chance against Hebrew as our lingua franca for the twenty-first century. That language war is over, modern Hebrew holds the field, and mamma-loshon has been routed. Still the jargon persists in showing vital signs.

Touring Australia a few years ago, I learned that Melbourne had a Yiddishist school, and I insisted on seeing it. Imagine, Yiddish persisting down near the Antarctic! Sure enough, I met Aussie boys and girls who talked my Bronx Yiddish. There were no skullcaps on the boys, no religious reminders on the walls, just pictures of Shalom Aleichem, Chagall reproductions, and Israel posters. Compared to the main Hebrew day school with its playing fields, auditorium, library, and green campus, it was tiny, small even compared to the nearby Chabad institute where Hassidic Yiddish, very different from Yiddishist Yiddish, was being taught. The teachers were resolute young socialist ideologues, throwbacks to another time, and more power to them! To me every Yiddish speaker they produce is precious.

Rearguard Action

In Israel's early years, the language war was still going on. Doctrinaire Zionists frowned upon Yiddish as a vestige of a degraded ghetto past that had to be forgotten. Most of them from Ben-Gurion on down could speak perfect Yiddish, but they were resolved to make Hebrew the national tongue, and they choked off the mamma-loshon in their throats.

Once in those days I saw a Yiddish musical comedy imported from Argentina in a Jerusalem theater, and I found myself back on Second Avenue; same old plot of the clash of generations, same coarse comedians, same mushy lovers, all in spicy mamma-loshon. I loved it, and I mentioned this at dinner that night to one of Israel's great Zionist ladies. "You mean you went to that thing?" she sniffed, with a disbelieving look down her nose. "*Really?* And you *enjoyed* it?" It was as though I had confessed to seeing a pornographic movie. Maybe she really did disapprove, though I half-suspect that she rather envied me, but couldn't risk being seen at a Yiddish show. Nowadays things are different in Israel, of course. "*In victory, magnanimity,*" wrote Churchill. There are chairs of Yiddish in the universities.

A belated recognition that an inheritance has been disintegrating has arisen in America, too, and a campaign is on to keep it from vanishing utterly. Most of the energy goes to preservation—museums, exhibits, lecture series, Yiddish-speaking circles, university courses, and massive rescue collections of discarded crumbling old books. Scholarly research continues, and doughty new writers even produce fiction, poetry, and essays for the shrinking audience. All this is to the good, but a true revival is not in sight. What life Yiddish has in the United States outside religious enclaves today comes from the residual momentum of a language that traversed ten centuries, and from a brilliant classical literature resembling Mendele's prophetic figure, the *Klatche*, an obdurate old nag which refuses to lie down and die.

The Classics

As Yiddish leaves the scene as the nexus of our culture, only schol-ars will know much about that literature, but three giants will defy oblivion, I am sure: Mendele, Shalom Aleichem, and Isaac Leib Peretz. Great Yiddish writings pale in translation, but enough of their power comes through to guarantee them a posterity. More important, I believe their writings guarantee a posterity to the lan-guage.

The nineteenth-century father of Yiddish literary art, Mendele the Bookseller (*Mendele Moykher Sforim*), was a sharp unforgiving satirist, with an original style oddly combining surrealist dreami-ness with harsh daylight realism. The greater Aleichem always deferred to him as a disciple, and Mendele was harsh with disciples, too. On reading Aleichem's first effort he threw it in the fire, say-ing, "Now you have progressed, you have burned a novel."

Earlier Yiddish fiction, I gather, tended toward vulgar potboil-ing romances for housewives and simpletons, while pious readers uncritically devoured wonder tales of Hasidic saints. Mendele introduced into Yiddish the antiromantic grittiness that in the west began with Cervantes. He also wrote in Hebrew, veering between the two languages, but his absolute seriousness in Yiddish was something new and trailblazing, mingling a modern critical stance with Talmudic lore and acerb social observation. Aleichem's eye was just as penetrating, but his heart was warmer, his pen kindlier, and he caught not only the pain and grime of life in the Russian Pale but the indomitable comic spirit of that oppressed embattled Jewry.

Shalom Aleichem has been called the Jewish Mark Twain, and there is in fact one indisputable parallel between them. In their masterpieces, *Tevya the Dairyman* and *Huckleberry Finn,* both hit on the identical creative stroke, the telling of a first-person story by an artless nobody, within his limited range of words and ideas. What on earth, one might wonder, could a Jewish dairyman in

Czarist Russia and a river boy from a small Missouri town possibly have in common? The answer is *gallantry*. Tevya breasts his fate as the drudging father of five daughters, beset in the hopeless poverty of the Pale but never losing faith in his old Jewish God; Huck lights out from a slave "sivilization," and defies Southern law and an unjust social order by rafting down the Mississippi with a black runaway. Worlds apart, both rise to themes of enduring grandeur. Concealing the highest art in the subtlest plain talk, Huck approaches a comic Jeremiah, Tevya a comic Job.

By a minor miracle, the Broadway show *Fiddler on the Roof* caught a spark of *Tevya*. Music and dance can conjure up truth where translation fails. Essentially an elegy on the extinguished life of the shtetl, *Fiddler* still enjoys international success. The dancing, singing Tevya has become the lovable epitome of the vanished shtetl Jew, even as the brave, pathetic vanished Anne Frank has become the Jewish heroine of the Holocaust. On receiving the Nobel Prize, the Yiddish author I. B. Singer said, with a razor edge of irony which may have escaped his applauding audience, that he was being honored for giving voice to ghosts.

The world takes to its heart ghostly Jews like Tevya and Anne Frank. With Israel's living Jews, and their abrasive refusal, like Mendele's Klatche, to lie down and die, the world has problems. Still, it does seem to be getting used to them, albeit grudgingly. *En brera,* Israelis say: "no choice."

The Key

Of the three immortals, Peretz is the sophisticate. More redolent of European literature than of Mendele's folk art, his style breaks out of the confines of Hebrew and Yiddish, though he was a master in both. His grasp of Jewish problems is profound, and he writes with haunting Haskalist pessimism about the convulsive transitions around him. Peretz also writes memorable, occasionally even light-hearted, Hasidic tales, authentic in substance if ambivalent in outlook. When Peretz re-creates folklore, which he does superbly, it is with willed naiveté, as it were, and the effect is one of artful rather than artless simplicity.

In Peretz's work, as in most Yiddish literature I have read, there runs a deep fault between the folkish and the secular. One might fancifully argue that through this very fault, opened by the earthquake changes in nineteenth-century Jewry, the sudden brief glory of great Yiddish writing erupted. All these authors, Aleichem included, produced fiction, poetry, and plays of current life with the folk element muted or absent. Why not? A man may as well write as he pleases in a language which offers a small audience and meager earnings, unless one hits it big with the non-Jewish public in translation, as Shalom Asch did with his Christian trilogy. Nevertheless, the rare stuff that rings like gold, and resists time like gold, is the folkish vein. Aleichem discerned this early, mined that vein till he died, and never hit it big—though the creators of *Fiddler* did—but the day he died work stopped in most Jewish workplaces in New York, and hundreds of thousands turned out for his funeral. The Jewish people, *Amkha*, knew what he had done for them.

An acid unbeliever of recent times, the poet and storyteller Itzik Manger, touches classic stature in his satirical *Humesh Lieder* ("Pentateuch Ballads") and the raucously funny *Book of Eden,* because the substance is so intensely Jewish. His love lyrics and poems of personal angst seem to me thin, by contrast. Lately I have been reading Chaim Grade, a contemporary of mine now deceased, who much like the old Haskalists, was torn between modern culture and the yeshiva *mussar* ("ethics") movement in which he grew up. What gives Grade's work its force is precisely this wrestle in his soul with the Yiddishkeit which both stifles and fires his gift.

In a word, the lifeblood of Yiddish literature is in Yiddishkeit.

That is the key. Isaac Bashevis Singer was a mischievous hedonist like Manger, and he made no bones about it, but it was the saturated Yiddishkeit of his work that won him the laurel crown.

Excursus: Cutting *Kriah*, or Rending a Garment

When the old shokhet out on Long Island cried to heaven for "Yiddishkeit" as opposed to "Jeedaism," was this what he had in mind, the folkish content of the writing of a cynical apikoros? Hardly, but it is what I have in mind. The other night I opened the Talmud a shade wearily to daf yomi. The rocket ride happened twenty years ago, and the old zest is not always there, though it can be rekindled, as it was when I read an arresting comment by Rashi on a sugya in the treatise *Shabbat*. The sugya may seem far afield, but it defines Yiddishkeit for me, and I have long been groping for just such a definition.

In dealing with prohibited work on the Sabbath, *Shabbat* examines the thirty-nine basic labors which went into building the Tabernacle, as described in the Book of Exodus. The sugya includes *kriah,* the act of tearing, and touches on "cutting kriah," rending a garment at the death of a loved one by a gash of one's clothing with a razor or knife. In its freehand way, the Gemara enumerates Jews beyond the immediate family for whom one should also cut kriah, for instance, a *talmid hakham* ("great scholar"). Rather surprisingly, it lists as well any Jew at whose death one happens to be present, relative or not. Drawing an analogy to the rule of cutting kriah when one sees a Torah scroll go up in flames, Rashi spells out the analogy in these marble words: "... *for there is no Jew however empty who does not have in him a trace of the Law and the Commandments.*"

I was studying the daf that night in a volume from a small Talmud printed in Stettin one hundred and thirty years ago. It was once my grandfather's, and when he made aliya he gave it to me, saying, "*Tommer vest du a mull geben a porkeh.*" ("Maybe you'll poke into it some time.") I make notes in margins of my large Talmud, but this one, with its remarkably clear print and durable yellowing paper, I never mark. However, I did underline that one unforgettable Rashi comment, by which I will here define Yiddishkeit: *There is no Jew however empty who does not have in him a trace of the Law and the Commandments.* Yiddishkeit, I submit, is that trace.

I have known some pretty empty Jews. An acquaintance of mine, a famous comedian whose forte is pungent Jewish clowning, converted to Catholicism to marry a lady of that faith. When reproached for his apostasy, he is reported to have quipped, "It was the funniest thing I could do." There is forlorn Yiddishkeit in that joke, it is a wry authentic Jewish *vitz*; the self-mocking twist, the subtle denial of any real turncoat intent, and the awareness that a Jew remains a Jew to the world and himself until he dies, no matter what he does. If I happen to be there when this eminent funny man expires—which is unlikely, since our paths seldom cross and he is my junior by decades—I may cut kriah for him, now that I know the law. At least I will think about it.

The Bell Curve

Such a definition of Yiddishkeit will go down hard with the observant. If I did not have Rashi to rely on, I might not proceed along this thorny path.

Yiddishkeit to the faithful, and I am one, ordinarily means living by the halakhah, nothing else. A social scientist plotting a bell curve of Yiddishkeit by that much broader definition, would show observant Jews nowadays as a decidedly minor statistic, well down the right-hand slope toward a terminus in a saint like Rav Moshe

Feinstein. At the low end of the other slope, there would be, let us say, the comedian who thought that apostasy was the funniest thing he could do. In between would be all the Jews of the world, at the latest count some thirteen million, down from the sixteen million before the German massacre. The bell curve would locate each of us as a statistic—assimilated, intermarried, unaffiliated, Hasidic, Zionist, post-Zionist, Orthodox (*haredi),* secular, Modern Orthodox, Conservative, Reform, Reconstructionist, traditional, not so traditional, very traditional, learned, ignorant, humanist, and so on—all of us would fall somewhere on that curve. In the middle, at or near the rounded top, I think I would find one of my oldest friends, the editor of the Columbia *Spectator* in 1934, when I edited the *Jester.*

Those were the days of the Great Depression, when he and I were on opposite slopes of another bell curve, the range of political opinion at Columbia. He was an earnest radical, covering strikes in the Kentucky coal mining country at some risk of his neck, while I was making jokes about everything, including radicals who went rubbernecking to strikes in Kentucky. He became an author of note on public affairs, exposing and attacking American radicalism and the Soviet system. About forty years after we graduated, he took it into his head to write a critical analysis of my books.* We met often for this project, and I learned only then that my old chum could speak flawless Yiddish, and knew more about the literature than I did. At college, neither of us had given a hint of our Yiddishkeit to each other, except perhaps by showing up at Jewish fraternity dances. That was how we Jews behaved then at Columbia.

Now here was a man who had the heritage in his grasp, at his fingertips, and who not only masked it during four college years but chucked it all in "marrying out." Yet today, past eighty, he loves to reminisce in Yiddish and to throw off recondite Talmudic

---

Herman Wouk: The Novelist as Social Historian by Arnold Beichman (New Brunswick, N.J.: Transaction Books, 1984).

phrases. Whether he regrets not transmitting his rich Yiddishkeit to his children and grandchildren, I cannot say, but there is a wistfulness about him when we talk Yiddish that is unmistakable. Perhaps, though, he is only feeling rueful about what time has done to both of us.

I place him at the midpoint of the bell curve because he is aware of the tradition, has lost his hold on it, remembers it well, and if I am not mistaken, might now wish to have kept more of it in his and his children's lives. That is about where, on average, American Yiddishkeit seems to be. Israeli Yiddishkeit is a totally different story, to which we will come shortly.

The Archipelago

Not a few American Jews will find my depiction here of Yiddish and Yiddishkeit far too dismal. They and their children speak Yiddish as well as they do English. Among them are doctors, lawyers, real estate developers, small businessmen, computer experts, financiers, shopkeepers, poets, painters, and university professors. What they have in common is living by the halakhah, and they dwell in enclaves where nearly everybody else lives the same way. Around New York such islands of intense normalized Torah existence include Monsey, Crown Heights, Borough Park, and Far Rockaway, and a sort of archipelago of such environs dots the country in or near big cities, offering small-town *heimish* ("homey") milieus for the faithful. Restaurants and pizzerias are kosher, shops are geared to Orthodox taste and practice, women's styles are modestly modish, day schools, synagogues, and yeshivas abound, local weeklies feature religious and Israel news, and factions and rivalries keep things lively.

Hasidim are found there in force and are much publicized, since the media finds them photogenic. The less conspicuous

Misnagdim, however, may well be the majority. In their vigorous *yeshivishe velt* ("yeshiva world"), the old Lithuanian learning goes on with impassioned earnestness from Brooklyn to Los Angeles. This velt is producing notable new editions of rare works of Torah scholarship, also high-quality Hebrew-English volumes of familiar classics—prayer books, Pentateuch, Mishnah, Talmud, Rambam— much in demand and running to several editions. A feel of eastern Europe lingers in these enclaves. They sprang up around Hasidic Rebbes, or old-country giants of Lithuanian learning called *Gedolay Hatorah.* These founders have passed on. In the archipelago grand-children and great-grandchildren tend to speak English among themselves, and some are at home in spoken Hebrew too, but Yiddish remains bedrock.

Whether Yiddish literature has any future in this community is another matter. This is the real surviving Yiddish audience, yet the lit-erature originated, after all, in the Haskalist rebellion against the old ways. In our little Palm Springs synagogue, the discourses of the late Lubavitcher Rebbe line the shelves, and the rabbi reads them all the time. For him they are holy text. I have read them too, and the com-plex rabbinic Yiddish is exceedingly distant from Peretz and Shalom Aleichem. That such a gulf can be bridged seems unlikely. Thus, a rich literary legacy impregnated with truthful Jewish experience, reli-gious and secular, may well go a-begging. I hope with all my heart that I am indeed being too dismal.

Yiddishkeit: An Afterword

An Israeli general I have known for many years recounted an argu-ment he had with another general, to whom he quoted a comment of Rashi. The other looked blank. "The trouble with you," my friend told him, "is that you lack Yiddishkeit." He is no saint him-self, not at all, but he was using "Yiddishkeit" in the sense that I suggest here. The term in that broad sense takes in all of us poor sinners. I know Reform Jews and humanist Jews too, who have worked all their lives to build Israel and to rescue Jews, sometimes laying their lives on the line. To assert that such Jews have no Yiddishkeit is unintelligible to me. The cardinal mitzvah of *ahavat Yisrael,* love of fellow Jews, has filled their days. Who among us can say that of himself? And if a man dresses in black, prays with deep devotion, punctiliously observes Shabbat, eats only glatt kosher, and despises Jews who have learned less and observe less, in my view his Yiddishkeit is deeply flawed by his lack of *ahavat Yisrael.*

This discussion has been leaving out a major sector of our people, the Sephardim, since Yiddish is not part of their tradition. In America, remarkably close-knit and vigorous communities from Sephardic lands like Syria, Iraq, and Iran maintain their own synagogues and schools, with customs, liturgy, and music that differ quite a bit from Ashkenazic practice. Their origin is Spanish-Portuguese, and they have their own jargon, called Ladino, based on Spanish. The principal of a Sephardic yeshiva happened to be in Palm Springs not long ago for a weekend, and we did daf yomi together. I was writing this chapter, and wondering what term the Sephardim employed instead of Yiddishkeit, so here was my chance to find out.

"What word do you Sephardim use," I asked him, "to describe the concept of Jewishness, or Judaism? We say Yiddishkeit. And you?"

"Yiddishkeit," he said.

Sixteen

Ivrit and Zionism

The Smoke-Filled Room

My bar-mitzvah pocket watch, a slender white-gold Waltham given to me by the Minsker Congregation of the Bronx, lies here on my desk seventy years later, both of us still ticking away. It brings to mind another rite de passage of my boyhood, the first Zionist meeting I attended. My father brought me there, and to this day I am not sure why.

The scene is preserved in my memoir-novel, *Inside, Outside*. It was on a Friday night, the air in the place was gray with tobacco smoke when we walked in, and plates of sandwiches were laid out for refreshments. Papa cautioned me about the sandwiches—not that he had to, I well knew the look of school lunchroom ham—and he joined with zest the boring wrangling in English and Yiddish. I was repelled and puzzled. By then Zaideh was living with us, and I wondered how Papa could tolerate such gross goyishness, let alone drag me into it. I loved him and let it go at that, my mind being occupied with teenage matters, but it was many years before I really changed my view of Zionism, formed that Shabbat evening in the smoke-filled room.

When I grew up I called myself a Zionist, attended fund-raising dinners, and even spoke at some, gave money, knew the patter, and believed in the need for the homeland I first visited in 1955. My sharp-witted mother had been going there off and on to see Zaideh. "Israel is inspiring," she once said, "but when you go away it fades." So it was with me in 1955. I came home to a jarring critical fuss about *Marjorie Morningstar*, and Israel faded, Ben-Gurion and all. A year later Israel's army surprised the world by a dashing capture of the Sinai in the Suez War, but the British and French bungled their part of the attack, the Soviet Union rattled rockets, Eisenhower harshly ordered Israel out of the Sinai, and the whole thing was a historic fiasco. I was briefly stirred by the Israelis' exploit because they were the home team, though it came to almost nothing.

Agnon

One lovely June morning in 1967, when I arrived at the Georgetown Synagogue to daven, the rabbi greeted me with, "Agnon is here." Agnon! The Israeli author had just won the Nobel Prize for Literature, shared with the poet Nelly Sachs. In the sciences, Jewish laureates abounded, but Shmuel Yosef Agnon was the first in my own game of prose literature. I wangled invitations for myself and my wife to the luncheon where Agnon was speaking. Israel's ambassador appeared at the outset to make an impromptu fighting speech which brought a thousand Conservative rabbis cheering to their feet, for it was another touch-and-go moment in the Middle East. The Egyptian dictator Nasser had ordered the UN peacekeepers out of the Sinai, they had meekly obeyed, and he had then poured armored divisions into the peninsula up to the Israeli border. Now he was closing the Strait of Tiran, choking off Israel's Red Sea shipping lane, and proclaiming in fiery public speeches that the end of "the Zionist entity" was at hand.

Agnon's talk was a grievous letdown. It was hard even to see this aged little man in a big black yarmulke, with a microphone blocking his face, and the pages of his speech held up to his eyes. While he was droning on in Hebrew amid restless noise, an embassy aide approached us. The ambassador had planned a dinner for the great author that night, but because of the war situation, could we entertain him instead, since we were kosher? My wife at once agreed. Agnon didn't eat meat, the aide added, and would like to bring a friend or two. No problem, she assured him.

General Geva

Agnon showed up with a bareheaded man he cheerfully introduced as "my son the apikoros [atheist]," and ten other people, including Israel's military attaché, a handsome broad-shouldered general. Not a whit fazed, my wife just put another leaf in the dinner table, being used by then to Israeli informality. Her main dish was a quiche, and Agnon wolfed portion after portion, saying that since arriving in America he had been subsisting on bread and salad.

"This is better than Stockholm," he declared in Hebrew, insisting that I translate to my wife. "They served me on plates of gold. The king assured me that the food was kosher and the gold plates too. I thanked him, and I didn't eat." Invited to lead the grace after the meal, he asked for a cup of wine, and when he finished he passed the cup to her, an antique custom Rashi mentions in Genesis. The military attaché kept jumping up to answer telephone calls, obviously war-related, then he would rejoin the talk with debonair calm. This broad-shouldered general, whose name was Josef Geva, would in time cost me years of my working life.

I drove Agnon back to his hotel, where he chatted with me for hours, quaffing French brandy and complaining of insomnia. In Israel I had tried in vain to converse in Hebrew, but the Israelis' rapid rattling of their Ivrit (modern Hebrew) lost me, and they said I spoke like a Bible character. Yet I understood Agnon, he seemed to understand me, and after a while I almost forgot we were talking Ivrit. He was unhappy with the goodwill tour the government had foisted on him. The money being thrown away was scandalous. "I am a penniless man," he said, gesturing around at the hotel suite, "and look how I am living!"

From his long weary rambling I began to glimpse something of his intellectual stature. This quaint little skull-capped Jew with a mottled face and old-fashioned manners had a devilishly acute humorous mind, and his artlessness was not a pose, exactly, but a self-created persona of a literary Tevya. "We are storytellers, Herman Wouk," he admonished me, with a waving forefinger. "Remember—pictures, pictures, no thoughts! And write only what you want to write. Never think about sales."

When he finally let me leave, he said at the door, as we shook hands, "I expect great things of you."

"How is that? You said you don't know my work."

"My neighbor bought three copies of your *Mered* [*Mutiny*] to give to friends, and she is no fool," he said with a shrug and a very straight face.

(*"Never think about sales!"*)

In the three years before he died, I saw Agnon each time I returned to Israel, and I came to love this plain, remote, old Jew of multiple masks. And now about that war, and about Josef Geva.

Brief Honeymoon

The Six-Day War exploded, and Israel's astounding victory threw the world media into a tizzy. The stooped despised Wandering Jew had doffed the shtetl caftan, straightened up, and seized the sword of the conquering Joshua, et cetera. Such extravagant imagery seemed plain fact, as Jews from all over the world—including me and my little family—thronged to the Promised Land to joyride down to Jericho and up to the Golan Heights, to sing "Jerusalem the Golden," to walk the Temple Mount, and to pray at the Wall, in its spectacular new plaza setting. It was a honeymoon of history that lasted six years, then Egypt and Syria simultaneously invaded on Yom Kippur, and caught the conquering Joshua flat-footed. For a week or more, things looked very black for the Zionist dream. A bloody turnaround victory forced Egypt, by far the largest and strongest Arab foe, to the peace table. But General Josef Geva, who had become a good friend, said to me, "In the Yom Kippur War we lost our virginity." A foreseeable outcome of honeymoons.

All those events rolled over my head while I was racing the calendar to write *The Winds of War* and *War and Remembrance,* never sure to the last that I would finish the task before I died. But I did, and a new challenge confronted me, a work of fiction measuring up to the troubled marvel of Israel. For a central theme, the Yom Kippur War would be perfect, I thought, encapsulating highs and lows of the Zionist adventure—heady triumph, near-catastrophe, gutsy recovery, and morning-after sobriety. I tried the idea on Geva, by now a grizzled industrialist, telling it rather like a film writer pitching a story to a studio head. He heavily sighed when I finished, and in his measured response, a judge was reluctantly sentencing a pathetic defendant to a long term at hard labor.

"Don't write about one war," he said, "and don't start in 1948. It's a hundred-year story."

Indeed I could not portray Zionism in one war, it turned out, nor even in one novel. In writing *The Hope* and *The Glory,* I served the whole sentence, but I did start my story in 1948.

The Battle of Latrun: "*Voss? Voss?*" (What? What?)

Driving between Tel Aviv and Jerusalem nowadays, you speed past a hill called Latrun, where a memorial to the Armored Corps displays all the tanks that have fought in Israel's wars. Here at Latrun in 1948, when the War of Independence began, Yiddish-speaking immigrants fresh off the boat were given rifles and water bottles, and thrown into combat against a fortress manned by the British-trained Arab Legion. In the peppery way of Israeli polemic, the occurrence at Latrun sometimes gets magnified to a colossal disaster in which thousands of hapless refugees were mowed down by Arab cannon. The best estimate is that some seventy-nine recruits may have died, a few from heatstroke and dehydration, for it was a day of *hamsin,* fiery desert wind.

When I learned about Latrun, I was transfixed by the detail of the language gap between the Israeli officers and the bewildered recruits. "*Voss, voss?*" ("What, what?") the miserable newcomers kept shouting in Yiddish at their superiors and each other, as the bullets flew all around them. Here surely was Zionism epitomized, it struck me: the leap from the shtetl to the Holy Land, from Yiddish to Hebrew, recorded in the blood of the *voss-vossim* (as they were then and there dubbed), who did not panic but kept marching up the hill under fire from the fortress, until their leaders managed to convey the order to fall back.

The wisest of my consulting experts, the late eminent economist Ernst Nebenzahl, who was for decades the Comptroller of Israel, exclaimed when I showed him my opening chapter of *The Hope* about Latrun, "Oh, you're not making it an army story, are you? There's so much more to Israel than the army!" True enough. The Land, like the Torah, has seventy faces. In Israel's first years, though, only one other face mattered as much: Ivrit.

Ivrit

Five million Israelis today read Ivrit papers, watch Ivrit television, and talk Ivrit among themselves. All the operations of their redoubtable army, navy, and air force are conducted in this modern Hebrew.

Israelis take their Ivrit as much for granted as we Americans do our English. The hoary tongue has been magically transformed in an eyeblink to raffish youth, like the aged Faust in the opera.

Colloquial Hebrew is a racy, slangy, spicy speech, with many American loan-words and a few Arab expressions jostling a host of phrases from Talmud and Tanakh. Hebrew purists may cringe, but the grandchildren of the voss-vossim work, play, and sing in their jangling native Ivrit, updating it as they go. The language that my Yiddish-speaking parents called *Hebrayish,* and my grandfather *Lush'n Kaydesh* ("holy tongue"), has passed in my own lifetime from the bookcase, the bet midrash, and the synagogue to the strong open sunlight of the Land; to everyday street use, university lecturing, fighter pilot communication, and the whispers of young lovers. The vocabulary of the Bible and the rabbis has been stretched to handle science, politics, business, technology, warmaking, homemaking, and journalism. Aspiring authors write not the smooth Hebrew prose of the Rambam or even Bialik, but what comes naturally to them, Ivrit.

Yet to the father of political Zionism, Theodor Herzl, what today seems so natural was only the vaporous hopeless dream of a few besotted philologists. "Can you imagine," he once said scornfully, "ordering a railroad ticket in Hebrew?" (Actually, it's easy. "*Cartis la'rakevet, b'vakasha.*") In his book *Old-New Land,* a visionary tract in the form of a novel, Herzl portrayed the coming Jewish homeland as a cosmopolitan little utopia, set down on the sands of the eastern Mediterranean, a polyglot Mitteleuropa in the Holy Land, complete with such amenities of high culture as cafés, operas, theaters, smart shops, and leafy promenades, its Jewish citizens speaking French, Italian, possibly even English or Polish, depending on where they came from, but of course mostly German, the international tongue of Herzl's native Mitteleuropa. Hebrew? A joke.

Excursus: Herzl

At the majestic flawed figure of Herzl, let me pause. Israel has no Mount Rushmore. If it did there would be not four heads carved on the cliff, but one—Theodor Herzl.

Everything was wrong with Theodor Herzl's scrappy, fragmented, chaotic political creation called Zionism, except that it worked. It still works. It teetered on the brink of self-defeat until the day it shakily prevailed. It continues to be its own worst enemy. In its ever-boiling factionalism, all parties manage to agree on only two points: (1) Israel should survive, and (2) Israelis should talk Ivrit. Extremists can be found who will dispute those points, too. Jews will be Jews.

A few Jews today still decry Herzl's memory. Too many have never heard of him. Who was this giant? An assimilated minor Austro-Hungarian playwright and journalist, a *comme il faut* Viennese man about town, until he covered the Dreyfus trial in Paris for his newspaper; and then he was so stung in his numbed Yiddishkeit that he became charged with a megalomanic vision as by a lightning stroke. The Jews had no future in the diaspora, their one hope was to found a Jewish State in Palestine, and he would lead the founding himself! At the time Theodor Herzl was so ignorant of Jews and Judaism that he did not know Zionism was already fermenting in Russia, sending pioneers to Palestine to farm the Land, and to create, side by side with the small religious yishuv, a new modern Jewish presence there.

Herzl saw in Dreyfus's ordeal, and in the volcanic social upheaval it was causing in France, a red-light warning, a signal that Emancipation was a delusion, a dead end, and a possible deathtrap for Europe's Jews. He did not foresee the Holocaust—who of sane mind could?—but he did sense an oncoming horror, and he was inspired to cry danger. To point the way out, he dashed off in a few weeks a fervent manifesto, *Der Judenstaat* ("The Jewish State"), turning overnight from the scribbling of ephemera to grappling

with life-and-death issues of the Jewish nation. This urbane unbeliever, until then a lightweight Viennese literary dandy, had found
his life's historic mission.

In rising to this quasi-prophetic call, the transfigured Herzl
uncovered in himself leadership genius and fantastic stores of
energy. Nowadays the fashion among Israeli literati is to debunk
Zionism's heroes, and Herzl is eminently debunkable, as most great
men are. But the debunkers are having their say in Israel, and in
Ivrit, because Theodor Herzl lived his last seven meteoric years creating and leading the first Jewish political resurgence since A.D. 70.
He died in 1904 of heart disease at only forty-four, but by then he
had made the Jewish State possible, by calling the Zionist movement into being with sheer personal force. Buried at first in
Vienna, he lies today on a hillside outside Jerusalem, called Mount
Herzl. That is Israel's Mount Rushmore.

Ben-Yehuda and "Uganda"

Twelve years before the Dreyfus trial, while Herzl was still insou-
ciantly strolling the boulevards of Vienna in top hat and frock coat,
the man who made Ivrit possible arrived in Palestine, a newlywed
of twenty-three. On stepping ashore in Jaffa, so the story goes,
Eliezer Ben-Yehuda told his wife that henceforth they would com-
municate only in Hebrew. They were pioneers, coming to work the
desiccated soil amid the Arabs and the ancient ruins. He and his
family never really spoke again in another tongue.

His Jewish background was as full as Herzl's was scanty. Born a
Chabad Hasid, he passed a boyhood immersed in Lithuanian
yeshivas, then broke from the religion to become a hard-bitten
unrelenting Maskil. Reviving the language was his singleminded
passion. He spearheaded the effort till he died. He wrote the first
comprehensive modern Hebrew dictionary, a monumental task

brilliantly carried out. Ben-Yehuda much resembled Herzl in his fanatic willpower. Conceivably, it was this shared trait that drew both men—otherwise poles apart—to support "Uganda," a movement to settle the Jews in the land we now call Kenya. This project all but aborted the Zionist movement at the outset, and might have killed the idea of a Jewish State for another two millennia.

Ask an ordinary Israeli schoolboy what Uganda means, and you will hear all about the Entebbe raid, a sensational rescue by Israel's armed forces of Jewish hostages held in an Air France plane, hijacked by terrorists and parked in a Uganda terminal two thousand miles from Tel Aviv. An A-plus schoolgirl might also mention the almost-fatal rift in Zionism over the proposal to locate the Jewish State in "Uganda," at the equator in darkest Africa. The ironies of the Uganda crisis are manifold, the details a tangle of disputes beyond unraveling, but the large picture is clear enough. It is Josef Geva's "hundred-year story" in miniature.

Herzl and "Uganda"

Russian Zionism was a grass-roots movement, sprouting despite harsh Czarist police surveillance. Herzl's Zionism by contrast sprang from the brain of one man, free as air in emancipated Vienna, his smart-set existence void of Judaism and untouched by the brutish truths of shtetl life. This difference generated the Uganda crisis. The Russian Maskilim, however irreligious, were soaked in the tradition they had shrugged off. When Herzl brought to the annual Zionist congress a British offer to grant the Jews a homeland—not in Palestine, for that was under Turkish rule, but on a grassy plateau near Lake Victoria, then part of Uganda, today within Kenya—he ran into a fire wall of Russian opposition.

This offer came a mere six years after Herzl summoned and presided over the first Zionist Congress in 1897. In that short time he had gained international stature as a spokesman for the Jewish people. Tall and courtly, with deep-set blazing eyes and imposing black beard, he fully looked the part. Into the highest political and financial circles Theodor Herzl strode as though he belonged, and as such he was received. His goal in one word was a *charter,* an internationally recognized grant of territory to the Jews, for a place on earth of their own. That this place could only be the Holy Land was the essence of Zionism, Russian and Herzlian alike.

But this meant dealing with the Turks, which Herzl took upon himself. After years of sickening discouragement and postponement, costly bribes spent in vain, and interminable Levantine double-crossing, he actually penetrated the maze of the Turkish court in Constantinople and managed to see the Sultan himself. Herzl's diaries on this whole business make fascinating but melancholy reading. What he got from the Sultan, whom he never saw again, and from his minions thereafter, was the runaround.

Yet he was indefatigable and unstoppable. He met with the German Kaiser to seek support in his dealings with the Turks, only to encounter more runaround, of the straight Teutonic rather than the devious Byzantine variety. He confronted England's most eminent Jew, Lord Rothschild, and failed to sway him from his frigid hostility to the Zionist idea, shared by nearly all wealthy diaspora Jews. He even made his way into high Czarist circles, and obtained from the powerful minister Plehve, an avowed anti-Semite, some small leeway for legal Zionist activity in Russia.

With the Sixth Zionist Congress approaching in 1903, for all this dazzling darting about on the world stage which had won him the adulation of the Jewish masses, Herzl had nothing tangible in hand to bring, and he was suffering badly from his heart trouble. The Russian Zionists, a major bloc of delegates at the Congress, had been following his lead, though vexing him by sending the *halutzim,* pioneers, to Palestine. The numbers were insignificant, a few thousand at most, but Herzl viewed this "infiltration," as he termed it, as demeaning to the Jewish cause and an incitement to the Turks.

The trouble was that under a surface of common Zionist enthusiasm, the two ideologies were at cross-purposes. Herzl had a western journalist's grasp of politics, he knew what statesmanship was, and he was going to the sources of power like a statesman. The Russians were intellectuals, *luftmenschen,* short on savvy about statecraft, and long on complicated midnight theorizing in cellars, but they were bitterly aware that murder, rape, and looting were ever-present dangers to themselves and their families. They knew one thing: *Jews had to get out of Russia,* and had to go somewhere. For those Zionists that meant Palestine and Palestine only, Herzl or no Herzl, Turks or no Turks.

Kishinev

Easter, 1903.

Mobs rampage through Kishinev for two days, and while a garrison of five thousand Russian troops stand by and do nothing, dozens of Jews are killed, and the damage mounts to immense sums. A world outcry goes up. President Theodore Roosevelt sends a letter of protest to the Czar. It is not accepted. The British Foreign Office considers allowing an emergency settlement of Russian Jews around El Arish in the Sinai. Herzl is thrilled and exalted at the news. The Jews of Kishinev have not died in vain, a CHARTER is in sight, in a place abutting on Palestine! Alas, the notion is soon withdrawn, and the Uganda offer surfaces instead.

How serious was the offer, and why was it made? A befogged subject for scholarly delving. Could it possibly have been implemented? An exercise in fruitless fantasy. The fact is, Herzl seized on "Uganda" as a great step forward, an achievement to bring to the Congress. It blew the Zionist movement apart, and it hastened his death, if it did not kill him outright. He won the vote, but the issue was not "Uganda, up or down," only a tepid motion to send a delegation to survey Uganda for its suitability. Two years passed before the money was raised and the delegation actually went. Their report was negative, but by then Herzl was dead, and so was the issue. The noncommittal vote in fact had been just a sop to the defeated and ailing Herzl. Strangely, a large bloc of religious delegates had swung to him and saved him from crushing humiliation. To the end, the Russian Maskilim fought against any consideration whatever of a homeland outside Palestine. After the vote, they walked out, though they later walked back.

Was Herzl grasping at a straw? Not so, not exactly. The Uganda offer—at a minimum—meant acceptance by the world's most powerful empire *of the principle of a Jewish homeland.* Even if the bizarre scheme had come to pass, with the resettlement of some Russian Jews in Uganda, it could only have been a stopgap. More likely, it would have remained a talking point, a moderately strong card, in the long political game to pry a Jewish homeland from the Sultan. Such was evidently the faltering leader's reasoning, and his statesmanship was not wholly misguided, but he reckoned without the gut issue of Yiddishkeit. The Russian Maskilim had all lisped in their childhood at the Passover seder, "Next year in Jerusalem," and even the most rabid apikoros among them had those words in his blood.

Zionism was the modern revolution in the Jewish spirit, the will to live on resurging, to prevail over everything else in Judaism, in a time of threatened extinction. Herzl's Zionism was newfound Yiddishkeit of brain and heart. The Russians' Yiddishkeit reached back through the centuries to Yavneh, the Talmud center that came into being as the Second Temple burned. Yavneh prevailed.

Collapse of the Pioneers

But how could Eliezer Ben-Yehuda, the father of Ivrit, conceivably have been in favor of Uganda? Yet he was, and so were most Jews of the *First Aliya,* the pioneer immigration wave in Palestine.

Of all the little-known facts of this dust-covered record, this remains the most baffling. These people had acted out Zionism with their calloused hands, their toil-worn backs, and their blood spilled by Arab marauders. They had worked the holy soil all their adult lives. They were the *doers,* the "practical Zionists," while Herzl and his western cadre were the mere *dreamers,* the "political Zionists." Such had been their slogan and their rationale. Then how could these ultra-Zionists, these *halutzim,* have forsaken their ideals in favor of a preposterous Jewish "homeland" in equatorial Africa, twenty-five hundred miles from Palestine?

When this anomaly surfaced in my research, I telephoned an Israeli author and activist I have known for decades, Arie Lova Eliav, a crusading peacenik who may know more Israeli history than the historians, having made a lot of it himself. I put the puzzle to him, and here is what he told me, pretty much in his own words.

> Ben-Yehuda was a broken man by then. So were many of the First Aliya people. Their idealistic "practical Zionism" had been a terrible lifelong disappointment. Nothing had worked out. The farming of the poor soil was difficult and unprofitable. Arab harassment was a constant worry. The Turkish authorities were hostile and corrupt, and gave little protection. Thanks largely to the philanthropic support of Baron Rothschild, who had been subsidizing them down the years, their hard existence had been barely endurable. But the Baron was unreachable off in Europe, and the settlers felt more and more like slaves of his heavy-handed local bureaucrats, who told them what to do and how to do it, and used the Baron's money to whip them into line.
>
> Their plight was a tragedy, but good came of it, all the same.

A new wave of Zionists was springing up in eastern Europe, the Ben-Gurion generation, carrying forward the Zionist-socialist program. Spurred by the Uganda fiasco, and the collapse of the First Aliya, to come to the rescue and settle the land, those Second Aliya Zionists were the prime builders of Israel.

So it was that Eliezer Ben-Yehuda, who allowed no utterance but Hebrew to pass his lips once he reached Palestine, could advocate a homeland for the Jews in Africa. The Russian delegates at the Congress in Switzerland, amid the civilized comforts of Basel, could maintain an iron front of Zionist idealism, but the Jews of the First Aliya were there on the ground in Zion. Disillusioned, shattered in spirit, they had had it with idealism.

Nobody asked the Jews of the old religious yishuv what they thought of Uganda. They were Yavneh.

The Charter

"Nations are cold monsters," Charles de Gaulle once put it, a neat phrase for realpolitick. After the Uganda botch and Herzl's death, history had to produce a cold monster to support the groping Zionist movement, and so it did. A crack in time opened when the Turks entered the First World War on the German side, and the Middle East as a result became a war front. When the British invaded Palestine, their Foreign Office under Lord Balfour determined, for wartime policy reasons—a buffer for the Suez Canal being high among them—to issue the famous Balfour Declaration of 1917. Here was Herzl's dreamed-of *charter!* Or as close to it as the Jews would ever come, until they themselves wrote the one that mattered most, the Declaration of Independence of the State of Israel; which like the American Declaration, reviewed the historical background of the people and the land, and concluded with a stark proclamation that an independent Jewish State once more existed in the Holy Land.

In turn, the efficacy of that Declaration hung on the calculated act of another cold monster, the Soviet Union. After the Second World War, in order to edge the British out of the Middle East, Stalin in 1947 ordered the communist bloc in the UN to vote en masse for the partition of Palestine, to the great shock and rage of the Arab countries. This vote enabled Israel to run up its flag in May 1948, when the British pulled out. Thereafter Stalin became a snarling advocate of all Arab positions, but meantime Israel had won its Independence War against five invading Arab armies, and America, not the Soviet Union, had moved into the political void left in the Middle East by the departing British.

And so the Jewish State was born. If there was a miracle in any of this, it was that after millennia of stateless wandering, the Jews were not only still around, and still aspiring to return to the Land, but at this point were ready to fight for it, as they had not been since the Bar Kokhba revolt, the last flicker of armed Jewish resistance to Rome, crushed out by Hadrian in A.D. 135. They were enabled to reenter history because of two world wars and the clashing of great powers, but to the glory of Herzl and of Zionism, when that conjunction of the stars occurred, they were prepared to seize the moment.

They have had to fight many wars since, about which I have written two long novels. Half a century after the Declaration, there are some signs that their Arab neighbors may at last be growing semi-reconciled to this tiny island of the west in the vast sea of Islam. The late greatly admired King Hussein of Jordan, in a broadcast to his people after the Six-Day War, said, "It is the will of Allah." If there is another explanation, I do not know it.

Footnote: Truman

At the time of the Declaration, President Truman's Secretary of State was General George Marshall, who had masterminded America's victorious strategy in World War Two. With all the force of his immense prestige, he advised the President not to recognize the Jewish State, for Marshall's job, as he saw it, was to calculate American national policy in cold realistic terms. David Ben-Gurion read the Declaration at exactly midnight in the Middle East. Eleven minutes later in Washington, President Truman recognized Israel. The Chief Rabbi of Israel, visiting the United States some months afterward, was invited to the White House. "God put you in your mother's womb," he told the President, "so you would be the instrument to bring the rebirth of Israel after two thousand years." It is recorded that Truman wept.

Seventeen

YOSSI

Mea Shearim

An army man some thirty years my junior, whom I met in my research on Israel's wars, has become my own personal Eliezer Ben-Yehuda. All I know in the military line is sea combat, and in my writing of *The Hope* and *The Glory*, he educated me about land warfare as Israel fights it, from the platoon level to general staff planning. In return, I have taught him a little Talmud, a most advantageous exchange for me. He is fluent in English, but at the outset he ruled that we would talk and correspond in Hebrew. With a few lapses, we have really done so. It was a tough but wise decision. Otherwise, I might not have managed to write those novels, for I had to talk to many, many Israelis, not like a Bible character but in Ivrit. His name is Yossi Ben Hanan, and we have become the closest of friends over the years.

We happened to meet for the first time a few days before *Simhat Torah*, the Rejoicing of the Law. Outside Israel, the holiday runs two days and nights, but there the second night is given over to musical merriment—trumpets, drums, clarinets, what have you, all amplified to deafening volume—since by their religious calendar it is a week night, and playing of instruments is permissible.

Yossi invited me to come walking with him that night in ultra-Orthodox Mea Shearim. "Something to see," he assured me, and indeed it was.

In Mea Shearim's main square men and boys by the hundreds, in the black garb of pietists, were dancing under blasting loudspeakers and blinding spotlights. Crowded on the sidelines, their bewigged wives and mothers, some with babes in arms, and long-haired girls in skirts to their ankles, looked on and gossiped while numberless children boiled underfoot. Yossi wore his colonel's uniform, and I was dressed like the blatant American tourist I was and still am, but nobody looked twice at us. My new friend said, as we threaded our way through the women and children, "This is what we're fighting for. They keep the flame." From a senior Israeli army man such words were not usual, and I began to sense common ground.

I followed him to join with yeshiva youths cavorting in a huge second-story study hall, in suffocating sweaty circles eight or ten deep, shaking the floors and the walls with their exuberant stamping, in a white glare of neon and an ear-splitting blare of saxophones. After that we sedately danced and sang with old fur-hatted, golden-robed Jerusalemites in a small tumbledown synagogue, softly shuffling hand to hand with them as they took us into their rounds. So we went from one place of rejoicing to another, until at last—that night, and for years thereafter, for this became our annual *hazakah* (commitment)—we ended up at the yeshiva of an ancient Kabbalist, Reb Areleh, famed for his unique ecstatic dancing on Simhat Torah. Clasping a small Torah scroll in his arms, Reb Areleh's custom was to race with a strange gait around and around the floor of the dazzlingly lit *bet midrash*, study hall, igniting among his followers frenzied rhythmic handclaps and jubilant shouts, while visitors like us were permitted to watch, perched precariously on wooden benches stacked along a back wall.

When we left the yeshiva that night, Yossi pointed out a poster in Yiddish, plastered on the old stone wall:

GOD-FEARING PARENTS!!
Forbid your children to speak the "Ivrit" of the Zionists!
It is a desecration of the holy tongue!
It will corrupt their pure souls!
Your sons will wander into evil ways, God forbid!
YOUR DAUGHTERS' VIRTUE WILL NOT BE SAFE!!!
Command them to talk only Yiddish, the speech of our fathers!

"What do you make of that?" asked my personal Eliezer Ben-Yehuda.

"Full circle," I said.

Yossi rose to become Chief of the Armor Corps. When he retired, he went into the Defense Ministry, in a post involving international trade. Today his duties keep him on the move around the world. Now and then, he telephones me from places like Warsaw, Beijing, or Hanoi. I have given up the little apartment in Jerusalem where I wrote much of *The Hope* and *The Glory.* We no longer wander in Mea Shearim on "second Simhat Torah," as we did for some twenty years, and Reb Areleh of blessed memory is long since gone. I think of that poster as the last shot fired in the language war.

The Smoke-Filled Nightclub

"You don't want to do that," said Yossi. I was asking him, when we had known each other for years, for a tour of Tel Aviv's night life.

"Why not?"

"Because Friday night is *the* big night in Tel Aviv, and it's solid *hillul Shabat* [profaning of the Sabbath]."

Yossi likes the religion, knows a lot about it, studies it off and on, observes it when inclined, and otherwise does exactly as he pleases. Nothing could be more Israeli. About my observance he is over-tender, so I told him I was writing a chapter in *The Glory* about just such a scene. On that basis, he reluctantly agreed to do the tour. This was shortly after the controversial Lebanon War ended. Yossi had fought in the war and had narrowly escaped an ambush in which a brilliant friend, touted as a coming chief of staff, had been killed. Many soldiers were still deployed up there, none too happily, but life in Israel—or at least in north Tel Aviv— was back to normal. So early one Friday afternoon, we holed up for Shabbat in a small hotel, and sallied out in the evening to cruise the hot spots on foot.

For someone new to it, Friday night in Tel Aviv, especially north Tel Aviv, is a real eye-opener—and a far cry, my good believing friends, from Shabbat candles, Kiddush, table hymns, and Torah talk over gefilte fish and noodle soup. For total blithe unawareness of the Sabbath, north Tel Aviv on Friday night might as well be a side street off Times Square, except that people talk Ivrit. The *in* spot that year was a place called Mandy's, which got going only after midnight. When we entered, Yossi cut a swath through the lobby into the crowded bar, where big-shot politicians of both parties were milling about in a great noise, drinks and cigarettes in hand, instantly recognizable through the tobacco haze. Israel's chief spectator sport is politics, and photographs and caricatures of the main players are in the papers all the time. The women tended to be plump, middle-aged wives, with here and there a sharp, slender young creature clad with Israel's flair for eye-catching couture.

Everybody greeted Yossi with the beguiling warmth of Israelis. When he introduced me, some people yelled compliments about my books, and I bellowed my thanks in Ivrit, bringing surprised grins. This went on for half an hour or so, and then we were back out on the sidewalk in the humid summer air of Tel Aviv, amid the electric signs of nightclubs, and young and old Israelis roistering along the streets. We walked in silence for a while.

"Not Mea Shearim," I said.

"You asked to see it."

"I wouldn't have missed it."

I told him of a talk I had had that day with a soldier of the Golani elite unit, which had captured the Beaufort Castle, a fortress just inside Lebanon, at the start of the war. Claimed by the government as an almost bloodless victory, the operation had in fact been a murderous botch. This soldier's anger at the false claim, and at the pointless death of his comrades, was chill and hard. "I don't think this country is worth dying for," he said. He has, in fact, since become a neurosurgeon in New York, and shows no signs of going back.

Yossi was silent. I prodded him. "Well, is it?"

It was a while before he spoke up. "In all our wars so far, about twenty thousand fighters have fallen," he said. "That's as many Jews as were gassed in Auschwitz in two days." A long pause, until we entered the darkened hotel. "Do you remember the Kishinev pogrom? Does anybody? The whole world was in an uproar because fifty Jews were killed. That was in 1903. Later, Jewish lives became cheaper." He gave me a brief strong hug. "*Shabbat shalom.*"

With some difficulty, I said, "*Shabbat shalom.* Thanks for the tour."

"No problem. Is Israel worth dying for? Was Zionism a good idea, or a foolish dream? Depends on your Yiddishkeit."

During the writing of this chapter, Yossi's son, a tank company commander, was severely wounded on patrol at the Lebanese border. After all, I think I know why my father took me to that smoky Zionist meeting in the Bronx.

Part III

THE JEWISH RESURGENCE

Who among you will give ear to this?
Who will heed for the time to come?

—ISAIAH 42:23

Eighteen

The Miracle

When Israel raised its flag I was thirty-three, and forty when I first came there, in 1955. At that time Ben-Gurion said to me, "We need four million Jews here, then we will be safe." In my last epilogue to *This Is My God,* written in 1987, I commented, "They will be there before the century ends, with more coming. Such at least is my instinct." The count as I write in mid-1999 is about five million, with more coming.

This resurgence of Jewry in the Holy Land is nothing but phenomenal. In 1955, a winding two-lane asphalt road climbed from Tel Aviv to Jerusalem. Wrecked trucks, buses, and improvised armored cars of the War of Independence convoys were rusting away along the sides. As the road was improved and widened, many of these were removed, and those that remained were coated with bright red antirust paint, no longer wrecks but memorials. Today, Tel Aviv–Jerusalem traffic roars up and down a six-lane highway, where a few wrecks are still perched here and there, forlorn reminders of bygone heroic times.

What surprises me each time I go back is the building, the *building*! It seems never to slacken. The papers there talk of an economic slowdown, but everywhere the tall cranes swing and snort;

hammering and drilling are the discordant music of Jerusalem. Whole new suburbs, which I could swear weren't there last time, now crown the old desiccated hills around the holy city. As for Tel Aviv, where Herzl envisioned a leafy little Vienna-by-the-sea, the urban sprawl of gray concrete is hardly beautiful, but startling in its vast extent and tall spiking towers.

My chapter about Israel in *This Is My God* is naively rapturous, and maybe I should wax rapturous here, but I am aiming only at the truth. There used to be a wonder about the whole experience of arriving in Israel, in an airliner of the Jewish State: the first glimpse of the sacred coast, the El Al captain's announcement in guttural Hebrew and heavily accented English, "We are about to land in Tel Aviv," the start-up of a tape of rousing Israeli songs, the thud of wheels on the Holy Land. Time and again, as we rolled to a stop, I would make the blessing on good news with profound joy. Nowadays I still make the blessing, but rather as I do three times a day over bread.

What has changed beside the passage of years? The precariousness of Israel has changed, the tentativeness, the fight against odds for existence itself. The "Zionist entity" has matured as a peculiar but solid little nation on the Mediterranean littoral, formally recognized as such by the world, even by some Arab neighbors. Perhaps for the seventy-odd percent of American Jews who have yet to set foot in Israel—an astounding and sorry statistic, but true—the thrill still awaits them. After all, a Jewish State established on biblical soil remains a marvel, even if it is a familiar marvel, like the pumping of one's heart. Yet we who lived through Israel's first cliffhanging fifty years knew a suspenseful excitement which—we devoutly hope—the Jews who come after us will never experience.

"Is—Is It Safe?"

The other day my Palm Springs pharmacist, booked to go to Israel with his temple group, asked me in a confidential low tone, "Is—is it safe?"

What a question for a Jew to ask! Far safer for a tourist, I would venture, if one goes by crime rates, than Washington, New York, or Los Angeles, or for that matter Rome or Athens. Random terrorism is a world fact, but Israel has excelled in suppressing it. My pharmacist will be safe because the Arabs have compelled Israel to learn war, to create a brilliant intelligence service (which can fumble like any other), and to organize a first-class police force. Neither Graetz nor Herzl could have pictured Jewish air squadrons streaking Holy Land skies or brigades of Merkava tanks rolling over the sacred earth. Yet except for an occasional sonic boom of a lone patrol plane, the pharmacist will have no inkling of this martial might. It is invisible, off on military bases, or out in remote drill areas, or manning the borders.

In fact, except for the signs in Hebrew, Israel's cities look very much like peacetime America: crowded restaurants, prospering shops and malls, jammed-up traffic, and throngs of pedestrians hurrying about their business. The romantic beauty of Israel is in its green mountainous north dotted by super-modern industrial parks, and its arid red-brown desert south, an Israeli Palm Springs awaiting developers. Always for newcomers there are the Bible resonances, in the look of the land and in the fabled places: Sodom, the Dead Sea, Bethlehem, Rachel's Tomb, Masada, Nazareth, and above all, evocative, magical Jerusalem.

One aspect of Israel still thrills me, though I will refrain from rhapsodizing: the young people. There have not been young Jews like these for aeons, and there are none quite like them in America, nor anywhere in the diaspora. Some are in army uniform, some in the worldwide youth costume of sloppy jeans and badly tied worn sneakers. They play rock music on portable boxes, and laugh and flirt and fool around. They are not free of drugs, or draft-dodging, or callow cynicism. They can be swept by disconcerting fads. They are creatures of their time. Yet there is something different about them: a bearing, an air, a carriage, a collected manner, not characteristic of young people elsewhere. Each one is somebody, to himself or herself. The continued existence of Israel rests on their shoulders, and deep in their hearts they must know it. It is they who are at risk. My pharmacist's temple group will be safe. The one abiding question is whether Israel is safe from itself.

For the Sake of Heaven

From the Talmud treatise *Ethics of the Fathers,* a handbook of accessible wisdom:

> Every dispute that is for the sake of Heaven, in the end will be resolved and endure. . . . What manner of dispute is for the sake of Heaven? Hillel and Shammai . . .

Israeli society is a patchwork of ongoing Hillel-Shammai confrontations. There are four main clashes, with branches and eddies beyond numbering, and all four in my view are for the sake of Heaven; that is to say, for the survival of God's people in a time of almost intolerably rapid and wrenching transition. The differences are passionate, and one is dangerous. By living there I have come a very long way from my simple outlook of 1955, and by my years of research for the novels, I have learned enough to write a bit about Israel's "cauldron of contradictions."

To begin with, Israel was founded as an egalitarian socialist society, and that foundation has crumbled away. As the government tries to bridge from old collective structures to a market economy, angry protests rise that the transition is too fast or too slow, too drastic or too weak, too political or too impractical. Every yard of forward change is fought over between the modernizers and the old-line socialists.

A second economic clash of a different and deeper sort is in substance ethnic. Though the Sephardim are only fifteen percent of world Jewry, within Israel they have equaled the Ashkenazim in numbers almost from the outset. Their different customs and education, and their stubborn religiosity, slowed their absorption into the secular Zionism of Ben-Gurion's day, and the disparity of status and opportunity has been so marked that they have been called "the second Israel." Still, an Iranian Jew has just been appointed Chief of Staff of the armed forces, climbing that very greasy pole to the top. Similar advances all across the society, with marriages among the young people (love is a wonderful thing), are moderating the gap. The Sephardim are now old settlers, after all, compared to eight hundred thousand Russian newcomers. Nevertheless, such social change is slow, and few Sephardim would say that equality is in sight.

In politics, a third rift goes down to the bedrock of Zionist philosophy and policy, and at that rift two secular power groups, Labor and Likud, have ceaselessly ground away at each other. The dovish Laborites have been the inheritors of Ben-Gurion's collectivist outlook, the hawkish Likudniks the disciples of the nationalistic Begin and Jabotinsky. The peace party plunged the country into the Oslo Agreements. Their opponents unseated them when the public, euphoric at first, became disenchanted by terrorist bus bombings, and by the suspicion that soft concessions were being made in the face of Arab intransigence and bad faith. In the latest election, the Israeli public once again has turned to a Labor led coalition, and the party system is in considerable disarray.

Since the two major parties have been so nearly balanced, the splinter religious factions have held a powerful swing vote between them, causing unseemly horse trading in election years, government by complicated alliances, and cries from the huge secular majority in Israel that they live in a "theocracy"; which is nonsense, of course, but very angry inflammatory nonsense. The tenacious religious parties for their part have unashamedly used their position to push their religious agendas and their claims on the Treasury. Long ago, the late President Chaim Herzog called this antagonism, the fourth rift, a greater danger to Israel's survival than the Arab armed forces. His words were prophetic, for it was this explosive clash which spilled the lifeblood of a Prime Minister.

Friendly Fire

It sometimes happens in war that two battalions on the same side make contact in the night, mistake each other for the enemy, and inflict bloody havoc on themselves in a blind firefight. That is exactly what is going on in Israel. The secularists and the pietists are on the same side in Jacob's eternal struggle to stay alive among the nations. Both are serving according to their best lights. Neither is wholly wrong nor wholly right. Neither can identify the other as a friend. In the navy in World War II, we had a signal device called IFF—*Identification, Friend or Foe*—and would that I, who move freely in both camps, could improvise some such code, which could flash between them to call off the blind firefight! Let me at least try.

The first thing to consider is that in the new Jewish State, *both sides have most of what they want.* The religious have the so-called status quo: rabbinic authority over ritual matters, Sabbath restrictions in pious neighborhoods, exemption from the army for bona fide yeshiva students, religious festivals observed as national holidays, and armed forces that eat kosher food.

But rabbinic authority extends hardly further than personal status matters—marriage, divorce, conversions—and certification of kashrut. The secular party holds the whip hand. They have the land.

It is theirs. They are so far superior in numbers to the believers that they swamp elections, national and local. Freedom of speech and of the press, of dress, of entertainment, of an utterly free lifestyle limited not by the Torah but only by one's purse, are all taken for granted. When two such different cultures must live together cheek by jowl in a very small country, talking the same language, using the same streets, obeying the same traffic signals, paying into (or getting around) the same tax system, there will be rubs; but—

(*At this point, two phantom argumentative Israelis break in, burning with impatience.*)

Maskil and Matmid

Interrupts the maskil: "Stop trying to whitewash the theocracy, because that's really what it is. You don't live here. You are not nagged at every turn by antiquated rules and restrictions that you don't believe in. You can't picture how that infuriates people like me. We have a Jewish land and a Jewish language. I feel I'm a complete Jew here, more so than these benighted bigots who despise the government, who mostly don't serve in the army which protects them, their wives, and their swarms of kids, and who believe the universe was created six thousand years ago—"

Strikes in the matmid: "They are so ignorant of Yiddishkeit that I can only pity them. They don't know who they are, where they came from, or what makes them Jews. Their newspapers and their advertisements are pornographic. They care for nothing but pleasure and money, their children grow up like wild animals, and our main worry is to keep our own children from being contaminated. They have no Jewish past but a few wars, and no Jewish future, because their children in the end will all go to America or Europe or anywhere else they can get in. Why should they stay here, if it isn't the Holy Land of their fathers?"

The two camps have split between them—so it seems to me—the three essential and enduring truths of Jewish nationhood: land, language, and learning. Call these the three L's of Jewish survival, if you will. The secularists hold to two of those truths, land and language. The pietists know one final truth, learning that teaches observance, though some are fervid settlers of the land as well. It is a fact, as the humanists would have it, that in the world at large nationhood rests on land and language; and, therefore, they reason, they are authentic and complete Jews in the reborn Jewish State. The pietists cling to the lifeline reaching back to Sinai, convinced that there is no other way to be authentically Jewish, today as for thousands of years.

Talks with a Rising Star

In my research, I came to know the military commanders well, and few officers were more totally secular than a staff general, considered a rising star, whom I first met at the home of Yitzhak Rabin. In two conversations at his office, each lasting more than an hour, he shed much light on my task, and I was excited at finding such an able Jewish mind in high place and heading higher. He has since become a prominent political leader, and no wonder. Here was a junior staff officer at home in world literature and world history, with the course of all Israel's wars at his fingertips, delivering a conspectus of the country's development, with a dynamic projection of its long-range future.

"The only twentieth-century revolution that has succeeded is the Jewish revolution," he summed up at one point, having traced the decreasing effectiveness in the enemy forces war by war, including the Yom Kippur War, in an absolutely convincing narrative sweep. "As for our conflict with the Arabs, it seems like a Sisyphus stone, but it is not." (I had some trouble with his Hebrew pronunciation of *Sisyphus*, until he gestured the uphill rolling action.) "There will be peace, and until there is, we will win whenever they turn to the military option. In the long run we have to achieve two things, a standard of living equal to that of western Europe, and the continuing flow of our best youth into the military elites. Then the nation will be on firm ground. The economy is moving up toward that level, and so far, our youth vie with each other to be accepted into the elites. So we can be hopeful about the future."

The mix of military analysis and social vision stirred me. Before we parted, I launched into an unconsidered spate of my own thoughts, which the reader already knows. The final truth about Israel, I suggested, was that it was a miracle, and that this sense of the miraculous had to be preserved, once the pressures of war were off and peace came. Otherwise, living in Israel would be just one option for the young, with a great magnetic world outside drawing them away. The general looked uncomfortable at this, and shifted the subject. These talks occurred about twelve years ago. In his present eminence, he appears to be taking a second look at the religious element of Israel, which is only prudent. His name is Ehud Barak.*

Off-Off-Broadway

Recently in New York I met the daughter of an old Knesset leader, a man of intellect and a great Zionist. She works backstage in off-off-Broadway theaters, loves off-off-Broadway, and has no thought of ever going back to Israel. I asked her whether that troubled her father. She shrugged. "It's my life. Israel is all right, I grew up there and served in the army, but New York is *fascinating*." Her boyfriend,

---

*This passage was written in 1998. As I edit my book for the press, Ehud Barak has just become Prime Minister.

another Israeli, wore large earrings and had a shaven head. He was in the moving-van business.

Whenever I return to Israel, there are certain people I never fail to see, and one of them is Eliakim Rubinstein, a character in *The Glory*, mentioned by his right name as an aide to Moshe Dayan in the Camp David peace process. Today he is Israel's Attorney General. Like me he wears a kippah, but unlike me he is a profound Talmudic scholar. During this last visit, I told Eliakim about my encounter with the off-off-Broadway daughter. Eliakim lowered his voice, much like the pharmacist asking "*Is—is it safe?*" In a deeply worried tone he murmured, "That is a very sensitive subject, the secular youth."

"Oh, look, for that matter," I said, "religious youngsters leave Israel, too."

He shook his head. "Not a problem."

Legal minds like Eliakim's are trained to worry about the worst possibilities. Young Israelis do love to travel, especially when they finish their army service. Some of them discover the great world and decide to try their luck out there. Most come home, and of those who linger outside a number eventually come home, too. All the same, the young woman so contented in off-off-Broadway is a figure to be reckoned with. This Israeli worry is a mirror image of the diaspora hand-wringing over intermarriage. The concern is the same, the detachment of the new Jewish generation from its roots. Will it be a generation worth mentioning? Or are the ashes of Eichmann, scattered on the Mediterranean, rising up like the dry bones in Ezekiel, to contemplate with spectral satisfaction what is happening to the young in the Jewish State and in America, the two surviving bastions of the ancient people he did his utmost to destroy?

By Way of Correction

This book purports to be only a sketch, and no passage is sketchier than what I have written so far about Israel. For instance, I have referred to "pietists" and "secularists" as though there really are two such entities, which is foolishness. On the religious side alone there are a dozen sub-factions. There are *haredim* (themselves splintered), *datiim* (also of several varieties, both Ashkenazic and Sephardic), *masortiim* (differently defined by every third *masorti,* I sometimes think), and of course the Hasidim, devoted to numerous Rebbes of varying tendencies. The large secular majority, the *hilonim,* range from humanists who know the Tanakh and the Talmud in scholarly depth, through a broad spread of viewpoints to the "post-Zionists," mostly extreme Marxists undaunted by the collapse of communism, who—so far as I understand their rhetoric—try to remain ultra-radical by being "post" whatever Israel and Judaism stand for. Post-Zionism strikes me, after some study, as unserious academic posturing, but there it is, the infra-red of the secular spectrum. In politics too, quite aside from the tactical co-opting of small religious parties, both Labor and Likud are actually rickety structures of several nailed-together factions, always subject to the threat of breakaways.

It is certainly remarkable that such a fragmented society and such jerry-built governments have so far held their own in war, and what is harder, in peace. Irreconcilable Arabs have seen the Jewish State right along as an ephemeral episode like the Crusades, a thorn in the flesh of Islam to be gradually and surely extruded, as much by internal weakening as by external force. The Crusaders too were a motley discordant lot, they point out, with conflicting loyalties to different kings and nobles; and "Outremer," the Christian State they set up around Jerusalem, lasted a mere ninety years. On that analogy Israel has only forty years to go, and Rabin's assassination may well have been taken by them as an encouraging sign of inner decay. An Arab expert recently said to an Israeli writer I know, "You Jews in the end will chase yourselves out of the land."

Self-Portrait of a Country

Israel's weekend papers come out Friday afternoon, easily as thick as New York's Sunday *Times*. These fat Friday editions, with multi-colored shrieking headlines, get to Palm Springs a few days later. Half a world away, I leaf these newspapers to try to stay in touch. Skewed as the image of Israel is in the world media, it is not much worse than the way the Israelis portray themselves in their popular press. The staid *Ha'Aretz* (*"The Land"*), with a modest circulation and a more elevated style, is less shrill but hardly less self-castigating. The magazine sections especially can get me down, preoccupied as they sometimes seem to be with rock singers, billionaires, movie stars, sex crimes, political scandals, fashion models, and the like; the usual content of Sunday papers everywhere, but a bit out of key in the jazzed-up language of Isaiah and the Mishnah. Able and witty columnists blast their country and their countrymen, week in week out, with unrelenting sardonic negativism.

Of course the truth about the Israelis is as different from this journalistic self-portrait as Jerusalem is from Los Angeles, and one can find penetrating articles and searching interviews on current affairs amid the scoffing and the fluff. Still I cannot quite be easy about the effect on Israeli fiber of this heavy infusion of American pop culture. In the world at large, governments rail about it, but Israelis seem to revel in it, almost as though their Jewish identity were invulnerable. I hope they are right.

Nor can I overlook the cultural impact of the Arab ambience that surrounds this little land, infiltrating its bureaucracies and its politics with a tinge of the Levantine. The influx of a horde of Russians who know nothing of Yiddishkeit, or as an Israeli might term it, *Yahadut,* is another diluting element, for all the undeniable wealth of manpower and education they bring to the country. A bright young politician, not over-religious, remarked to me in an anxious tone and with wrinkled brow, "We have to absorb eight hundred thousand pork eaters. It's serious."

Then what sort of image am I myself sketching here, after all, but a decidedly dark one? What was the theme that began to surface when Yitzhak Rabin fell to three shots fired by a fanatic in a kippah?

Amkha

Eliakim Rubinstein said to me, shortly after the assassination, "Those three bullets not only killed a great man, they destroyed the tolerance that has been building between us and the secularists for a generation. When I came into Golda's government, my job was at risk because I wore a kippah. It will be twenty years before we get back to where we were a month ago."

It has not worked out that way. The old disputes go on, but no man's job is less secure today for his wearing a kippah, and in the universities and the army, it is less and less a bar to advancement. One highly placed kippah-wearer commented on the aftermath of the assassination, adjuring me not to quote him by name, "The truth is Yitzhak Rabin is becoming a Christ figure. He died to save Israel from civil war." An exaggeration, no doubt, with a whiff of the apikoros, but in all truth the country has absorbed the terrific blow, recovered itself, and gone forward on the tortuous road to peace, and to its destiny, foretold by Balaam, to "dwell alone among the nations."

How has this happened? I ascribe it to the one facet of Israel that gets scant scrutiny in the media, is not news in its very nature, and at bottom remains an ancient mystery: Amkha, "Your people," the nearly five million inheritors of the Covenant. Whatever the froth of headlines and sound bites, they go about their daily lives, the invisible secret of Israel's greatness. While the leaders shrill at each other, Amkha patiently gets the day's work done. While Knesset members fulminate in a rowdy very Jewish version of parliamentary democracy, Amkha attends to the army service, the public utilities, the open-air markets, and all the thousand ongoing processes of a nation's life. Whatever power Israel wields—and that power is formidable—it is based on Amkha.

"Go out and see what the people are doing," is a surprising Talmud expression. The sages in effect give up on a puzzling point and consult the folk wisdom of Amkha. At no turn in modern Jewish history has that dictum been more apt, for in the Holy Land the warm middle masses are its stabilizer. They have fought side by side in wars, *hiloni* and *dati* alike. Whatever the belief or unbelief of their neighbors, they respect them for their sons and daughters who are manning the bases, the borders, the missile boats, the tanks, and the planes, and they love them for the children they have lost in battle. The media, and writers like me, tend to generalize about Israel from the noisy visible fringes—the post-Zionists, the haredi rock throwers, the celebrities in the fizzy weekend supplements— but in the heartland, after a heroic period that established the country, the old Jewish people are there, working their way through to a new national identity still eluding definition.

Amkha is moving toward that definition, better than the leaders. Extremists aside, most non-believers have an affection for the old tradition and a willingness to go along with it, though not themselves bound by it, and though irritated by things like a national airline that doesn't fly on Shabbat. Most believers understand that we are in a revolutionary time, and that men of good will are looking for a modus vivendi. Within Amkha there is far more love of the land and of fellow Israelis than there is hatred at the fringes. But it is the hatred that spills into the streets, alerts the media, and draws the TV cameras.

Nakhamu: The Theme

"Nakhamu, nakhamu ami!" ("Comfort, comfort my people!") So begins Isaiah 40, always read on the Shabbat after the Ninth of Av. *Consolation Shabbat,* we call it, and it happens to be approaching this week as I pen these words.

Every thinking Jew knows that the heritage is threatened. That is no theme, except for heavy-hearted pessimists who must pour out their forebodings no matter what. The death of Yitzhak Rabin woke me to the fact that my own lifetime has spanned one more instance of the supernatural resilience, recorded in Scripture and in Graetz, of the Jewish people, and also of its age-old precariousness. Nothing can surpass the harsh eloquence of Ezekiel, and the narrative of Ezra-Nehemiah, as a picture of our threatened heritage, at the lowest ebb to which the nation has ever sunk. That was when the building of the Second Temple began.

The jacket picture on this book is the work of a winner of two Pulitzer prizes in photography, David Kennerly, an old Gentile friend. Once he said to me, as we were traveling around Israel together, "I have been everywhere, and this is the most exciting place on earth." So I have found it. So the more than three million American Jews who have not visited the reborn Jewish State may yet find it. As for my pharmacist's temple group, I know they will be safe, and I hope they will glimpse the miracle.

Nineteen

AMERICA:
THE WHISPERING EMBER

In the dispersions of the exile there are yet remote cities
Where our old lamp smokes, hidden;
Where our God has left us, for a great deliverance
A whispering ember in the ash pile.
  —BIALIK, *THE MATMID*

An Encounter in Minsk

Back in 1967, touring the battlegrounds of the Soviet Union for a
month to research my World War II novels, I made it a point to
visit Minsk, the birthplace of my parents, one of the first big cities
overrun by Hitler's invasion. There to my astonishment I came
upon a living relative. The massacre of the Minsk Jews was an early
horror of the Holocaust, and we did not think any of our family
could have survived, but this man had escaped eastward ahead of
the Germans with his wife and children, and had spent the war in a
camp behind the Urals. On returning to Minsk, he had had no way
to get in touch with us, Soviet conditions being what they were.

Soviet Minsk, rebuilt after the war's devastation, was an unlovely Stalin-era grid of new, yellow concrete buildings. The only trace of its once populous and famous Jewry was a single wooden synagogue on the outskirts, hardly more than a fenced hut, with a crude little Star of David in an attic window. I went there to daven, and found a bare minyan of old men in dilapidated prayer shawls and moldy-looking phylacteries. Nobody spoke to the bizarre American stranger until the Torah reading, when I was asked in Yiddish for my Hebrew name, and was called up for an aliya. Afterward, a gray-faced little man limped over to me, leaning on a cane. "So you're Haym Zelig, and your father was Abraham Isaac? Then your mother's name was Esther Shayna, and I'm your uncle Gershon."

Gershon had a life story to match his melancholy countenance, which he told while the old men were laying out vodka and cookies after the service. He had scraped up the money and gone to America when my mother did, only to be turned away at Ellis Island because of an ear infection. A brief glimpse of the Statue of Liberty and the skyscrapers, and he sailed back to wear out his years in Minsk and behind the Urals.

Over the vodka, the minyan men warmed to me and pelted me with questions about America and Israel. After a while, they shyly asked to have a good look at my beautiful tefillin. Around the table the phylacteries went. Since I traveled with a spare set, when they were returned to me I handed them to Gershon. They were from Jerusalem, I told him, and they were his. Gershon's woeful look passed from incredulity into radiance, almost as though he had at last made it through Ellis Island. The other old men regarded him with awe. He was holding a fistful of diamonds.

Amkha Arrives

Most American Jews are descended from Ostjuden like Gershon who, unlike him, got past Ellis Island into the land of the free. We are a brand snatched from the burning. Driven by the eternal Jewish vital force, the will to live on of Amkha, our parents and grandparents left Europe in a rapid massive population shift just ahead of the storm, to create here a great diaspora like none known before. They were by no means the first Jews to come here, of course. Some Spanish and Portuguese families dated back to Dutch New York, well before the Revolution. A sizable German community was already entrenched with Reform temples, and the Hebrew Union College. A few of those families like the Schiffs and the Guggenheims had even made it big, and had become philanthropists and art patrons.

These eastern European Jews were a different breed, a tidal wave of humanity two million strong, with an intense Yiddish character and a terrific charge of pioneer energy. On Manhattan's Lower East Side, there sprang up overnight, as it were, a Yiddish-speaking little world of tenements, pushcarts, sweatshops, and synagogues, wretched in reality but electric in promise, which lasted only until they could move on. And move on they soon did, scattering through the land, clustering in the great cities, braving the coolness of the settled Jews and the anti-Semitism of nativists to weave themselves into the fabric of our open society. Amkha in America was exuberant, unstoppable, pumped up by the adrenaline of freedom. FREEDOM! Freedom to travel or settle anywhere, freedom from government oppression, freedom from special laws for Jews, freedom in fact from the Torah itself, requiring no Haskalist revolt, just the freedom to fall away.

Falling away was all the easier, because when the great migration was taking place, the rabbis by and large had lagged behind, preferring their accustomed miseries under the Czar to the spiritual risks of that glittering Sodom, Trefe America. The Reform temples, with their churchlike organs, bareheaded rabbis, and truncated services in English, were not for such Ostjuden, so Amkha found itself at first in something like a religious vacuum.

Conservative Judaism

At a yeshiva high school I briefly attended to please Zaideh, I learned of an evil place called "Schechter's Seminary." Pious Jewish lads aiming for the rabbinate went on to Yeshiva College, I was told, while wavering ones greedy for easy money defected to this seminary, where they learned practically nothing, but acquired suave talk and manners to equip them for pulpits in lush Conservative temples. This was in the 1920s, when Conservative Judaism was growing up all over the land like Iowa corn in July. The Orthodox regarded this burgeoning movement askance or assailed it outright. They had no more power to stop it than the Vilna Gaon and his followers, two centuries earlier, had been able to halt the spread of Hasidism. For better or worse, a goodly part of Amkha was discovering a way to go on being Jewish in America that suited them, though the strictly observant might deplore it.

Solomon Schechter, the master thinker of Conservative Judaism, was a scholar of the German historical school, *Wissenschaft des Judentums,* "Science of Judaism," but unlike its leading lights, he was observant in conduct and belief. He writes in his key work, *Some Aspects of Rabbinic Theology:*

> Whenever any influence, no matter by whom advanced or by whatever power maintained, developed a tendency that was contrary to a strict monotheism, *or denied the binding character of the Torah** or aimed to deny the unity and character and calling of Israel, although it may have gained currency for a time, the Synagogue finally succeeded in eliminating it as noxious to its very existence.

---

*Italics mine.

Schechter won world renown by discovering and translating Hebrew manuscripts of the Cairo *genizah*, a treasure trove in an ancient Egyptian synagogue of worn discarded sacred books and scrolls, some dating back to Gaonic times. Invited by wealthy American leaders in 1901 to preside over a recently organized rabbinic institute, the Jewish Theological Seminary, he held the post until his death seventeen years later. There he molded an innovative pattern of worship, and Amkha has voted in massive numbers, with memberships and with money, for Conservative Judaism. My fellow believers who happen to read this description will not like it much, but it is what happened.

The Conservative Compromise

To denounce the Conservative leadership and laity as compromisers, to call the movement kosher-style Judaism, to equate it with Reform and assimilation, in short, to consign much of American Jewry to the devil, strikes me as irresponsible. In writing this, I part company with some exasperated old friends. The Jewish Theological Seminary has produced important Talmudic scholarship, and has graduated many rabbis who are observant as well as smooth-spoken. In my novel *Inside, Outside,* in the character called Holy Joe Geiger, I portray another sort of Conservative rabbi, perhaps with a touch of mischief in the picture, but with affection, too, for the man who was my model lived a sad life, and was a warm friend of our family.

Conservative Judaism took shape as a blend of Reform and tradition. Amkha may have found the borrowed Reform departures a bit off-putting at first, but in time not uncomfortable. The seating of men and women together, the use of English to lighten up a shortened liturgy, the soulful organ music, and perhaps as important as anything the parking lots, with special permission to drive to services, all made observance less burdensome, and for some more attractive. My own parents joined a Conservative temple for a while when we moved to Manhattan, hoping that their three rebellious teenagers would prefer it to being dragged to an old-style synagogue. My father in his activist way even became a trustee, much to Zaideh's displeasure, though when the board voted to pass the plate on Friday night, he bowed out. By then, it was clear that my sister, my brother, and I were unimpressed. We knew the religion, and whether we were conforming or not, Holy Joe Geiger offered no real alternative to Zaideh's authentic Yiddishkeit.

Nor for most of Amkha did the Reform of the German Jews. Not at first. I remember, for instance, being ordered to take off my yarmulke when I went to a Reform temple for the funeral of a friend's father. That sort of thing must have gone down hard for the Ostjuden, not to mention the brief mostly English liturgy, and the ham in the social hall buffet afterward. Amkha was not ready for such explicit throwing off of the yoke.

Orthodoxy Rebounds

The low point in American Orthodoxy came after the First World War. There were small synagogues all over like my father's Minsker Congregation, and in wealthy neighborhoods they might even rival the temples in size and elegance, but the trend was toward the less demanding modes of worship. When the rabbis did start to come to America in force, they had little success in exhorting Jews who were tasting freedom and loving it to return to strict halakhah. Some nimble rabbis took Conservative pulpits instead, bringing to Amkha Orthodox scholarship, if not Orthodox practice.

In 1928 Zaideh arrived to become rabbi of the Minsker Congregation. By the time he left for Israel, twenty-three years later, his flock had dwindled until there were empty rows of seats even on Yom Kippur. Partly this was due to the drift of Bronx Jews to Manhattan or the suburbs. Partly he blamed himself. "I should have learned Turkish," he said as I taxied with him to the ship that would take him to the Holy Land. That was what he called the English language. "But the sound of it was so harsh to me!" Years before that, when I was a new ensign en route to the South Pacific, I encountered a Jewish navy chaplain in San Francisco, a Reform rabbi, who assured me in all friendly earnestness that in twenty years Orthodoxy in America would be dead. I tried to argue, but on the facts it was not then an irrational forecast.

Yet today does it not look fatuous? From coast to coast, the archipelago of the faithful prospers and expands. The day schools turn out smart young learners who go on to universities, and then to rewarding professional careers. In a separate track yeshivas flourish, where Talmud and halakhic codes remain the basic curriculum, transfer to university is discouraged, and some students go on learning well into married life. Hasidism too, with its separate schools and its intensive disciplines, has made itself a home here. Kosher food has become a multibillion-dollar industry, much patronized by non-Jews too, and keeping to the laws has become simple if one cares. Even I am somewhat less of a strange duck than I used to be.

What turned the tide? Mainly the Nazi horror. Some important rabbis and yeshivot of eastern Europe took the alarm and got out barely in time. Observant refugees crowded in from western Europe, too, infusing their means and numbers into the synagogues. Besides, Orthodoxy was learning Turkish. Talmud study in English was becoming routine, and a rabbinate was emerging which could hold its own with the graduates of the Seminary and Hebrew Union College; especially since powerful intellects had been at work, forging Orthodox philosophy in a modern idiom.

Torah has been taught in many ages, many languages, many modes of thought. When a new context arises, there is confusion and defection until it is articulated in a living frame of reference, or as the Talmud puts it, "in the language of men." European thinkers like Franz Rosenzweig and Samson Raphael Hirsch, and in America the great Rav, wrote incisive works which gave this new young rabbinate a serious fresh viewpoint to popularize.

Meantime Conservatism and Reform were encountering the penalties of success. Since many of their practices overlapped, convenience as much as conviction was influencing memberships. Intermarriage was hitting Reform hard, and eating into Conservatism as well, while Orthodoxy had more or less stabilized, what with its larger families and even a minor *ba'al tshuvah* movement, a return to observance. An upbeat mood spread among the Orthodox, which the others irritably termed "triumphalism." An aggressive Orthodox lay leader I know well, a law professor and investment expert, said to me a few months ago with cheery confidence, "Reform and Conservatism are on the ropes."

A Worm in Horseradish

"On the ropes?" I had no idea of the actual figures, so I got hold of the American Jewish Year Book for 1997. The actual statistics jolted me like one of our Palm Springs earthquakes. Here were the numbers, rounded off:

Conservatism	40%
Reform	39%
Jewish but not affiliated	13%
Orthodox	8%

How in the name of heaven, I wondered, could my friend, immersed as he is in current Jewish affairs and active in the controversies, have come out with such a remark?

My mother, who lived to be almost ninety-five like Zaideh, and had a lot of his moxie, was fond of a Yiddish saying, "*The worm lies in horseradish, and thinks there's nothing sweeter.*" It is a state of mind one can fall into, this delusion that one's milieu is all of reality. To showbiz people, for example, nothing else truly exists. I know, because I have now and then succumbed to that seductive lunacy. Until I saw those yearbook figures, I was a bit of a triumphalist myself, a bookworm in horseradish. For thirty years, writing huge historical works in the isolation of my lair, I had been seeing little of general Jewish life. Robust youthful Orthodox congregations, the fruit of the day school movement, dot the land. If one worships only in those, one can remain unaware of those crushing statistics. That happened to me. But the law professor is a man of the world, and knows the figures. He could only have meant that Reform and Conservatism were losing their children en masse, and were ruefully becoming aware of it.

Orthodoxy or Doom?

Some believers therefore regard both movements as transient aberrations of the open society, doomed to disappear, and they make no distinction between the two. In fact, a clear clash of doctrine separates them. Solomon Schechter's dogma that the Torah is binding prevails at the Seminary, if variously interpreted; whereas it is a founding dogma of Reform that the halakhah no longer binds our ancient people. If in practice the denominations appear to be moving closer, that can happen when reality treads down theory.

Certain stern public figures in Orthodoxy are unrelenting in their absolute condemnation of both movements, going so far as to call them deviant forms of the Jewish religion, like Christianity. Hard words! But Yeshiva University itself, a citadel of Orthodoxy, is not without problems, in some Orthodox views. The president of Yeshiva University, for instance, tells of asking a rigorous Hasidic

Rebbe pointblank whether he, the president, and his family belonged in *Clal Yisroel*, that is, could be considered Jews, and the response was, *"Doctor, you have asked me too difficult a question."* So there it is. No matter how far to the right one moves in Orthodoxy, one may still end up on the trefe side of somebody even stricter.

Yet there are counter-tendencies among the black hats. Let me cite the young Hasidic rabbi of Palm Springs, who appears on page 1 of my first chapter. Since I wrote that page, he has had two more children; no, three, come to think of it, since his wife, an able school principal, recently produced twins. Family life, and perhaps desert life, together with prison chaplain experiences, have mellowed our Palm Springs Hasid. When he first came, he would not set foot inside a Conservative temple building. Just the other day, he told me he had invited the new Reform rabbi to his home for Shabbat dinner. "We must get along with them," he said. "They are also Jews."

"Rabbi, you mean we are also Jews," I replied. "Do you know the figures?"

He somberly nodded.

Against the Grain

Orthodoxy or doom for American Jewry, is that truly how the land lies? If so, our remarkable diaspora is in trouble. American Jews resist being bound by halakhah because it cuts against the tenor of their lives, the air they breathe. The right of individuals to go their own way, work toward their own goals, make their own choices, is the very grain of the tree of liberty. Whatever preachers may say against material success, the United States is rich in opportunity, and success is sweet. Moses warns against that sweetness in Deuteronomy: "*. . . lest thou say in thy heart, by my power and the strength of my arm have I gained all this fortune . . .*" Translation: "I have this house, this family, this stock portfolio, this high-flying career. I'm living the American dream. Observance is your shtick? Fine, just leave me alone. If you have nostalgia for Minsk, I don't."

And so the Melting Pot is beginning to work on Jewry. Its effect was deferred in the passing century by the shock of the Holocaust and the rise of Israel, but today the Holocaust is an academic subject, and Israel is no longer a beleaguered underdog. Amkha in America is not dying, it is slowly melting, and those are very different fates. Dying is a terror, an agony, a strangling finish, to be fought off by sheer instinct, by the will to live on, to the last breath. Melting is a mere diffusion into an ambient welcoming warmth in which one is dissolved and disappears, as a teaspoon of sugar vanishes into hot tea. Far from feeling strangled, assimilating Jews may well feel even freer than they did in their parental households, however dim the Yiddishkeit there may have been. All that is finished, closed off, done for, just a "heritage" to be talked about now and then with nonchalant pride, by the intermarried or assimilated Jew.

That is a change, since formerly an assimilated Jew's identity was something to be shucked off or lied about. Jewish identity is a distinction nowadays because of Israel's international stature and the amazing achievements of Amkha in America. Why not modestly acknowledge kinship with the Jewish State's redoubtable armed forces, with all the Nobel laureates in the sciences and the celebrities in the arts, with world figures like Albert Einstein and Yitzhak Rabin, with captains of industry, presidents of Ivy League universities, Secretaries of State, senators and congressmen, governors and mayors, television comic stars and famous filmmakers, especially since none presents a disquieting persona of halakhic observance?

The Whispering Ember

The real question here, the one that cuts to the bone, is *why should parents care?* They made their free choices in their time. Now it is the children's turn, and if they choose to deep-six their Judaism in the warm soup of the Melting Pot—Reform, Conservative, and Orthodox children too, because disenchantment with strict halakhah can and does happen—so what? Is not the freedom to choose in matters of religion as American as apple pie? And yet, *and yet*, as we pass into the new century, the unease of the older generation is a discernible truth of American Jewish society. Only a few are indifferent. Most care, some deeply.

My final chapter is about this whispering ember of Yiddishkeit in the heart of American Jewry today. Amkha of the years since Ellis Island is hearing a still small voice warning that it may prove the last generation worth mentioning, that half a century after Der Fuehrer's gasoline-soaked remains burned like rubbish outside his bunker, set afire by his bodyguards under a rain of Russian shells, he is at last on his way to winning his war against the Jews. Nor is that all the ember whispers. If I am not enormously mistaken, it whispers a feeling of loss, of hollowness at the core of self, of a lack of purpose, of a bleared focus in the life of Amkha in America at the very crest of success.

If so, I think I know the reason. The impressive national infra-structure of organizations and institutions—still entirely alive and hardworking—found fulfillment until now in the work for Israel, in the creation in America of community centers, hospitals, temples, museums, old folks' homes, and in the dogged maintenance of Holocaust awareness. In these ways the will to live on has done wonders. And if American Jewry should eventually melt away except for a few hundred thousand Orthodox—something I do not for the moment foresee—it would still have written a record of responsible deeds worthy of the children of Abraham. The unselfish outpouring of treasure and energy for Israel in its desperate struggling years will remain the crown of American Jewry's twentieth-century history.

But all that is the work of yesterday. What of the century that is upon us? In the pages that remain, I write my far from confident personal views, for the judgment of those who care.

Twenty

THE BREATH OF THE CHILDREN

Flashes from Jerusalem

A surgeon who once probably saved my life phoned out of the blue and asked me to talk to a nephew of his, on a visit to Palm Springs after a year of study in a Jerusalem yeshiva. I could not say no, and into my office there soon came a well-favored youth in chino slacks and a polo shirt, with a fresh open countenance, an engaging manner, and alert smiling eyes. This was not my notion of a Jerusalem matmid, so I asked him where he had done his learning. At a "Conservative yeshiva," he told me, three or four years in existence, where some thirty-five young men and women had been learning Talmud together.

Ecclesiastes says there is nothing new under the sun, but this sounded pretty new to me. To size him up, I talked a little Talmud with him. A regular yeshiva *bokhur* could have cut him to ribbons, yet in a fashion he knew his stuff. More important, it became clear as we chatted about Israel and the religion that he had an eager appetite for Yiddishkeit and for learning. He said he was returning to Harvard for a post-graduate course in political science, but I inferred that he had left his heart in Jerusalem and was contemplating aliya. As I walked him out to the gate, he thanked me for inspiring him. I should have thanked him for inspiring me, with a sense that something new might really be going on in Amkha.

Later that day, an expert on the sociology of American Jewry telephoned me from Jerusalem, to answer my e-mailed inquiry about those jarring yearbook statistics. A long time ago at Columbia University, he and a son of mine, together with a classmate who has recently been Israel's ambassador to the United Nations, started a Jewish off-campus residence, the *Bayit* ("House"), which still flourishes. Today, he is a professor at the Hebrew University. He amiably confirmed the yearbook numbers, but when I quoted my friend's view that Reform and Conservatism were on the ropes, he fired up. "I can't say about Reform, but Conservatism on the ropes? Ha! The Solomon Schechter day schools are exploding all over the country. It's a new era."

He was a fervid Conservative of the traditional wing, it turned out, active in the tug-of-war against the majority of rabbis pulling closer to Reform. With some passion, he went past my query to volunteer his view of Jewry worldwide. What worried him most, he declared, was the waning "sense of peoplehood," an invented concept but one vital to our survival. Everywhere Jews were thinking and acting more as individuals, and less as members of the Jewish people, the mystical continuum across the centuries embodying our history, religion, and culture. I interrupted to ask what he meant by that odd phrase, an invented concept, to describe Jewish peoplehood. "Man-made, of course," he said. And there it was, the old gulf between the believers and the enlightened, gaping across the ten time zones between Jerusalem and Palm Springs.

The Torah calls us a holy people, chosen by God to bring his light to the nations. That is the message of all our prophets. Either it is the truth, or the whole structure that has stood three thousand years falls to the ground, does it not? Not at all, not necessarily, according to Conservative and Reform thought, of which I am admittedly no master. By means of a variety of man-made concepts, I gather, some of them advanced and ingenious, Jewish identity and continuity can be preserved without the supernatural God of the Mosaic revelation. My sociologist plainly took this for granted, so I shut up and listened, as is my wont, and he promised to send me some of his writings on the theme.

Forty years ago I asked a hard-bitten atheist, then my attorney, to read my first draft of *This Is My God,* to test how the book might go down with the enlightened. So telling was his response that I inserted it into the book word for word, where it stands today. *"Judaism as wisdom, as a source of identity, as noblesse oblige, as survival machinery, yes,"* he wrote to me. *"If only you leave out the supernatural God, we might have a meeting of the minds."* The sociologist's phrase *"man-made"* recalled to memory that astute demurral, and I have been thinking about it a lot.

The Challenge

If I were asked today by an intimate whether, in the forty years between the writing of the two books, my thinking about Judaism has changed, I would reply, "Hell, yes." If he then asked whether my belief in a supernatural God and his Torah has changed, I would reply, "It is stronger." Both responses would be honest. After forty more years of turning over the entire Torah once a year, wrestling with its difficult aspects, working through the classic commentators, I remain a believer in the Law of Moses and in its binding commands for me, and for all Jews who come to understand what Moses taught. But as the Jewish condition has meantime radically altered, so have my views on our present and our future.

Despite all the clarity and force of the narrative part of Torah, understanding the *mitzvot,* the commandments, is a hard challenge nowadays, for those not raised from the cradle to take them as the norm. One trouble is the very accessibility of the Five Books in English. Anybody can read excellent new editions, translated commentaries and all, like a Sunday paper or a novel. Why then should there be any difficulty in understanding the Torah's laws? If the humesh and the commentaries make little or no sense to so many readers when it comes to the commandments, are the readers to blame, or are those ancient precepts simply irrelevant in a time of a global economy, moon walks, probes to Saturn, and satellites—including some Israeli hardware—hovering overhead, so that a professor in Jerusalem can chat with a novelist in California about Jewish peoplehood?

If I could offer a convincing way to meet this challenge, I would be a new Ezra. Five centuries before the Christian era began, Ezra returned to Zion with a small contingent of the exiled Jews to reclaim the Holy Land, while most remained in Babylon. Scripture records a historic turning point, when Ezra assembled the returners in Jerusalem and read the Torah to them, expounding it with such effect that in those Jews Ezekiel's prophecy was fulfilled: *I will take away your heart of stone and give you a heart of flesh.* Such power to restore Amkha's living heart is beyond the likes of me, but I can at least describe how my view of all this has changed in forty years.

Toward a Meeting of the Minds

When *This Is My God* came out in 1959, Adolph Eichmann was still hiding in Argentina, safe and prosperous. The Six-Day War lay well in the future. Most American Jews regarded Israel with detached sympathy and some lent it charitable support, while a few doctrinaire Zionists and anti-Zionists shrilled at each other with futile vehemence. The millions of Soviet Jews were silenced prisoners, living in terror and prohibited from practicing all aspects of their religion and culture. Elsewhere Jews lived free, yet their interest in Judaism was weak and declining, and there was considerable discarding of Jewish identity.

That was really the origin of *This Is My God,* for I felt impelled to give an account of my contrary ways. Of course, I hoped that the book might prove an elementary tool for anyone who might want to think again about Judaism, but its popular acceptance astonished me, and even more my publishers, who had printed only a small run of copies. Evidently the ember was already faintly whispering, here and there. Even the atheist's comment, when I reconsider it, was echoing the whisper. He was offering to accept everything in Yiddishkeit, after all, except the final leap of faith, which in the end everyone must make alone, from an impulse of the soul. I might have tried then and there for that meeting of the minds, and if this new book has any purpose, it is just such a belated effort to do so. I have been reaching out my hand to interested Jews who cannot, or think they cannot, believe in the supernatural God of revelation, saying to them, "Come, let us study together."

The Odium of "Orthodoxy"

Certain readers may well hesitate to take my offered hand. I know that. The resistance among many American Jews to anything or anybody "Orthodox" is very striking, and warrants a word or two. Despite my disclaimer, some will scent here a "plea for Orthodoxy," and I can only wonder why. What need? The plea for my beliefs I wrote forty years ago, and I stand by it, but to reiterate it in another book would have been a weariness to me and a waste of what time and force I still have. I have been up front about my personal convictions in this sketch of our heritage, in essence a reach toward a meeting of Jewish minds.

Here in Palm Springs some years ago, my older son and a few friends founded a day school at the local temple, where my granddaughter has been getting a meaty Jewish and secular education. The school has had the usual money troubles, of course. Yet the most generous Jewish philanthropist of the town, advanced in age and religious in his way, stonily refused until his death to support the school because the principal was Orthodox. He himself could only have come from an Orthodox home, so something deep was going on there, a violent reaction to his own background. This kind of bitter obduracy surfaces on both sides. One well-known Orthodox rabbi publicly announced, for instance, during the recent fiery conversion controversy, that Conservative and Reform Jews were not Jews at all, period. This douse of gasoline on the fire was not well received.

Our Jewish census is shrunken enough after the Holocaust, God knows, three-thousandths of one percent of world population. This rabbi's dictum would cut our count down to about *one ten-thousandth of one percent!* He too is of advanced age, and in his long lifetime he has no doubt observed with dismay the cascading of the old-country Jews from Orthodoxy to Conservatism in great numbers, and the further cascading of such Jews to Reform, and from there to indifference and assimilation. This spectacle has gnawed at him, and feeling impotent to contend with it, he breaks out in venerable rage.

In our Palm Springs shul, Jews of every stripe will show up to say Kaddish. One Shabbat, at the table where I was giving my dvar Torah, a well-dressed stranger of fifty or so sat listening with an angry unyielding look. Afterward he stayed on through the entire service, punctiliously reciting every Kaddish but not davening much. When it was over, he came up and said brusquely, shaking my hand, "At last, somebody I can relate to," and walked out. We never saw him again. In Jews like him *dos pintele Yid* has survived to whisper, "Say Kaddish, at least," and I hope that in this book such Jews may find someone they can relate to.

The Scrolls

Meantime some mild mellowing seems to be going on in Reform. At a Reform bat mitzvah of my nephew's daughter, which I attended out of family affection, I wore not only my kippah but my old-style woolen tallis. So did a couple of other men, and nobody ordered us to desist or leave. The girl did a star turn with her Torah verses and blessings. The liturgical music was a rock-and-roll guitar trio, singing and swinging in Hebrew and English. Later the rabbi, with understandable pride, showed me the Torah from which the girl had read some lines. It had been contributed by a wealthy member at high cost, a new scroll written on beautiful parchment by a Jerusalem scribe, a masterwork of Hebrew calligraphy. The temple's Holy Ark already contained several Torah scrolls, but naturally another was welcome. That scroll will last a very long time, though it will never be read straight through unless it passes into other hands, since in a Reform temple only brief excerpts are used.

Walking back to the hotel where Sarah and I were staying for the weekend, I wondered whether the rabbi ever gave any thought to this. Reform temples must have holy scrolls even for those excerpts, but where are they to come from? Multitudinous Torahs in Europe were desecrated or destroyed by the Germans, and an Israeli committee went to great pains to rescue and restore some, but these went out at once to communities eager for them. The question persists, *where are the scrolls in the Reform and Conservative temples to come from?* Torahs do wear out, or are ruined by fire, water, or vandals, and these movements will never produce them. Even should a young man like my Conservative visitor decide to make the writing of scrolls his life work, he would have to turn "ultra-Orthodox" to qualify. Reform and Conservative rabbis might examine their utter dependence, in this regard, upon a father-and-son guild who in matters of doctrine they would dismiss as antiquated fanatics.

Halakhah requires every Jew, if he can, to write a Torah scroll during his lifetime. I once aspired to do this myself, thinking all it needed was enough time and application. When I lived in Israel, I spent days with Jerusalem scribes, studying the process. As I gave up on slaughtering fowls, so I abandoned this fanciful ambition, once I understood what it entailed. One can pay a scribe to write a Torah as one's surrogate to perform the mitzvah, and that is what I did. My Torah has traveled far and wide with me, and its present way station is here in the desert, where it is read on Shabbat.

The Will to Live On

The Book of Ezekiel opens with a dazzling mystic vision of a Chariot, a *Merkava,* the divine seat of the presence of the Lord. The Talmud cautions against speculation on the secrets of *Maaseh Merkava,* The Work of the Chariot. After some probing into Gershom Scholem's books I have taken heed of the warning, and left Ezekiel's Merkava alone. Nowadays *Merkava* designates Israel's world-class battle tank. The father of the Merkava, Major General Israel Tal, has remained on active duty into his seventies, as Admiral Hyman Rickover did in America's nuclear submarine program. Tal was assigned the Merkava project because the Soviet Union was furnishing first-line tanks to the Arabs in swarms, while no country would sell any to the Jewish State.

I first met General Tal long ago, when he was advocating peace policies which even today the Oslo Agreements only approach: a paradoxical fellow, an aggressive fighting general, a pioneer inventor of heavy munitions, and a crusading dove. In *The Hope* there is a portrait of Tallik, as he is nicknamed, accurate if a touch warm. Tallik once told me pridefully that though his forebears were Talmudic scholars, he had never in his life set foot inside a synagogue. Maybe he wanted to shock me. I replied offhand that the Talmud for millennia had been the guarantor of Jewish survival, and that in our day the Merkava tank was his Talmudic commentary, and not bad at that. Tallik took this in silence, with an enigmatic grin.

From the scribe who writes scrolls to Tallik who builds tanks, what most Jews have in common is at least the will to live on as Jews, and that is not man-made. That is the lifeblood of Amkha, in some of us pulsing and red, in some sluggish and anemic, but the Torah scroll and the Merkava are both the work of that vital force. For the scribe, writing a Torah is a task requiring infinite pains. One miswritten letter, one *psul*, renders an entire scroll unusable. I have seen many a Torah abruptly rolled up in mid-service and put aside for repair. The Merkava too, in model after model produced by General Tal, has required infinite pains. One misconceived structural element, one flaw in assembly, and under battle stress a faulty model could fail and cost the lives of tank crews, or even lose a war. The extremes meet in meticulous devotion to excellence, for the sake of God's people, on the battlefield where the scribe does not fight, and in the synagogue where Tal does not set foot.

In Israel, the issue of survival is clear-cut. The Israelis have Land, Language, and Learning, and an amazing efflorescence of Torah writing and publishing is going on. Sacred study is not for everybody, but life for all is intensely Jewish, while one of the world's premier armies stands guard against an enemy no longer at the gate but still unreconciled. Under God, Israel will endure. The diaspora is another matter. Our task is to preserve those who will come after us as generations worth mentioning, and to accomplish that we have been groping for a new direction.

The Leadership

If I thought Orthodoxy could give that direction, I might try to seize the flag myself, quietist though I am, and rush forward with a hurrah, but I well know that my fellow believers are focused on preserving their own way of life, to the extent of limiting their contacts, communal and cultural, with the rest of Jewry. Even within the fold, there is a tendency toward ever greater strictness, and closer scrutiny of each other's piety. Counter-trends exist in some outreach programs, but I discern no inclination toward national leadership. I understand why this is so, and what I write here is not critical but realistic. Nor, in my view, can our diaspora look for leadership to the Conservative or Reform movements. Both seem to me responsive rather than forward-looking, accommodating their doctrines and practices to social changes as they develop; hence the mellowing of Reform, if I judge right, and on the other hand some vigorous pulling away in Conservatism from what is deemed "too Orthodox." These observations can be corrected by my readers for any myopia they believe they discern in the writer.

Happily, the folk instinct of Amkha has created here in America an efficient nationwide engine of leadership, which for decades has been setting and meeting the year-by-year goals of Jewry. The names of the organizations are many, the purposes diverse, the convictions sometimes at odds, but the energy of all has been funneling into one mainstream. An awareness now grows in that notable leadership that it is moving along mainly on past momentum, that the will to live on is less and less satisfied, and that while American Jewry is far from dying it is, in navy parlance, dead in the water.

That at any rate is how I see it, and therefore my last pages are addressed to those leaders. It is they who are at the helm and can turn us to our new direction. It will be at best a very slow process, as when a supertanker, changing course on the open sea, bears ahead for many miles before starting to answer to the rudder.

"What Are You Learning?"

The new direction has for years been coming into sight, and is today much talked about among our leaders. If I may be allowed one more analogy from navy days, Clausewitz said that in war the basic things are simple, but the simple things are very difficult. So it is with leadership. A massive turn to Jewish education appears to be inevitable, but this turn will be very difficult indeed. For to call a spade a spade, our leaders by and large are not learned, yet it will no longer suffice for them to give or to raise money. Money is needed, lots of it, but dedication of the heart is more urgently needed, and there's the rub. How do these admirable men and women lead a drive to reclaim the Yiddishkeit they themselves may lack, and have had little thought or hope of ever acquiring?

Again, the answer is simple but very difficult: *by starting to learn.* What they learn, when they learn, how they learn, is each individual's responsibility. If I am right, the will to live on has been a collective imperative for all of them. Loyalty to their Jewish past, to family memory and inherited ethnic identity—in short, a sense of noblesse oblige—has been energizing them to lavish time, effort, and money on our people's causes. The demands of the future are harder, but in the end may offer more reward. Jewish learning undertaken in good heart has magic in it.

Whether the commitment is to conversational Hebrew—which I consider of prime importance—or the prayer book, or the Mishna, or simply the Hebrew alphabet if one doesn't know it, or the weekly sedra, or Yiddish, or Kabbalah, or Graetz, or for the ambitious the whole range of Jewish thought and law, the thing is *to make a start.* Compared to such personal commitment, listening to weekly Sabbath sermons, or to lectures on Judaism by people like me, are of small account. Such passive experiences leave little or no residue. Reb Moshe Feinstein stamped on my spirit this urgency of personal commitment. Years might pass before I would see him, but whenever I did, he would ask straight off, "What are you learning?" as in olden times adults would ask a child, "What is your *posuk* [Torah verse]?" If I happened to be slacking off, as was too often the case, I would feel the gentle query like the flick of a whip.

So let me put my aspirations for American Jewish leadership in one visionary image. In some not too distant day, at the local conclaves of these organizations, and at the grand annual gatherings, they will be greeting each other, men and women alike, with "What are you learning?" High on their yearly agendas will be *Reclaiming the Heritage Through Learning*; a sort of nationwide Manhattan Project of education on a scale unimaginable today, into which funds and work will be pouring as they once poured to Israel in her years of peril. For the stark fact is that in the new century already upon us, we will be fighting against our own peril, a slow slump to oblivion.

Yet here in the United States, for all the scary attrition I have pictured, we are still a community over five million strong. That is more than the population of Norway. We live in the world's greatest nation, speaking the world language, and our material and intellectual resources are impressive. At a far stretch of my hopes, our descendants could one day be a diaspora comparable to Babylonia. At the moment, of course, that is beyond rational expectation. We have to concentrate on lasting at all. And the ultimate reason for that—to write down the unthinkable—is that if by some unforeseeable future horror Israel goes down, we will be the last bastion of God's people on earth.

But that is mere nightmare. Israel will survive by God's grace into an era of uneasy peace as world Jewry's spiritual center, even as Palestine was in the time of Yavneh, though the Babylonian Jews were more numerous, and possibly more learned. The Talmud we study, after all, is Babylonian. Smaller communities in places like Canada, Australia, France, Mexico, and South America are showing surprising tenacity, and Russian Jewry, almost throttled by the fallen Soviet system, is reviving as a reservoir of redeemable souls, perhaps in the millions. Ours can become a leading diaspora of sinewy promise and power, if we will be strong and of good courage, and will acquire the vital grip we need on Language and Learning.

Amkha can be aroused by its leaders to move mountains, but heart has to speak to heart. The Talmud says that in the world to come we are asked three questions: *"Did you negotiate in good faith? Did you try to raise a family? Did you have a set time for Torah?"* Not, mind you, "Did you observe the Sabbath? Did you keep kosher? Did you daven three times a day?" The sages probably took such observance for granted, but in any case they were delving to the bare rock of Jewish survival: *right conduct, children,* and *Learning.*

> Resh Lakish quoted Rabbi Judah, "The world is sustained only by the breath of the children in the house of learning."
> Rav Papa objected to Abayi, "What about you and me at our learning?"
> He replied, "Do not compare breath tainted by sin to the breath of the sinless."
> —TALMUD, SHABBAT 119B

The leaders now in their adult vigor will serve their day and pass on. The octogenarian hand that moves this pen will have gone well before them. Our future lies with the children. The ember whispers and smolders, and if it is not to die here in America, it can only be blown into flame by the breath of Jewish children at their Learning.

AFTERWORD

So my task ends.

Turning the last page, a skeptical reader may well muse: "*Quite moving here and there, lots of information, but I still wonder how this author, who reads Spinoza and Schopenhauer, and moves in the jazzy worlds of literature, film, and theater, can really accept these antique documents as divinely inspired and binding on his conduct*"—or in Irwin Edman's words, I may seem to such a reader a prime instance of the power of a dream.

Long ago, in *This Is My God*, I stated the case for my religious beliefs and conduct, and perhaps I brought a fresh note to some very old arguments, judging by the book's continuing acceptance among a variety of readers. It was not my intent then, and has not been in this book, to persuade others to believe or behave as I do. My aim in both works has been to break through the crust of prejudice, and reawaken clearheaded thought about our magnificent patrimony. Apropos, let me adduce here an excerpt from *This Is My God*:

> Following an interlude after college which had been all chase and no thought, I moved into a freely chosen observant life. I was gambling my whole existence on one hunch: that being Jewish was not a trivial and somewhat inconvenient accident, but the best thing in my life, and that to be a Jew the soundest way was the classic way. Living this way, on a gamble, I learned things about Judaism that no other procedure could have taught me.

The faith might have remained a closed book to me—except as childhood nostalgia—had I not made the experiment. There are many things that you can come to know only by trying to do them.

And that is the simple truth. Singularly lucky though I was in my father and my grandfather, I never really submitted to their authority. I was a Yankee Doodle boy, and not until my mid-twenties did I figure out for myself that they had endowed me with a treasure which I would make my way of life.

Here in the land of the free one comes to live by the Torah in one of two ways: either by growing up in a pious environment where authority reigns and observance is the norm—though even that, in an open society, may not keep all the young within the fold; or else one makes an individual choice, whatever one's background may be, to try to take on the commitments and rewards of a Torah existence. Of course, the more one knows and learns, the more possible it becomes to do that. In the end, every American Jew, however brought up, makes a choice. This book advocates only that it be an informed choice.

Moses himself admonishes us in Deuteronomy, as he concludes the Torah, "I have set before you this day life and death . . . choose then life, that you and your descendants may live to love your God and to cleave to him, for he is your life and the length of your days." At the time Moses was speaking about the life and death of our folk, but the folk consisted of individuals, and each one had to join in that momentous choice, set before them on the banks of the Jordan by the departing Lawgiver.

A patriot of the American Revolution, Samuel Adams, once said: *Driven from every other corner of the earth, freedom of thought and the right of private judgment in matters of conscience direct their course to this happy country as their last asylum.* The hoary Jewish spirit, preserved by centuries of conformity to a Torah-centered social structure, has been adapting exuberantly to a New World of free choice, because the bone-deep individualism of our people has always been there. *Two Jews, three opinions,* runs the old saw. Even the Talmud, hammering out the line of prevailing halakhah, is a battleground of sharp wits and strong opposing views.

Among those who care about eventual Jewish survival, our free-choosing folk is very slowly gravitating back to the magnetic tradition. That seems clear to me, but beyond that, I cannot pretend to foresee how our future Jewry will take shape. If this book in any way helps readers to rethink the matter for themselves, I will have done, to the best of my ability, what I set out to do. In a word, I have tried to write a book that my father would have found up to the mark.

Between them, my father and grandfather exemplified the two ways of Torah life in America which I have just described. Zaideh arrived from the Soviet Union a Hasidic rabbi in his hale sixties, and he never deviated from halakhah by a hair. He organized his existence on a Torah basis from the outset, took a little apartment a few steps from a synagogue, found a slaughterer he could trust—providing he himself supervised the killing of his Sabbath fowl—and went on teaching and preaching in old-country Yiddish, exactly as though he had not been transported ten thousand miles to a new continent. He could do this because my parents supported him. He did not learn English because he did not have to.

My father came here a fugitive from compulsory service in the Czarist army. He arrived penniless. In order to eat he worked on Shabbat. So did most of the Russian Jewish immigrants, religious or not. As time passed and he painfully worked up to a decent standard of living for our family, he resumed the halakhic ways of his upbringing. In this he differed from most of the other immigrants. That was his free choice. My memoir-novel *Inside, Outside* I call a kaddish for my father, and here is a key passage from this, my favorite book among the works I have written:

Now and then Pop came to Zaideh's flat to join in our study. How wistful his weary face would be, as he listened to our sharp exchanges, never cutting in, only listening! I had my moments of rebellious disgust with this burden, I must tell you. Once I told Pop in no uncertain terms how tired I was of this interminable Talmudic brain-twisting over laws two thousand years old.

"I understand, Yisroelke," he said. "But if I were on my deathbed, and I had breath enough to say one more thing to you, I would say, 'Study the Talmud.'"

Not Zaideh's star quality, I now realize, but Pop's attitude, kept me going. He had yielded me into Zaideh's hands, so that I would get more religion than he had the time or the learning to give me himself. Zaideh was a commanding personality, but in his quiet way, so was Pop. For a long time I thought of Zaideh as the one who shaped me most. Wrong. It was Pop, always Pop. All my life long, I have only been trying to be like my father.

תנצבה

May his soul be bound in the bond of everlasting life.

HERMAN WOUK
1994–1999
Palm Springs

NOTES

The amplifying Notes that follow are offered mainly as sidelights, for my book is over. Footnotes in a work sweeping through thirty centuries of our history, literature, and tradition, would have been impractical, and after all, the book addresses not the scholar but the common reader. Yet I trust that scholars who glance at my pages will discern an arduous effort to be accurate, and in matters of controversy, balanced. Nor have I relied on my own research. Authorities in varied fields have reviewed the manuscript, and at the end of these Notes I offer my acknowledgments to them, together with a Glossary of Hebrew and Yiddish terms, and a list of Biographical Names.

Prologue

Page 4 *The lone assassin . . . justified his act by morbidly misquoting the Talmud:* Rabin's assassin defined the Prime Minister, because of his peace policy, as a *rodafe*, that is, "a pursuer bent on murder." This twisted nonsense cost the Jewish people the life of a great man, and devastated his bereaved family.

Page 7 *. . . my deeply mourned friend Yitzhak Rabin:* When he was the Israeli ambassador to the United States I was living in Washington, writing my World War II novels. He and his wife Leah came often to our home, and we were frequent guests at the embassy. Rabin was a shy man, taciturn and hard to know, but in the end we became true friends. His broad knowledge of American history was only one unexpected facet of this many-sided quiet sabra, who will live forever in the chronicle of Jewry.

Page 7 *. . . Moshe Feinstein, the great Torah master:* His son-in-law, Dr. Moshe David Tendler, was my rabbi and consultant during the writing of *This Is My God*, and so I came to know Moshe Feinstein. The kindly sage admitted me to his elementary Talmud *shiur* (seminar), and at forty I sat among the eighteen-year-olds, keeping up with them as best I could. I became a sort of *ben bayit,* "son of the household," in the Feinstein home, a memory I cherish, and an influence not to be measured.

Chapter 1. The Rebbe and the Historian

Page 13 . . . *the scrawny, new mini-country was tottering under the imposed load of half a million refugees:* With these expulsions the Arabs doubled Israel's manpower at the outset. Against their own interests, they have almost consistently strengthened Israel's hand during her first fifty years. In 1947 they rejected the UN partition plan, which would have given them a sovereign Palestinian State then and there. By threatening Israel with a second Holocaust they incurred the defeat of the Six-Day War, which brought the Jewish State on the world stage as a formidable new small power. Their surprise attack on Yom Kippur ended in a turnaround victory for Israel which forced Egypt to the peace table, the first Arab power to recognize the Jewish State's right to exist.

Page 17 *American Jewish publishing seems to expand and prosper:* The most popular Hebrew-English religious library today is the Artscroll series of the Brooklyn-based Mesorah Heritage Foundation, offering the classic works in excellent editions, within a frame of strictly Orthodox scholarship (fair warning to freethinkers). Magazines of Jewish interest multiply, and local weekly newspapers flourish, coast to coast.

Page 21 *Heinrich Graetz's* History of the Jews: This monumental masterwork, evoking the saga of our people from the days of the Patriarchs to the late nineteenth century, is inexplicably out of print as I write. I hope some alert publisher will bring it out again soon, for it is wonderful and irreplaceable.

Chapter 2. Running on Empty

Page 24 *All those leaders at her annual conclave:* In 1998 the General Assembly of Jewish Federations held its annual meeting in Israel, and the keynote speaker was the renowned Talmud scholar Rabbi Adin Steinsaltz. A few years earlier it would have been unthinkable for this secular North American body to assemble in Jerusalem, let alone to feature an Orthodox activist of Steinsaltz's stature, a vivid instance of "the gravitating to the magnetic tradition," which I believe I discern.

Page 26 *Only with the Six-Day War in 1967, fifty years after the Balfour Declaration, did there come the abrupt mass turn to Zionism:* Those six days altered the focus of my own life and work. Until then I had called myself a Zionist. At that point, in my fifties, I became one. In my novel *The Hope*, turning on the epochal Six-Day War, I depict the political and social bombshell the victory was in the United States.

Page 27 *"The first thing Israel has to do . . . is tear down Yad Vashem":* Every Jew alive should at least once visit Yad Vashem, a compound of buildings in Jerusalem of somber architecture and terrific emotional impact, memorializing the destruction of the European Jews. Mr. Thomas Friedman of the *New York Times* is the subject of this anecdote.

Page 29 *The Man on the Cruise Ship:* Nothing I might invent could equal this experience of the two brothers in Poland. It is a true story, told here without the slightest embellishment.

Chapter 3. The First Destruction

Page 35 *. . . the burning of the Talmud and even of Jews was still going on:* These savageries persisted, in various European countries, into the eighteenth and nineteenth centuries. (See *Encyclopedia Judaica*, "Auto da fe" and "Burning of the Talmud.")

Chapter 4. The Second Destruction

Page 48 *. . .* apikoros—*in Yiddish* apikayress, *is a term for an aggressively and irredeemably Godless person:* A Yiddish anecdote, no doubt apocryphal, tells of a notorious atheist, "the Odessa Apikoros," and of a rebellious yeshiva *bucher* who decides to seek him out, so as to study real Godlessness under him. Searching through the Odessa Jewish quarter, he is directed to a small *bet midrash*, where to his amazement he finds the Apikoros sitting in tallis and tfilin, murmuring over a Gemara. "So, you want to learn to be an apikoros?" the famous unbeliever welcomes him cheerfully. "Sit down, sit down, my son. It will take you about five years."

Even in Godlessness, the Hebrew spirit remains moralistic. To the epicurean, the gods exist, but they are ethereal beings uninterested in, and irrelevant to, human affairs. The apikoros, on the other hand, defines himself by formally declaring, "*Let din v'let dayan!*" Translation: "There is no justice, and no Judge!" Implication: there should be, but there is not! The epicurean will take part in a religious ritual if he happens to enjoy it. The apikoros, never! *L'hakhis,* to provoke anger, he may well make a point of eating ham on Yom Kippur. He is a serious Godless person. Very Jewish.

Page 48 *. . . Epicurus . . . his was an elevated philosophy of enjoyment of life's transient good things:* In appreciation of the good things of this world, the Talmud has some surprising sallies which an epicurean might almost endorse.

> Samuel said to Rav Judah, "Snatch and eat, snatch and drink, you sharp scholar, for this world we are leaving is a wedding!"
>
> Rashi elucidates: "If you have the means to enjoy yourself, do so. Don't wait until tomorrow, when you may die. Like a wedding, this world is here today and quickly gone."
>
> Rav said to Rav Hamnunah, "My son, if you have the means, be good to yourself. Death does not tarry! And if you think, I must leave means for my son, who will tell you in the grave what is happening? Men are like the plants of the field, these grow up when those wither."
>
> Rashi: "Don't worry about your son, let him look to himself. As he grows up, so will his livelihood."
>
> —ERUVIN, 54A

Eruvin, a treatise about an arcane aspect of Sabbath law, is known for its difficulty. You never know what you may find in the Talmud until you learn it.

Page 53 *. . . the historian Josephus . . . Himself a commander in the battles, though hardly an admirable one:* For anyone interested in the action and color of ancient times, Josephus's writings are enthralling, though the Jews of his day despised him as Graetz does, for his tricky turncoat performance as a military man. Even giving himself the best of it in the Jewish Wars, he discloses that at the siege of Jotapata, he convinced the last-ditch resisters to commit mass suicide, rather than yield to the Romans, by drawing lots and slaying each other. Then, contriving to be one of the last two left, he persuaded the other fellow to join him in surrendering. Not exactly your Masada-style hero, Josephus. He wrote fine battle scenes, though.

Page 54 *. . . Jochanan ben Zakkai acted in time . . . to preserve Jewry:* The Talmud gives a moving account of Jochanan ben Zakkai on his deathbed. He is in tears, and his sorrowing disciples want to know why he is weeping. Ben

Zakkai tells them that he fears facing God to answer for his life work. Barry Freundel, my rabbi and a consultant on this book, suggested in a striking talk on Tisha B'Av that Jochanan ben Zakkai doubted, to his last hour, whether he had done right in abandoning besieged Jerusalem for Yavneh, thereby diverting Judaism forever in a new direction.

Page 55 *This once resplendent Jewry:* Professor Louis Feldman of Yeshiva University, an authority and writer of note, demurs from my picture of their extinction:

"The decline of Egyptian Jewry was due largely to the loss of 50,000 in Tiberius Julius Alexander's repression of riots between Jews and Greeks, and of uncounted thousands (probably hundreds of thousands) . . . in the revolt of 115–117, led by a would-be messiah, Lukuas Andreas. So far as we can tell, Hellenistic penetration was not a major factor in the loss of numbers . . ."

My view that the Hellenizing of those Jews weakened their community is an impression gathered from my inexpert delving in this recondite field. My learned adviser is surely right in his factual analysis.

Chapter 5. The Third Destruction: I

Page 57 *. . . this account now traverses a time tunnel of mind-numbing length—no less than one thousand seven hundred years:* A consultant challenged me, "I wonder why you omit the Middle Ages, particularly the Spanish Golden Age . . . the Inquisition and the role of the Conversos, the disputations between Jews and Christians, etc. Surely these play a crucial role in the evolution of the Jew into modern times."

After much thought I opted for the time tunnel because of the theme of my book. Nothing that happened between the fall of the Second Temple and the present day, not even the Spanish tragedy, ever matched the German onslaught as a threat to eliminate the Jews from human history, a threat under which—in my judgment—we still live. The story of the Spanish Jews has been told in brilliant depth by Graetz.

Page 58 *. . . the flames of the Inquisitions:* The Inquisitions were purportedly established to root out heretics and heresy, not to torture and burn Jews. But they were preceded by terrible periods of forced mass conversions, mainly around 1391 and 1412. The Jews therefore had a difficult choice. They were threatened with expulsion if they did not convert, and if they did become Conversos, they were subject to the Inquisition.

Page 59 *"From the Gaonate to the Haskalah"*: Professor David Berger is the author of the relevant essay, "Judaism and General Culture in Medieval and Early Modern Times," contained in a collection entitled *Judaism's Encounter with Other Cultures: Rejection or Integration?* (Jason Aronson, 1997).

Page 62 *Among his philosophic labors he [Mendelssohn] tried to reconcile Hebraism and the reviving Hellenism—an intellectual feat akin to squaring the circle:* Mendelssohn's great predecessor in this effort was Philo of Alexandria, whose work harmonizes sacred Scripture with Greek philosophy through radical exegesis and allegory. The late Harvard philosopher Professor H. A. Wolfson held that Philo's bridge between the two worldviews lasted for seventeen centuries, until Spinoza tore it down. Wolfson's searching studies of Philo and Spinoza are both masterpieces.

Page 69 *Anti-Semitism . . . was expounded in leftist thought . . . by none other than Karl Marx himself, descended from a line of rabbis:* A curious little book published forty years ago, out of print and probably to be found only in research libraries, is *A World Without Jews,* by Karl Marx; actually a reprint of a long essay reviewing a book by a well-known anti-Semite, Bruno Bauer (*The Jewish Question,* published in 1843). Marx's disquisition runs to eighty-three pages, and is unbelievably vituperative about Jews and the Jewish religion. The translator, writing in 1959, states that the Soviet authorities are expunging from Marx's works his worst anti-Semitic ravings. Possibly in Russia today this bowdlerizing is being corrected, if anybody there is still concerned with the writings of Karl Marx. (Dagobert D. Runes, translator, Philosophical Library, New York.)

Page 71 *. . . Pobedonostsev, spoke for the aroused Russian rabble, as well as for the Czarist government . . . "one third of the Jews will convert, one third will die, and one third will flee the country":* He was far off the mark. One third did flee Russia, my parents among them, but conversions were almost nil, and the Jews who remained did not die. On the contrary, millions survived the worst that the Czars and the communists could do. Russian Jewish emigration to Israel now approaches the million mark, and among those who remain, some hold key positions in government and business. Their Jewish identity and awareness may be near zero, but that they survive as Jews, after seventy years of Soviet asphyxiation of Jewish culture, is marvel enough. An American scholar in this field sent me a roster of fourteen such Russian Jewish leaders: bankers, cabinet ministers, media moguls, heavy industry tycoons. Pobedonostsev's grave must rumble with his turnings.

Chapter 6. The Third Destruction: II

Page 75 *. . . local firing squads:* It is a fact, obscured but gruesome, that in countries like Lithuania, Rumania, and Estonia, the German bloodlust spread to the native population, and recruits were not lacking for the wholesale shooting of their Jewish compatriots and neighbors.

Page 76 *. . . it was toward these two magnetic poles [Newton and the Baal Shem Tov] that the vital forces of Yavneh had been flowing in opposite directions:* I owe this insight to the writings of the late social historian Jacob Katz of Hebrew University. Before he died in his nineties, I was privileged to meet with him twice in Jerusalem for long talks. A spare little man in a yarmulke, he lived in a flat on the fifth floor ("It's good exercise," he told me), and he would welcome the out-of-breath visitor with coffee and cake. His lucid books transmute the conventional picture of Judaism as a monolithic life pattern, based in Talmud and crystallized in the *Shulkhan Arukh,* into a vision of an inspired dynamic religious structure, surviving in exile by successfully coping with change. Katz supplements Graetz with a whole second epic of Jewish social life and halakhah, on the move through the centuries. Nothing escapes his eye, certainly not the challenge of modernity. Among his main works:

> *Tradition and Crisis: Jewish Society at the End of the Middle Ages* (New York: Schocken Books, 1993).
>
> *Exclusiveness and Tolerance: Studies in Jewish-Gentile Relations in Medieval and Modern Times* (West Orange, N.J.: Behrman House, Inc., 1983).
>
> *From Prejudice to Destruction: Anti-Semitism, 1700–1933* (Cambridge: Harvard University Press, 1980).

I was first attracted to Jacob Katz by his autobiography, *With My Own Eyes,* published by Brandeis University Press, a stimulating introduction to the outlook of an important Jewish thinker.

Page 79 *In private conversation, a brilliant old friend of mine . . . took a position much like Hannah Arendt's:* The late Professor Walter Kaufmann of Princeton University, a noted Nietzsche scholar, was a rigorous thinker, a caustic critic, and a valued consultant on my World War II novels. Walter was severe on my first sketchy attempts to portray the Germans, for he tended to regard Nazism as an aberrant interlude of a terror regime, rather than a phenomenon deeply rooted in German thought, culture, and nationalism. After much study, directed by him, I disagreed; but the seriousness of my view on the matter in those books, I owe to his sharp strictures.

Page 80 ... *it is hard to understand how the intelligent author of* Eichmann in Jerusalem *could have been taken in:* A recent book about Hannah Arendt caused quite a flurry in the ivory towers of academia, by exploring her long love affair with the philosopher Martin Heidegger (*Hannah Arendt–Martin Heidegger* by Elzbieta Ettinger, Yale University Press, New London, 1995). The able tough-minded Arendt, who achieved wide acclaim with her *Origins of Totalitarianism,* turns out to have been a tremulous adorer of Heidegger, an arrant Nazi Party member during the Hitler years, who afterward escaped prosecution but remained under a cloud. The eminent professor, a married man, seduced this brilliant Jewish student of his when she was nineteen, and she never got over a slavish attachment to him, nor did he ever shake free of a hunger for her adoration and submission. Things became sticky when she rose to outshine him, even in Germany, in public recognition and book earnings, yet with ups and downs the relationship survived until his death. Heidegger's reputation, outside his notoriety as a Nazi, rests on his contribution to "Phenomenology," which commanded much attention as an aspect of the philosophical vogue called existentialism.

Did Arendt have a peculiar view of Eichmann because of her obsession with Martin Heidegger? Any bias in her writing about the trial would of course have been subliminal, but one may at least conjecture that her lifelong hopeless love for an ex-Nazi might have had something to do with it. Otherwise the puzzlement stands, and with it my very low opinion of "the banality of evil" as a philosophical insight about mass murder.

Chapter 8. Zaideh and the Humanist

Page 97 *At the center of this storm was Rabbi Moses ben Maimon, in Hebrew acronym the Rambam:* Because of his awesome mental powers and the towering authority of his works, the man has come to seem a legendary marble giant. In fact his days were very human and full of woe. Persecution drove the Maimon family from Spain, to lead a wandering existence in the Islamic countries of the Mediterranean; and he may have had to endure a temporary sham conversion to Islam, though the matter remains in controversy. Deep tragedy darkened his latter years, for a brother who dealt in jewels, entrusted with the family's fortunes, was drowned at sea with all their property. The sage was compelled to maintain self and family as a court physician to the great Saladin's harem, and to his vizier. A surviving letter of his describes with pathos the wearing burden of this service, plus the pressure on him from all Jewry as a supreme legal arbiter. The strength of mind and spirit that Maimonides demonstrated in producing his immortal works, notwithstanding his troubled life, brings to my mind a harsh realistic Talmudic word: "The load is according to the camel."

Page 99 ... *pagan thought was bursting forth from its long sleep under the blanket of Church dogma:* In the Middle Ages, pagan philosophy was available to Jewish thinkers mainly in Islamic paraphrase. Europe rediscovered the original ancient classics during the Renaissance centuries that followed, at first largely in Italy.

Chapter 9. The Sacred Story

Page 108 *Here we have the doctrine ... of eminent domain:* Charles Rembar, my legal counsel for many years, vetted my manuscript as an interested non-Orthodox Jewish reader. On "eminent domain," he comments as follows:

> Under the Fifth Amendment, the power of eminent domain may not be exercised "without just compensation." If the Bible is taken to be the supreme authority, it doesn't matter that one of the greatest of human documents expresses a different view. But then it is a mistake to use the human concept of eminent domain as a description of this passage in the Bible.

My usage of the term is indeed loose, but the concept of eminent domain long antedates the Fifth Amendment, and compensation was not necessarily, to my knowledge, a requirement in earlier times. Mr. Rembar is the author of *The End of Obscenity* and other well-known legal works. He is Norman Mailer's cousin, and he confirmed to me that my esteemed contemporary has not yet made it to the Promised Land, adding with commendable family loyalty, "But then, neither did Moses."

Chapter 10. The Fathers

Page 128 *Scripture amply bears out Jacob's melancholy judgment on his life:* My two-page summary of Jacob's history does no justice whatever to some of the most dramatic scenes in Scripture, for conflict, character portrayal, moral dilemmas, and sheer exactness and power of dialogue. In this sustained march of narrative, Laban, Jacob, Leah, Rachel, and the sons are delineated in strokes which in a secular author would be termed unmatchable genius.

Page 129 *The boyish crying of the disappointed, supplanted Esau compels sympathy:* At least it does mine, as the Torah tells the tale. The attitude toward Esau in Jewish tradition is almost uniformly hostile. His other name in Scripture is Edom, and the neighboring nation of Edom was for centuries a bitter enemy of the Jewish people. The Book of Psalms records the rejoicing of Edom at the fall of Jerusalem: "*Raze her, Raze her to the foundations!*" Yet the Torah enjoins warfare against Edom, "*for he is your brother.*" Herod the Great was a converted Idumean. In the Talmud "Edom" becomes a euphemism for the Roman Empire, and, in later rabbinics, for all oppressive regimes of the long Exile. A complex figure, Esau/Edom, and Midrash about him is abundant.

Chapter 11. The Law

Page 135 *. . . the Wannsee Conference:* This was a meeting of cabinet-level German officials with SS leaders, occasioned by a letter written by Hermann Goering, dated July 31, 1942, calling for a "final solution" of the Jewish question. Chaired by Reinhard Heydrich, deputy chief of the SS, with Eichmann as secretary, its proceedings were recorded in a document of the highest secrecy, the Wannsee Protocol. All copies were destroyed except one that turned up by chance in some captured Foreign Office files after the war. So the secret was bared to history. The meeting produced a plan for the destruction of the European Jews, by overwork and starvation as slaves in the east, the hardiest survivors to be "dealt with accordingly," i.e., exterminated. In my novel *War and Remembrance,* chapter 14, the detailed picture of the conference is a faithful rendering of the Wannsee Protocol.

Chapter 12. *Nakh:* The Prophets and the Writings

Page 145 *In half a century the Hexateuch has dropped off the screen of Bible scholarship:* Dr. David Noel Freedman, the Christian editor of the scholarly Anchor Bible series, and a generous consultant to me in his field of expertise, takes me severely to task for my joshing of the Hexateuch.

> You are being a little too scornful, not to say, derisive and dismissive. There was and is serious scholarship behind combinations such as a Hexateuch, and more currently the Tetrateuch, as well as the Pentateuch. If not as much is written about the Hexateuch, for example, it is not because the idea has been rejected, but rather that the insights have been incorporated into the current scholarship in other ways . . . you don't have to get into the debate, but you should not cast scorn on serious, often devoted and devout scholars. . . . As you may be aware from my little book *The Unity of the Hebrew Bible,* I have a different view of the whole matter. . . .

Professor Freedman's book might well set the teeth of Orthodox readers on edge, but his radical thesis is interesting, if very remote from a traditional understanding of Scripture.

Page 146 *. . . There is not a single law in all of the Prophets and Writings:* The Book of Esther narrates that the Queen and Mordechai decreed an annual reading of the Purim story. By rabbinic enactment, this decree became binding halakah. Like the post-Biblical holiday of Hanukkah, the Purim observances are *d'rabbanan* (precepts of the Sages).

Page 147 *Homer passes few moral judgments:* Not every Homer scholar would agree. Homeric scholarship, rather like Bible criticism, is an academic area of ongoing dispute, the consensus shifting with the decades. Between the "unitarian" and "analytic" schools, the question is still argued, whether a real poet called Homer wrote the epics, or whether the works are a compilation from several ancient sources. So in the Bible field we have the documentary theory of the Pentateuch. In *This Is My God,* I offer a detailed treatment of that topic, *"Wellhausen Theory: Higher Criticism."* At the time I wrote it I plumbed the subject to its origins, so as to deal with it seriously. An eminent old Bible critic, winding up a lifetime in the field, once remarked to me with weary candor, "When all is said and done, we can't go behind the text." An informed and not unreasonable conclusion.

Page 149 *. . . Job stands alone. Ascribed to no Jewish author . . . :* A Talmudic tradition ascribes the book to Moses. Among modern scholars, opinions are sharply divided about the book's origins, and no clear view emerges.

Page 151 *Ruth, a pastoral love story about . . . a righteous convert and the great-grandmother of King David, is the megillah of Shavuot, read at the start of summer:* Professor Feldman poignantly interjects:

> You should mention that Ruth is read on Shavuot because that holiday

commemorates the revelation at Sinai when Israel became a nation and was converted, so to speak; hence, a book about a convert to Judaism.

Page 152   *(Mene, mene, tekel, upharsin):* The words are difficult Aramaic, and have been variously translated and interpreted. The meaning however is fairly clear. *Mene, mene*—the root verb means "to count," and the emphatic repetition tells Belshazzar that his kingdom has been accurately surveyed, "counted," by the Lord. *Tekel*—root verb "weighed"—hence the King James expansion of the single word, "Thou art weighed in the balance and found wanting." *Upharsin* is partly a play on words. The verb root means "divided," but the root also refers to Paras, Persia. Summary: Your kingdom has been surveyed by the Lord, you have been found wanting, and your lands will be "divided" to the Persians. The English translation adds, "and to the Medes."

Chapter 13. The Talmud and I

Page 160   *... the Talmud has never since gone to press in any other page-by-page format:* In recent years Rabbi Adin Steinsaltz has been issuing a new edition of the Talmud, with a commentary in simple modern Hebrew that is a boon to all Jews, in Israel and in the diaspora. While he departs from the Bomberg pagination, a running head on every page refers the readers to that classic format. (I am reliably informed that he is reconsidering this departure.) Rabbi Steinsaltz has established yeshivas and teacher institutes in the lands of the former Soviet Union, to bring Yiddishkeit to masses of Jews dispossessed of their heritage by seventy years of malignant communism. Steinsaltz is a man in a million, and humble as a shoemaker.

Page 167   *Feynman listened carefully:* Richard Feynman once said, in a rare extemporaneous talk on religion:

> It doesn't seem to me that this fantastically marvelous universe, this tremendous range of time and space and different kinds of animals, and all the different planets, and all these atoms with all their motions, and so on, all this complicated thing can merely be a stage so that God can watch human beings struggle for good and evil—which is the view that religion has. The stage is too big for the drama.

This confession of awe at the marvels of Creation strikes closer to my own faith than many a synagogue sermon I have heard. I know lamentably little of what happens on Feynman's big stage beyond this little earth; but the

Bible teaches that no drama is too small for God to watch, starting with two naked innocents in a garden, and I believe it.

Page 169 *"You know, I had a lot of fun learning Talmud this past summer," she remarked:* One of the true breakthroughs of our time in Yiddishkeit has been the ever-growing participation of girls and women in serious learning. There are those who hold it an unwelcome departure from former ways. I could not differ more.

Chapter 14. Kabbalah

Page 173 *To all mysticism I am, and have always been, tone-deaf and color-blind . . . :* Rabbi Freundel enters a strong demurral to my treatment of Kabbalah:

> It is important to explain why mysticism is so powerful. I would include the sense of meaning that comes with every action and the possibility of bringing the Messiah. I would also talk about how living this type of lifestyle gives the adherent a feeling of connecting to G-d in very real and important ways. I might also mention the idea of sparks of G-d in exile as an answer to Jewish Diaspora and Jewish persecution.
>
> In short, I think a little more of the positive, meaningful side of Kabbalah, perhaps a little more of the system with at least a mention of the sefirot, and a little less of the criticism and the magical.

I am not unfamiliar with the imagery—Sefirot, Tzimtzum, Shvirat Hakelim, Partzufim, "Sparks of God in Exile,"and so on—but I cannot in good conscience undertake, despite Freundel's exhortation, to convey these mysteries with any success to the reader. For one who wishes to go more deeply into this field, I offer two reference works, of opposite nature. They are:

1. The "insider" view: *Mystic Concepts in Chassidism,* by Jacob Immanuel Schochet. Kehot Publication Society, 770 Eastern Parkway, Brooklyn, New York 11213.

2. The "outsider" view: *Major Trends in Jewish Mysticism,* by Gershom Scholem, Pantheon Books, 201 East Fiftieth Street, New York, NY 10022.

Scholem's book is a comprehensive standard work, hard going but accessible. Schochet offers a brief current handbook in English on the Hasidic approach, best studied with a well-versed teacher like Barry Freundel, for the concepts are strange and very difficult to grasp. I once heard the great Rav Soloveitchik himself expound on the theme of *Shvirat Hakelim* ("Breaking of the Vessels") with conviction and with passion. Something is surely there for those whom it reaches. Alas that *"my soul does not enter into their secret counsels."*

Page 187   ... *the fearsome Chmielnicki massacres:* The present Librarian of Congress, Dr. James Billington, a major scholar of Russian history and culture, read my manuscript, and urged me to take note of the Chmielnicki massacres, which in his view rival the Holocaust in cruelty and havoc, if not in scope. These events occurred in the Ukraine from 1648 to 1654, during an uprising of Cossacks and peasants against Polish rule. The history is complicated, but for the Jews the outcome was clear and stark; hundreds of communities destroyed, ravishing of women and loss of property beyond telling, perhaps as many as a hundred thousand Jews murdered, though the number remains in dispute.

I can recall from childhood days my parents referring to "Chmielnicki" as the ultimate in pogroms, but the German genocide had quite eclipsed Chmielnicki in my awareness, as it has in general memory, until Dr. Billington reminded me. The responsible Cossack leader, one Bogdan Chmielnicki, is to this day regarded as a hero in the Ukraine. The current *Encyclopædia Britannica* gives an ample account of Bogdan Chmielnicki's career, under the name Bohdan Khmelnitsky. The massacres of the Jews are not mentioned.

Chapter 16. Ivrit and Zionism

Page 221   *"Nations are cold monsters," General Charles de Gaulle once put it:* Machiavelli was there a little before de Gaulle with this insight in *The Prince,* the classic handbook for cold monstrous national policy.

With World War I, the breakup of the existing world system began. The Turks made the mistake of siding with Germany, which opened up the Middle East as a war front, and Palestine fell to the British with some useful help, it is said, from Zionist intelligence. Due to complicated reasons of state—not wholly excluding a trace of sympathy for the Zionist vision, and getting the weight of American Jewry on the Allied side—the British in November 1917 issued the Balfour Declaration, in the form of a letter from

Lord Arthur Balfour, the Foreign Secretary, to Lord Lionel Rothschild, the more friendly heir of the hostile Lord Rothschild. The exact language was the subject of long bitter dispute in the corridors of power, and influential anti-Zionist Jews had regrettable success in watering down the wording.

The sympathy of the British for Zionism is rooted in the King James Bible, which colors their culture like Shakespeare. The great Lord Palmerston was a friend of the Jews, and George Eliot's novel *Daniel Deronda* even envisioned the return of the Jews to Palestine. If the Uganda offer was based on a cold calculation of advantage—settling of the territory by Europeans, and the attracting of Jewish capital—it remained the only such gesture by a great power until the Balfour Declaration. At a low point of acrimony between the new Jewish State and Britain, David Ben-Gurion averred that the Jewish people must never forget the British role in aiding the historic Return.

Page 221 ... *the Declaration of Independence of the State of Israel:* That declaration, again, was made possible by a transient knotting of interests involving most of all the Soviet Union, the British Empire, and the United States; though in the United Nations partition vote, numerous nations large and small participated, barely passing the resolution by the needed two-thirds majority.

Page 222 *They* [the Israelis] *have had to fight many wars:* The decisive wars of Israel have been the War of Independence, 1948–1949, the Suez War of 1956, the Six-Day War of 1967, and the Yom Kippur War of 1973. These were in essence wars for survival. There have been smaller conflicts known in Israel as wars, though journalism and world history have taken little note of them, such as the War for the Water, the War of Attrition, and the "Peace in Galilee" action against terrorists based in Lebanon. For fifty years, the Arab countries have repeatedly attempted, each time with less success, to deny the rise of the new Jewish State by turning to "the military option," and one by one they have been making grudging peace with Israel. With the existence of long-range missiles and non-conventional weapons, Israel has to remain a nation on high alert, bearing a burdensome defense budget, to maintain world-class armed forces. My novel *The Hope* centers on the Six-Day War, and its sequel, *The Glory,* on the Yom Kippur War. Together, the books offer a picture of Israel's first forty years in war and peace, through the lives of four interconnected families.

Page 223 *It is recorded that Truman wept:* The incident is described on page 620 of *Truman,* David McCullough's superb biography (Simon & Schuster, 1992).

General Note on Chapters 15–16 (pp. 191-223)

Yiddish, Ivrit, and S. Y. Agnon

If the language war began when Eliezer Ben-Yehuda stepped off the boat, where do we locate the end of it? The rise of Ivrit was diffuse and gradual, but all wars do end, and seldom with the total destruction on one side. The defeated live on, subdued and diminished, as Yiddish is doing. Perhaps we can call the Six-Day War of 1967 the end, when a Hebrew-speaking armed force won a famous victory—the first since the time of the Maccabees—and Jewry's center of gravity irreversibly shifted.

Shmuel Yosef Agnon was born shortly after Ben-Yehuda disembarked in 1881, and died shortly after Israel routed all its foes in 1967. His lifetime therefore spanned the language war, as his works spanned the culture shift. Like his great predecessors, Mendele the Bookseller and Y. L. Peretz, Agnon wrote in Yiddish as well as Hebrew; but whereas they moved back and forth between the two languages, and did their most memorable work in Yiddish, once Agnon turned to Hebrew he stayed with it. He paid the price of relative obscurity for many years, but his reward was the Nobel Prize. I believe he sensed that Yiddish was going down, that the lifeblood of a culture is in its language, and that in this century Hebrew was destined to become a *sine qua non* of continued Jewish existence. Under Agnon's pellucid Hebrew, the cadences of his Yiddish origins make his style uniquely rich.

Chapter 20. The Breath of the Children

Page 268   Our Jewish census is shrunken enough . . . God knows, three-thousandths of one percent of world population: Winston Churchill once said about World War II, speaking of the time before the United States became a belligerent, "The only thing that ever frightened me was the U-boat war." He had faith in the indomitability of the British people and in the promise of Lend-Lease, but the sheer arithmetic of the sinkings threatened doom for England.

Strong as is my Jewish faith, the only thing that frightens me is the sheer arithmetic of our world predicament. Since the Holocaust reduced our numbers by one-third, we have barely been maintaining our numerical presence on earth, while the planet's population has been exploding. Whether the globe can indefinitely support such crowding worries the futurists, but the

Jewish arithmetic seems to me far more immediate and disquieting. The Mosaic Law, God-given or "man-made," kept us in identity down the millennia, but now we risk dwindling, within a century or two, below an ethnic critical mass. Every single one of us, observant or not, has become precious for our survival.

A valued Christian friend, whose minister son is married to a Jewish woman, once asked me why I am so concerned about assimilation. He loves his daughter-in-law, he said, she is happy, and she is informing her children about their heritage. Of all that I have little doubt, but she and they no longer count in the three-thousandths of one percent, which is carrying forward our history and our destiny in rapidly falling relative numbers.

Page 269   Meantime some mild mellowing seems to be going on in Reform: A noteworthy document of the Reform movement is "Renewing the Covenant: Our Reform Jewish Future," the Presidential address delivered at the Reform General Assembly in November 1997 in Dallas, by Rabbi Eric Yoffie. Six of the thirteen pages call for a detailed return to increased observance, including traditional Torah chanting in the temple and "reclaiming of Shabbat for Reform Jews." Rabbi Yoffie is by no means surrendering the Reform dogma that the halakhah is not binding, but he clearly has sensed that the lifeblood of Judaism lies, after all, in its traditions. I gather that his reception was decidedly mixed, one prominent leader even declaring that if Yoffie's views prevailed, "she would join the Unitarian Church."

"Renewing the Covenant" is certainly a far cry from the nineteenth-century Reform program, which emphasized universalist ethics and prophetic values, and which Solomon Schecter once brusquely dismissed as "nothing else but ham and a craving for assimilation." I am not inclined to be triumphalist about Rabbi Yoffie's views. Quite the contrary, I am struck by the sense of responsibility for the Jewish fate that he expresses. Reform has for generations been—so to speak—the Last Chance Café for Jews on the downward highway to assimilation. This new program undertakes to arrest and reverse the losses, and I honor Rabbi Yoffie for his concern, and for his courage in speaking out.

Afterword

Page 277   . . . I moved into a freely chosen observant life. I was gambling my whole existence on one hunch . . . that to be a Jew the soundest way was the classic way:

On Heresy

The word *heresy*, says *Webster's Unabridged*, derives from a Greek verb, *hairesis*, meaning choice. A heretic, then, is one who chooses his beliefs, instead of accepting those established by authority; rather an innocuous or even laudable sort of free spirit, one might say, but in certain times and places such choice has been a crime, even a capital crime.

When Samuel Adams wrote that America was the last refuge on earth of freedom of conscience, he was stating a fact of his day. In our day, with the worldwide diffusion of American culture, authority everywhere is being challenged, and freedom of conscience is emerging as a global ideal, if far from a norm. Immense areas of controlled opinion remain where Marxism shakily holds on, or religion engulfs politics, or an entrenched dictatorship terrorizes contrary thought. But the last world showdown between freedom and authority is over. Tocqueville predicted that America and Russia would one day divide the earth. For fifty years after World War II, the two hegemonies did in fact come head to head, with the extinction of the human race a horrible possibility. Freedom outfaced, outperformed, and outlasted its foe. All over the world now, whether or not the peoples are allowed to claim freedom, they aspire to be free. That is something new under the sun. Its impact on all religions has been immense. For the Jewish people, whose origin and continued existence are bound up with religion, it is an upheaval we are trying to cope with. When I made my own choice I had thought none of this through. I acted, as I have said, on a hunch.

Authority is a strong persisting aspect of all human culture. Sweep it out the door, and it may drift in through the windows. Humanism is a tolerant persuasion, and some of my best friends are convinced humanists, but humanism, too, can verge on orthodoxy in its fashion. It is almost a dogma of the humanists that serious belief in God and a religious structure betrays a mind either out of touch or second-rate. Yet there is another possibility; the mind may be that of a heretical humanist, so to say, making his (or her) free choice. Now and then I have had an encouraging signal from one or another famous humanist, like a winking light on a dark sea, spelling out, *I–don't–exactly–agree–but–you–are–on–to–something. Be–strong–and–of–good –courage.*

And so in my eighties, with so much still to do, I have written this book.

GLOSSARY

These thumbnail descriptions of terms, some of them complex and controversial, are only for ready reference. Fuller treatment is in the text of the book.

Aliyah—"Ascent." Wave of Jewish pioneers to Palestine, mostly from eastern Europe. The First Aliya occurred between 1882 and 1903, and five separate aliyot are discerned before World War II. Thereafter immigration tended to be continuous, if sometimes illegal, until the British withdrew in May 1948, and the State was declared. (Religious use of aliya: [1] a call to the Torah in synagogue or temple; [2] one seventh of the weekly sedra.)

Amora—"Commenter." An authority of the Gemara.

Ashkenazim—Jews of northern and eastern Europe and their descendants. (Also a current Hasidic term for Misnagdim.)

Chabad—Acronym of *C*hochmah, *B*inah, *D*aas, three synonyms for knowledge or wisdom. Denotes Lubavitcher Hasidim and their philosophy.

Daf Yomi—"Daily page." Custom of learning a leaf of the Talmud every day.

Daven, davening—Prayer in Hebrew, in the synagogue or at home.

Emancipation—The gradual freeing of Jews from restrictive laws in western Europe, beginning in the eighteenth century. In eastern Europe, Emancipation was never fully implemented before communism overwhelmed those countries, and restricted Jews in other ways.

Gaon/Gaonate—Supreme heads of learned academies, mainly in Babylonia, seventh to eleventh centuries. The office, which wielded considerable social power, is called by historians the Gaonate. The honorific term today means an eminent Torah authority.

Gemara—"Completion." Discussions in Babylonian and Palestinian academies of the Mishna, recorded in the Talmud.

Halakhah—"The Way." The body of Mosaic and Talmudic law, considered binding by observant Jews.

Halutz, halutzim—Literally, "girded." Zionist term for Jewish pioneers in Palestine.

Hasid, Hasidim, Hasidism, Hasidut, Hasidus—The term "Hasidim" is ancient, and has been applied to several sects in Jewish history. In Talmudic usage, a Hasid is a saintly person. Since the 1700s, the term has denoted a new mystical pietist movement within Orthodoxy, Hasidism, in Yiddish usage, *hasidus*. Its adherents are known as Hasidim, singular Hasid, devotees of charismatic dynastic Rebbes.

Haskalah—"Enlightenment." Intellectual and social movement in European Jewry, late eighteenth and nineteenth centuries, aimed at broadening Jewish life and culture beyond religion, to include secular learning, arts, and general interests.

Hebraism—Traditional culture, thought, and practice of the Jews, often used in contrast to Hellenism.

Hellenism/Hellenists—Ancient Greek culture and thought, and Jews deeply influenced by Greek ways.

Holocaust (Hebrew, *Shoah*)—The destruction of the European Jews by the German National Socialist government under Adolf Hitler, 1941–1945.

Humesh—"One-fifth." One of the five books of Moses, and by extension, a volume containing all five books.

Judaea and *Samaria*—Biblical names for the West Bank territory, disputed between Israelis and Palestineans.

Judaism—Orthodox, Conservative, Reform. Orthodox Judaism regards halakhah as a binding way of life for the Jewish people. Reform Judaism arose in nineteenth-century Germany as a liberalized response to the Enlightenment, and holds that halakhah is no longer binding. Conservative Judaism by doctrine adheres to halakhah, but adopts some liberalizing concepts and practices of Reform.

Kabbalah—"Tradition." Jewish mysticism, based largely on the Zohar, an extensive Aramaic commentary on the Torah. The Zohar is attributed by Kabbalists to a Talmud sage, Shimon bar Yokhai. Secular scholars ascribe it to a thirteenth-century Spanish Kabbalist, Moses de Leon.

Kashrut—The body of Jewish dietary law, including the removal of the sciatic nerve, in remembrance of the laming of Jacob by the angel.

Kibbutz—Communal settlement in Israel.

Kishinev—City in Moldava, Russia, site of a major pogrom in 1903, which raised a worldwide protest, and led to the Uganda Scheme.

Ladino—The lingua franca of Sephardic Jews, based on Spanish and written in Hebrew characters.

Lubavitch—A small town in Russia that was the original center of the Chabad Hasidim, devotees of the Schneerson dynasty.

Maskil—An adherent of the Haskalah. Loosely, a secularist.

Minyan—"Count." Quorum of ten men required for a formal prayer service.

Mishkan—"Dwelling." The portable Tabernacle in which the Divine Presence dwelled, during the desert wanderings of the Israelites under Moses.

Misnaged, Misnagdim (Hebrew, *Mitnaged*)—"Opponents." Traditional Talmudic Jewry, resistant to the rise of modern Hasidism.

Moshiakh—The Messiah.

Mysticism—Transcendental philosophy of life, found within the great religions in varying forms. Conceived as leading to direct experience of the Deity. (For Jewish mysticism, see *Kabbalah*.)

Nigleh/Nistor—Shorthand terms distinguishing Talmud learning (*nigleh:* "open, revealed") from Kabbalah (*nistor:* "hidden, esoteric").

Ostjude—German for an eastern Jew.

Phylacteries—(Hebrew, *tefillin*)—Leather boxes containing Scriptural passages, strapped on the head and left arm of men at weekday morning prayer. (See *Encyclopædia Judaica*, vol. 15, p. 898 ff, for an extended description.)

Pogrom—Anti-Jewish riots condoned by the authorities, mainly in Czarist Russia.

Post-Zionism—An intellectual movement rejecting the concept of a Jewish homeland.

Rabbi, Rov, Rav, Reb, Rebbe—Shared meaning, teacher. Today, *rabbi* is used by the clergy of the various Judaic denominations. *Rov* denotes a senior Orthodox rabbi. *Rav* is a Talmudic title applied today to such rabbis, especially to the late Talmudist and philosopher, Joseph Dov Soloveitchik, known as *the Rav* par excellence. *Reb* is a respectful form of address. *Rebbe* usually refers to a Hasidic leader, identified by the town of his dynasty's origin; thus, the Belzer Rebbe, originally from Belz, a shtetl in the Ukraine. A follower is a Belzer Hasid, or a Belzer.

Sanhedrin—Supreme judicial council of Talmudic scholars. In Jerusalem it sat in the Temple precincts, and after the fall at Yavneh and other locations, so long as Judea was under Roman rule. Napoleon convened a quasi-Sanhedrin to explore the status of French Jewry, with a view to Emancipation.

Sephardim—Strictly, Jews of Spanish and Portuguese origin. Loosely, Jews of Mediterranean countries.

Septuagint—Greek translation of the Hebrew Bible by Jewish scholars in Alexandria, third century B.C.

Shabbat—The Jewish Sabbath, starts before sundown Friday, and ends after nightfall Saturday.

Shoah (see *Holocaust*)

Shtetl—Diminutive of *shtot,* a town. Small town in eastern Europe.

Sugya—A Gemara discussion.

Tallis, tallit—A prayer shawl.

Talmud—"Learning." The Oral Law expounding the Law of Moses in two recensions, Babylonian and Palestinian (Jerusalem Talmud), circa 200 B.C. to A.D. 500. Consists of Mishna and Gemara.

Tanakh—Acronym for the three divisions of the Hebrew Bible, *Torah, N'*viim, *K'*tuvim (The Law, The Prophets, The Writings).

Tanna—An authority of the Mishna.

Targum Hashivim, Targum of the Seventy (see *Septuagint*).

Tikkun Olam—"Repair of the Universe." In the mystical system of Isaac Luria, every performance of a mitzvah by an individual Jew is an act of Tikkun Olam.

Tisha B'Av—The Ninth of Av, eleventh month of the Jewish calendar. A twenty-four-hour fast, mourning the destruction of the First and Second Temples.

Torah—"Teaching." The five books of Moses, and by extension, all Jewish law and learning.

Trefe—"Torn." Meat of a kosher animal killed by a predator, or by a non-kosher slaughter method, therefore prohibited. By extension, any unkosher food.

Tzome—A fast day.

Tzome Gedaliah—Annual fast day commemorating the assassination of Gedaliah, governor of Judaea appointed by the Babylonians, circa 586 B.C.

Uganda, Uganda Scheme—A 1903 British Government proposal to settle oppressed Jews of Czarist Russia in territory of central Africa.

Yad Vashem (Isaiah 56:5)—"Pillar and name," idiom for a memorial. A monumental group of structures in Jerusalem, commemorating the martyred six million European Jews, with the world's greatest Holocaust archive.

Yavneh—Coastal town in ancient Judaea, site of the Talmud school and Sanhedrin established by Jochanan Ben Zakkai, circa A.D. 70. Used in this book as a collective name for the Jewish religion and culture that survived the Second Destruction.

Yeshiva University—First Orthodox American center of higher learning combining religious and secular studies.

Yiddish—Contraction of Jüdisch-Deutsch. Dialect of German written in Hebrew characters, the lingua franca of the Ashkenazim of northern Europe. Also the language of much eastern European Jewish literature, and of Hasidic teaching.

Yiddishkeit—"Jewishness." Used in this book as a general term for traditional Jewish culture and identity.

Zionism—The modern political movement to obtain a Jewish homeland in Palestine, which led to the establishment of the State of Israel.

Zohar—Basic work of Kabbalah, attributed by Jewish mystics to the wonder-working Talmudic sage of the second century, Shimon bar Yokhai. Academic scholars ascribe it to a Spanish Kabbalist, Moses de Leon (1240–1305).

BIOGRAPHICAL NAMES

Agnon, Schmuel Yosef (1888–1970). Austro-Hungarian-born Israeli author, first Jew awarded Nobel Prize for literature (1966), shared with Nelly Sachs, Jewish poetess.

Aleichem, Shalom (1859–1916). Greatest of classic Yiddish authors, creator of Tevya.

Arizal (see *Luria, Isaac*).

Arnold, Matthew (1822–1888). English poet and critic.

Asch, Shalom (1880–1957). Yiddish author of a popular and controversial Christian trilogy.

Baal Shem Tov. Literally, "Master of the Good Name." Formerly a common term for wonder-working Jews. Today it principally denotes the founding saint of modern Hasidism, Israel Eliezer Baal Shem Tov (circa 1698–1760), known by the acronym, the Besht.

Balfour, Arthur James (1848–1930). British earl. As Foreign Secretary he issued the Balfour Declaration in 1917, stating the British Government's support for a Jewish homeland in Palestine.

Bar Yokhai, Shimon. Second-century Tanna of the Talmud, credited by Kabbalistic tradition with authorship of the Zohar.

Begin, Menachem (1913–1992). Prime Minister of Israel. Born in Russia, lifelong nationalist political fighter and leader, signatory of the 1979 peace treaty with Anwar Sadat of Egypt, which broke the united Arab front against Israel.

Ben-Gurion, David (1886–1973). Born David Gruen in Plonsk, Belorussia. Leader of the Zionist fight for independence in Palestine, head of the Labor party, Mapai. First Prime Minister of Israel, Defense Minister in the War of Independence and the Suez War.

Ben-Yehuda, Eliezer (1858-1922). Early *halutz* (pioneer in Palestine), first lexicographer of modern Hebrew, father of the rebirth of the language in the Holy Land.

Ben Zakkai, Jochanan. First-century A.D. Tanna of the Talmud, founder of Yavneh academy and Sanhedrin after the fall of the Second Temple.

Bialik, Chaim Nakhman (1873–1934). Hebrew poet, critic, and anthologist, key figure in the Hebrew revival in literature and speech.

Bomberg, Daniel (circa 1500–1553). Pioneer Christian printer of the Talmud and other Judaic classics in Venice.

Caro, Joseph ben Ephraim (1488–1575). Talmudic commentator, author of the definitive code of Orthodoxy, the *Shulkhan Arukh* ("Ready Table").

Chamberlain, Houston (1855–1927). British son-in-law of the anti-Semitic composer Richard Wagner. Wrote books of racial denigration of Jews, largely based on the theories of Gobineau.

Coleridge, Samuel Taylor (1772–1834). English poet.

de Leon, Moses (1240–1305). Spanish Kabbalist, credited by modern scholars with authorship of the Zohar.

Descartes, René (1596–1650). French philosopher and mathemetician, leading theorist of modern rationalism.

Dreyfus, Alfred (1859–1935). French Jewish army officer, convicted of espionage and sent to Devil's Island. The accusation was false, based on forgery and conspiracy, and after several trials Dreyfus was fully exonerated. His accusers committed suicide or fled. The Dreyfus case (L'Affaire) caused an immense upheaval in French society.

Eichmann, Adolf (1906–1962). SS colonel, key administrator of the German massacre of the European Jews, 1941–1945.

Feynman, Richard Phillips (1918–1988). American Jewish physicist, Nobel laureate.

Gobineau, Joseph Arthur (1816–1882). French diplomat and author whose theories of Aryan racial superiority were a source of modern anti-Semitism, as in the writings of Houston Chamberlain.

Graetz, Heinrich (1817–1891). German Jewish author of an epic history of the Jewish people, spanning three millennia.

Hasmoneans. Priestly family who led the successful rebellion against the Seleucid Greek kingdom, and reestablished an autonomous Jewish state in 164 B.C. The victory is celebrated in the holiday of Hanukkah. The

Hasmonean dynasty ruled Judea for more than a century thereafter, until abolished by the Romans. The Hasmonean story is recorded in the Book of the Maccabees, a work included in the Septuagint but not in the Hebrew Bible. A second "Book of the Maccabees" is in the Apocrypha.

Heine, Heinrich (1797–1856). German Jewish poet and critic, nineteenth-century apostate who returned in his final years to a reappraisal of his Jewish origins.

Herzl, Theodor (1860–1904). Austro-Hungarian, born in Budapest, Viennese journalist and playwright, founder of the Zionist movement.

Hillel and Shammai (last years of B.C., first of A.D.). Hillel was the greatest Talmudic sage, his thought and personality dominant in the Second Temple period. Shammai, his classic disputant, tended to the severe side of their disagreements. Two major "houses" of Talmud learning, Bet Hillel and Bet Shammai, carried on their divergence of relative leniency and strictness. Of both it was said, "These and these too are the words of the living God."

Ibn Ezra, Abraham (1089–1164). Preeminent Spanish Bible commentator, poet, and grammarian.

Jabotinksky, Vladimir (1880–1940). Early Zionist leader of Revisionism, a militant nationalistic program.

Josephus Flavius (circa A.D. 37–100). Classical Jewish historian.

Lamarck, Chevalier de (1744–1829). French naturalist. Lamarckism in biology is the hypothesis of the inheritance of acquired characteristics, to account for design in nature.

Lubavitcher Rebbe. Head of Chabad Hasidism. The late Menachem Mendel Schneerson, the seventh Lubavitcher Rebbe, was an eminent, sometimes controversial, leader in rescue work and Hasidic teaching.

Lueger, Karl (1844–1910). Anti-Semitic Austrian politician, mayor of Vienna prior to World War I.

Luria, Isaac ben Solomon (1534–1572). Kabbalist of Safed, Palestine, whose mystical system is the basis of modern Hasidism.

Maccabees (see *Hasmoneans*)

Maimonides, Moses (1135–1204). Medieval halakhic authority and philosopher, author of *Guide of the Perplexed* and the *Mishneh Torah.*

Manger, Itzik (1901–1969). Sardonic Yiddish poet and storyteller.

Medawar, Peter Brian (1915–1987). British geneticist (Nobel Prize).

Mendele Moykher Sforim (1835–1917). "Mendele the Bookseller." First of the great nineteenth-century Yiddish authors.

Pascal, Blaise (1623–1662). French philosopher, theologian, and scientist.

Peretz, Isaac Leib (1852–1915). Yiddish belle-lettrist.

Philo, Judaeus (circa 13 B.C.–A.D. 45–50). Alexandrian Jewish philosopher.

Pinsker, Leon (1821–1891). Russian Jewish doctor, author of influential early Zionist manifesto *Auto-Emancipation.*

Rabin, Yitzhak (1922–1995). Israeli military leader and statesman; Prime Minister when assassinated.

Rashi (1045–1105). Acronym for the French Talmudic scholar, *R*abbi *Sh*lomo *I*tzhaki, greatest commentator on Talmud and Bible.

Schechter, Solomon (1850–1915). Religiously observant Haskalah scholar, founder of Conservative Judaism.

Scholem, Gershom Gerhard (1897–1982). Pioneer in academic study of Kabbalism and earlier Jewish mysticism.

Shabbetai, Zevi (1626–1676). Kabbalist and false Messiah, born in Smyrna, Turkey, converted to Islam.

Sisyphus. Legendary Greek king, condemned to roll a stone uphill in Hades only to have it roll down again, for all eternity.

Soloveitchik, Joseph Dov (1903–1993). Preeminent modern Talmudist and philosopher.

Spinoza, Baruch (1632–1677). Jewish philosopher, apostate from Judaism.

Vilna Gaon (1720–1797). Elijah ben Solomon Zalman of the town of Vilna, in Belorussia. Intellectual and religious leader of Talmudic Jewry.

Zaideh. Rabbi Mendel Leib Levine, author's grandfather, born in Russia 1864, died in Tel Aviv 1958.